Meeting the Standards in Primary ICT

This practical guide to using ICT in the primary classroom addresses all the concerns of trainee and student teachers. It provides plenty of ideas and advice on how to incorporate ICT into classroom teaching on a daily basis. The authors bring together theory and practice to help prospective and newly qualified teachers (NQTs) acquire and develop the skills required for using ICT effectively and to develop the knowledge and understanding needed for Qualified Teacher Status.

Meeting the Standards in Primary ICT is split into three sections which will:

- Help you assess your ICT skills, knowledge and understanding
- Discuss ways of incorporating ICT for teaching across the primary curriculum
- Help you think about ICT and your own professional learning and development.

This book is not just limited to the use of ICT in the classroom but looks at the wider role of ICT in supporting effective professional development, so will be an invaluable resource that will benefit all trainee teachers on primary training courses. It will also be a reference for lecturers and mentors supporting trainees on these courses as well as NQTs in the early stages of their teaching career.

Steve Higgins is Senior Lecturer in Primary Education at the University of Newcastle upon Tyne. **Nick Packard** is an Educational ICT Consultant.

Meeting the Standards Series

Series editor: Lynn D. Newton
School of Education, University of Durham, Leazes Road, Durham, DH1 1TA

Meeting the Standards in Primary English
Eve English and John Williamson

Meeting the Standards in Primary Mathematics
Tony Brown

Meeting the Standards in Primary Science
Lynn D. Newton

Meeting the Standards in Primary ICT
Steve Higgins and Nick Packard

Meeting the Standards in Secondary English
Michael Fleming, Frank Hardman, David Stevens and John Williamson

Meeting the Standards in Secondary Maths
Howard Tanner and Sonia Jones

Meeting the Standards in Secondary Science
Lynn D. Newton

Meeting the Standards for Using ICT for Secondary Teaching
Steve Kennewell

Meeting the Standards in Primary ICT

A Guide to the ITT NC

Steve Higgins and Nick Packard

RoutledgeFalmer
Taylor & Francis Group

LONDON AND NEW YORK

First published 2004 by RoutledgeFalmer
2 Park Square, Milton Park, Abingdon, Oxon, OX14 4RN

Simultaneously published in the USA and Canada
by RoutledgeFalmer
1270 Madison Ave, New York, NY 10006

RoutledgeFalmer is an imprint of the Taylor & Francis Group

© 2004 Steve Higgins and Nick Packard

Typeset in 10.5/12.5pt M. Bembo by Graphicraft Limited, Hong Kong
Printed and bound in Great Britain by Bell & Bain Ltd, Glasgow

British Library Cataloguing in Publication Data
A catalogue record for this book is available from the British Library

Library of Congress Cataloging in Publication Data
Higgins, Steve (Steve E.).
    Meeting the Standards in Primary ICT : a guide to the ITTNC /
Steve Higgins & Nick Packard.
        p. cm. — (Meeting the Standards Series)
    Includes bibliographical references and index.
    ISBN 0–415–23047–0 (pbk. : alk. paper)
    1. Information technology—Study and teaching (Elementary)—
Standards—Great Britain. 2. Education, Elementary—
Computer-assisted instruction—Standards—Great Britain. 3.
Elementary School teachers—Training of—Great Britain. I.
Packard, Nick. II. Title. III. Series.
LB1028.43.H52 2004
371.33′4—dc22

                                                      2004006457

ISBN 0-415-23047-0

Contents

List of illustrations and tasks   vii
Series editor's preface   x
Acknowledgement   xiii

Welcome to your teaching career   1

PART I   Your ICT skills, knowledge and understanding   11

1   Auditing your own skills and understanding ICT
    capability   15

2   Text, pictures and multimedia   24

3   Managing and understanding information   33

4   Communicating with and through ICT   43

5   What does the research say?   52

PART II   ICT and teaching in the classroom   61

6   ICT for literacy and the teaching of English   65

7   ICT for numeracy and mathematics   77

8   ICT in primary science   91

9   ICT across the curriculum   104

10 ICT in the Foundation Stage   128

11 ICT and thinking skills   140

PART III   ICT and your own professional learning   153

12   Managing your professional responsibilities with ICT   157

13   Becoming a reflective practitioner   162

14   Applying for jobs and coping with interviews   167

Appendix A: Finding information on the web   175

Appendix B: Other sources of information   179

Appendix C: Glossary of educational ICT terms and abbreviations or *A Guide to Modern Geek for Teachers*   186

Appendix D: Legal, ethical and health and safety issues   200

References   204

Index   207

List of illustrations and tasks

Figures

1.1	Your initial ICT capability	18
1.2	Developing your ICT capability	18
3.1	A branching tree with questions to sort a collection of animals	36
3.2	An example of an interactive spreadsheet created using Excel	40
6.1	A Clicker Grid on homophones	66
6.2	PowerPoint presentation used to help children develop early phonic skills	67
6.3	Using DTP software for sorting and categorising activities	71
7.1	A screen from the ITP 'TellTime'	79
7.2	A screen from the ITP 'Number Grid'	80
7.3	A magic square activity based on a spreadsheet	87
8.1	A screenshot from the Digital Frog resources	97
8.2	A concept cartoon: 'I'll go fastest down the hill because I'm the heaviest'	98
9.1	The National Portrait Gallery archives	112
9.2	Crocodile Clips Elementary – virtual electronics kit	120
9.3	Animated satellite images of weather systems from the Met Office	122
10.1	Drawing and labelling a plant in a group discussion around the computer	132
10.2	Using ICT to develop sorting, planning and matching activities for young children	137
11.1	An integrated model for understanding thinking and learning	142
11.2	A screen from Number Grid	143

11.3   A further screen from Number Grid   144
11.4   A child's mind map created with Kidspiration   146
11.5   The Zoombinis meet the Fleens   149

Tasks

1.1   Skills, knowledge and understanding   19
1.2   Your own ICT skills and applying them to your teaching   19
1.3   Auditing your needs   21
2.1   Writing an assignment   30
2.2   Preparing resources   30
2.3   Planning for learning   31
2.4   Developing pupils' ICT skills   31
3.1   Using a spreadsheet   39
3.2   Using a spreadsheet or database for teaching   40
3.3   Developing pupils' information handling skills   41
3.4   Planning for learning with information   41
4.1   Exchanging information   50
4.2   Finding resources on the web   50
4.3   Developing pupils' communication skills   50
5.1   Finding relevant ICT research   59
PII.1 ICT in schools   63
6.1   Using ICT in whole-class literacy teaching   68
6.2   Using ICT in group or individual work in literacy   72
6.3   Using ICT to prepare resources for literacy   75
7.1   Using ICT in whole-class teaching for mathematics   83
7.2   Using ICT in group or individual work for mathematics   86
7.3   Using ICT to prepare resources for mathematics   88
8.1   Using ICT for recording in science   95
8.2   Using spreadsheets in science   96
8.3   Using ICT to demonstrate in science   100
8.4   Evaluating software and resources for primary science   101
8.5   Using ICT for research and information in science   102
9.1   Using ICT in teaching the whole class across the curriculum   111
9.2   Using ICT in group or individual work across the curriculum   126
10.1   Observing ICT in the Foundation Stage   133
10.2   Using ICT in the Foundation Stage   134
10.3   Using ICT to develop creativity in the Foundation Stage   136
11.1   ICT and children's thinking   143
11.2   Using ICT to develop thinking with the whole class   145
11.3   ICT as a tool for thinking   147
11.4   'Thinking skills' software   150
12.1   Organising your resources   159
12.2   Assessment and recording   160

12.3   Extending your professional knowledge   160
13.1   Why do I want to teach?   162
13.2   Reflecting on teaching with and about ICT   163
13.3   Developing an action plan   165
14.1   Applying for jobs   170
14.2   Creating a portfolio   171
14.3   Planning for interviews   173

Tables

1.1   An audit grid   20
4.1   Asynchronous and synchronous communication with and
      through ICT   44

Series editor's preface

This book has been prepared for students training to be teachers who face the challenge of meeting the many requirements specified in the government's Circular 02/02, *Qualifying to Teach: Professional standards for qualified teacher status* (TTA/DfES, 2002). The book forms part of a series of publications that sets out to guide trainees on initial teacher training programmes, both primary and secondary, through the complex package of subject requirements they will be expected to meet before they can be awarded Qualified Teacher Status.

Why is there a need for such a series? Teaching has always been a demanding profession, requiring of its members enthusiasm, dedication and commitment. In addition, it is common sense that teachers need to know not only what they teach but how to teach it most effectively. Current trends in education highlight the raising of standards (particularly in the areas of literacy and numeracy), the use of new technologies across the curriculum and the development of key skills for lifelong learning. These run alongside the early learning goals, baseline assessment, the requirements of the National Curriculum, the National Literacy and Numeracy Strategies, PSHE and citizenship work, National Curriculum Assessment Tests (NCATs), optional tests, GCSE examinations, post-16 assessment . . . The list seems endless. Such demands increase the pressure on teachers generally and trainee teachers in particular.

At the primary school level, since the introduction of the National Curriculum there is an even greater emphasis now than ever before on teachers' own subject knowledge and their ability to apply that knowledge in the classroom. Trainees have to become Jacks and Jills of all trades – developing the competence and confidence to plan, manage, monitor and assess all areas of the National Curriculum plus religious education. The increasing complexity of the primary curriculum and ever more demanding societal expectations makes it very difficult for trainees and their mentors (be they tutors in the training institutions or teachers in schools) to cover everything that is necessary in what feels like a very short space of time. Four of the books in this series are aimed specifically at the trainee primary teacher and those who are helping to train them:

- *Meeting the Standards in . . . Primary English*
- *Meeting the Standards in . . . Primary Mathematics*
- *Meeting the Standards in . . . Primary Science*
- *Meeting the Standards in . . . Primary Information and Communications Technology*

For those training to be secondary school teachers, the pressures are just as great. They will probably bring with them knowledge and expertise in their specialist subject, taken to degree level at least. However, content studied to degree level in universities is unlikely to match closely the needs of the National Curriculum. A degree in medieval English, applied mathematics or biochemistry will not be sufficient in itself to enable a secondary trainee to walk into a classroom of 13- or 16-year-olds and teach English, mathematics or science. Each subject at school level is likely to be broader. For example, science must include physics, chemistry, biology, astronomy, and aspects of geology. In addition there is the subject application – the 'how to teach it' dimension. Furthermore, secondary school teachers are often expected to be able to offer more than one subject. Thus, four of the books are aimed specifically at the secondary level:

- *Meeting the Standards in . . . Secondary English*
- *Meeting the Standards in . . . Secondary Mathematics*
- *Meeting the Standards in . . . Secondary Science*
- *Meeting the Standards in . . . Secondary Information and Communications Technology*

All of the books deal with the specific issues that underpin the relevant Teacher Training Agency requirements identified in Circular 02/02. The very nature of the subject areas covered and the teaching phases focused upon means that each book will, of necessity, be presented in different ways. However, each will cover the relevant areas of:

- subject knowledge – an overview of what to teach, the key ideas underpinning the relevant subject knowledge that the trainees need to know and understand in order to interpret the National Curriculum requirements for that subject;
- subject application – an overview of how to interpret the subject knowledge so as to design appropriate learning ·experiences for pupils, organise and manage those experiences and monitor pupils' progress within them.

The former is not presented in the form of a textbook. There are plenty of good quality GCSE and A-level textbooks on the market for those who feel the need to acquire that level of knowledge. Rather, the subject knowledge is related to identifying what is needed for the trainee to take the National Curriculum for the subject and translate it into a meaningful package for teaching and learning. In most of the books in the series, the latter is structured in such a way as to identify the generic skills of planning, organising, managing, monitoring and assessing the teaching and learning. The content is related to the specific requirements of Circular 02/02. The trainee's continuing professional development needs are also considered.

The purpose of the series is to give practical guidance and support to trainee teachers, in particular focusing on what to do and how to do it. Throughout each book there are suggested tasks and activities that can be completed in the training institution, in school or independently at home. They serve to elicit and support the trainee's development of skills, knowledge and understanding needed to become an effective teacher.

Dr Lynn Newton
University of Durham
May 2003

Acknowledgement

Microsoft, Excel, and Windows are either registered trademarks or trademarks of Microsoft Corporation in the United States and/or other countries.

Welcome to your teaching career

Teaching is without doubt the most important profession; without teaching there would be no other professions. It is also the most rewarding. What role in society can be more crucial than that which shapes children's lives and prepares them for adulthood?

(TTA, 1998: 1)

So, you have decided to become a primary teacher. You will, no doubt, have heard lots of stories about teaching as a profession. Some will have been positive, encouraging, even stimulating. Others will have been negative and pejorative. But you are still here, on the doorstep of a rewarding and worthwhile career. Without doubt teaching *is* a demanding and challenging profession. No two days are the same. Children are never the same. The curriculum seldom stays the same for very long. But these are all part of the challenge. Teaching as a career requires dedication, commitment, imagination and no small amount of energy. Yet, despite this, when things go well, when you feel your efforts to help this child or these children learn have been successful, you will feel wonderful. Welcome to teaching!

An overview of recent developments in primary teaching

As with most things, the teaching profession is constantly buffeted by the winds of change. In particular, the last fifteen years has been a time of great change for all involved in primary education. At the heart of this change has been the Education Reform Act (ERA) of 1988. The Act brought about a number of far-reaching developments, the most significant of which was the creation of a National Curriculum and its related requirements for monitoring and assessment which in turn have led to the development of the National Literacy and Numeracy Strategies.

Although there have always been guidelines from Her Majesty's Inspectorate (HMI), professional bodies (such as teachers' unions), local authorities and even official government publications, until 1988 teachers generally had freedom to decide for themselves *what* to teach and *how* to teach it. Different approaches to curriculum planning and delivery have proved influential at different times. As far as primary education is concerned, the most influential event before the ERA was probably the publication of the Plowden Report (Central Advisory Council for England, Education, 1967), with its now quite famous phrase, 'At the heart of the education process lies the child.' Children were suddenly seen as participants in the learning process, not passive recipients of it. Their active involvement, a consideration of their needs and interests, the matching of curricula and support to the needs of individuals and groups – these were all seen as significant developments in the education of primary children. However, by the mid-1980s there were those in education and in government who believed that the 'post-Plowden progressivism' had gone too far, and that there was a need to redress the balance, restore a structured curriculum and bring back traditional approaches in the classroom.

Blyth suggests that, as a consequence, over the last fifteen years or so:

> The relation between subjects and children's learning has preoccupied thinking about the primary curriculum especially since Plowden, and has unsurprisingly generated a very substantial body of professional literature.
>
> (Blyth, 1998: 11)

This preoccupation not only with the primary curriculum, but with progression in pupils' learning throughout the period of compulsory schooling and in all subjects, has resulted in the development of the idea of an official curriculum for England, Wales and Northern Ireland. Many other countries already had national curricula, so the idea was not new and there were models to draw upon.

In the second half of the 1980s, the government introduced the idea of a *Basic Curriculum* for all pupils of compulsory school age. At the heart of this is the *National Curriculum*, which is underpinned by a subject-led approach to areas of experience and their assessment.

The focus of the National Curriculum is a 'core curriculum' of English, mathematics and science. This core is supported by a framework of 'foundation' subjects: art, design and technology, geography, history, information technology, music and physical education. In Welsh-speaking areas of Wales, Welsh is also included as a core subject and as a foundation subject in other parts of Wales. Outside of the National Curriculum but still embedded within the broader framework of the Basic Curriculum are areas of experience, such as religious education, and a range of cross-curricular dimensions, themes and skills which allow for topic and thematic approaches in the primary classroom.

Initially grossly overloaded, the National Curriculum has undergone a sequence of judicious prunings to reduce the burden. The most significant of these was in 1995, when Sir Ron Dearing reduced and reorganised the content, placed more emphasis on the basic skills which all pupils should acquire and allowed the cross-curricular dimensions, themes and skills to disappear into the background. This generated a slimmed-down document which addressed some of the criticisms and concerns of primary teachers, and was accompanied by a promise that teachers would have a five year period of calm. Accordingly next National Curriculum revision was published in 2000, though for primary schools this revision was overshadowed by the introduction of the National Literacy and Numeracy Strategies which set out in considerable detail the expectations for attainment for pupils in aspects of English and mathematics.

The Standards debate

Parallel to the changing perspectives on curriculum has been an increasing emphasis on standards. There has, in essence, been a shift in perspective from *equality in education* (as reflected in the post-war legislation of the late 1940s through to the 1970s) to the *quality of education*, the bandwagon of the 1980s and 1990s.

The term 'standard' is emotive and value-laden. According to the *Oxford English Dictionary*, among other descriptors of a standard, it is first of all a weight or measure to which others conform or by which the accuracy of others is judged and second a degree of excellence required for a particular purpose. Both of these definitions sit well with the educational use of the term, where it translates as acceptable levels of performance by schools and teachers in the eyes of the public and the politicians.

Over the last decade the media have reported numerous incidents of falling standards and the failure of the educational system to live up to the degree of excellence required for the purpose of educating our young in preparation for future citizenship. We teachers have, purportedly, been measured and found lacking. It was this, in part, which was a major force behind the introduction both of the National Curriculum and the National Literacy and Numeracy Strategies.

In 1989, when the National Curriculum was introduced, the Department for Education and Science claimed:

> There is every reason for optimism that in providing a sound, sufficiently detailed framework over the next decade, the National Curriculum will give children and teachers much needed help in achieving higher standards.
>
> (DES, 1989: 2)

Underpinning the forces of change in primary education in recent years have been two major thrusts. The first is to do with the curriculum itself and the experiences we offer pupils in primary schools. The second, and not unrelated, is to do with how we measure and judge the outcomes of the teaching and learning enterprise. To achieve the appropriately educated citizens of the future, schools of the present must not only achieve universal literacy and numeracy but must be measurably and accountably seen to be doing so, hence the introduction of league tables as performance indicators. A cynic might observe that the mantra of *quality* in education has instead become an obsession with the *quantity* of education, at least in terms of the amount of assessment and testing that children in English schools are subjected to.

David Blunkett, then Secretary of State for Education and Employment, said in 1997:

> Poor standards of literacy and numeracy are unacceptable. If our growing economic success is to be maintained we must get the basics right for everyone. Countries will only keep investing here at record levels if they see that the workforce is up to the job.
>
> (DfEE, 1997a: 2)

While the economic arguments are strong, we need to balance the needs of the economy with the needs of the child. Few teachers are likely to disagree with the need to get the basics right. After all, literacy and numeracy skills underpin much that we do with children in the other areas of the curriculum. However, the increased focus on the basics should not be at the expense of these other areas of experience. Children should have access to a broad and balanced curriculum if they are to develop as broad, balanced individuals.

All primary schools are now ranked each year on the basis of their Key Stage 2 pupils' performances in the National Curriculum Attainment tests (NCATs[1]) for English, mathematics and science. The performances of individual children are conveyed only to parents, although the school's collective results are discussed with school governors and also given to the local education authority (LEA). The latter then informs the DfES, who publish the national figures on a school/LEA basis. This gives parents the opportunity to compare, judge and choose schools within the LEA where they live. The figures indicate, for each school within the LEA, the percentage above and below the expected level: that is, the schools which are or are not meeting the standard. This results in inevitable conclusions as to whether standards are rising or falling. Such crude measures as National Curriculum (NC) tests for comparing attainment have been widely criticised, notably by education researchers like Fitz-Gibbon (1995) who points out that such measures ignore the 'value added elements' – in other words, the factors which influence teaching and learning such as the catchment area of the school, the proportion of pupils for whom English is an additional language, and the quality and quantity of educational enrichment a child receives in the home. This idea of relative progress is an important one, as no judgement of the quality of teaching can be undertaken without identifying the relative progress that children in a school make. Davies (1998) suggests that:

> Dissatisfaction [with standards] is expressed spasmodically throughout the year but reaches fever pitch when the annual national test results are published. Whatever the results they are rarely deemed satisfactory and targets are set which expect future cohorts of children to achieve even higher standards than their predecessors.
>
> (Davies, 1998: 162)

There are also targets for initial teacher training, to redress the perceived inadequacies in existing course provision. These centre on a National Curriculum for initial teacher training which prescribes the skills, knowledge and understandings which all trainees must achieve before they can be awarded Qualified Teacher Status (QTS). It follows, therefore, that as a trainee for the teaching profession you must be equipped to deal with these contradictory and sometimes conflicting situations as well as meeting all the required standards. So how will you be prepared for this?

Routes into a career in teaching

To begin, let us first consider the routes into teaching open to anyone wanting to pursue teaching as a career. Teaching is now an all-graduate profession, although this has not always been the case. Prior to the 1970s it was possible to become a teacher by gaining a teaching certificate from a college of higher education. However, in the late 1960s and early 1970s, following a sequence of government reports, the routes were narrowed to ensure graduate status for all newly qualified teachers.

For most primary teachers in the United Kingdom this has usually been via an undergraduate pathway, reading for a degree at a university (or a college associated to a university) which resulted in the award of Bachelor of Education (BEd) with Qualified Teacher Status (QTS). Such a route has usually taken at least three and sometimes four years. More recently, such degrees have become more linked to subject specialisms and some universities offer Bachelor of Arts in Education (BA(Ed)) with QTS and Bachelor of Science in Education (BSc (Ed)) with QTS.

A smaller proportion of primary teachers choose to gain their degrees from a university first, and then train to teach through the postgraduate route. This usually takes one year, at the end of which the trainee is awarded a Postgraduate Certificate in Education (PGCE) with QTS. In all cases, the degree or postgraduate certificate is awarded by the training institution, but the QTS is awarded by the Department for Education and Skills (DfES) as a consequence of successful completion of the course and on the recommendation of the training institution.

Whichever route is followed, there are rigorous government requirements which must be met by both the institutions providing the training and the trainees following the training programme, before QTS can be awarded. In the 1970s and early 1980s, teacher training institutions had guidelines produced by a group called the Council for the Accreditation of Teacher Education (CATE). The guidelines identified key requirements which all Initial Teacher Training (ITT) providers should meet to be judged effective in training teachers. Alongside the CATE criteria were systems of monitoring the quality of programmes. Throughout this period, Blyth describes how

> ... the general reaction against the more extreme forms of child-centredness in primary education has been reflected in widespread and sometimes ill-informed criticism of all primary teacher education, and even of educational studies and research.
>
> (Blyth, 1998: 13)

During the late 1980s and early 1990s, there were a number of government documents which have moved initial teacher training in the direction of partnership with schools. This has involved school staff taking greater responsibility for the support and assessment of students on placements and a transfer of funds (either as money or as in-service provision) to the schools in payment for this increased responsibility. Alongside this responsibility in schools, staff have increasingly become involved in the selection and interviewing of prospective students, the planning and delivery of the courses and the overall quality assurance process.

More legislation has culminated in the establishment of the Teacher Training Agency (TTA), a government body which, as its name suggests, now has control over the nature and funding of initial teacher training courses. This legislation is crucially important to you as a trainee teacher, since the associated documentation defines the framework for your preparation for and induction into the teaching profession. So how will the legislation affect you?

The development of requirements for courses of initial teacher training

In 1997, a government Circular number 10/97 introduced the idea of a national curriculum for initial teacher training (ITT), to parallel that already being used in schools. This was to be a major development in the training of teachers. In the circular there was an emphasis on the development of your professionalism as a teacher. This implies

> . . . more than meeting a series of discrete standards. It is necessary to consider the standards as a whole to appreciate the creativity, commitment, energy and enthusiasm which teaching demands, and the intellectual and managerial skills required of the effective professional.
>
> (DfEE, 1997a: 2)

At the heart of this is the idea of raising standards. Circular number 10/97 had specified:

1   the standards which *all* trainees must meet for the award of QTS;
2   the initial teacher training curricula for English and mathematics; and
3   the requirements on teacher training institutions providing courses of initial teacher training.

Subsumed under the first set of criteria were groups of standards relating to the personal subject knowledge of the trainee, criteria related to his or her abilities to apply the skills, knowledge and understanding to the teaching and learning situation, and criteria related to the planning, management and assessment of learning and behaviour.

In May 1998, the DfEE issued Circular number 4/98, *Teaching: High Status, High Standards*, in which the Secretary of State's criteria were revised and extended. As well as generic standards for the award of QTS, the new document specified separate national curricula for initial teacher training in English, mathematics and science at both primary and secondary levels, and a national curriculum for the use of Information and Communications Technology in subject teaching to be taught to all trainees, regardless of phase focus. The fundamental aim of this new National Curriculum for ITT was to:

> . . . equip all new teachers with the knowledge, understanding and skills needed to play their part in raising pupil performance across the education system.
>
> (DfEE, 1998: 3)

These standards were subsequently revised and an updated version came into effect from 1 September 2002. *Qualifying to Teach: Professional standards for Qualified Teacher Status and requirements for initial teacher training* (TTA, 2002) is therefore an essential document for anyone preparing to teach in England.

So how does this affect you as a student teacher? In essence, it means that you must 'meet the standards' before you can be awarded QTS. One of the major tasks facing you as an entrant to the teaching profession is that of evaluating yourself against these professional standards relating to your skills, knowledge and understanding of teaching. As a trainee, you must show that you have met these standards by the end of your training programme so as to be eligible for the award of QTS. Courses in universities and other higher education institutions are designed to help you to do so, both in schools and in the institution, but the onus is likely to be on you to provide the evidence to show how you have met the requirements. Additionally it will be helpful to you to know the standards against which you will be assessed. This series of books, *Meeting the Standards in . . .* , is designed to help you with this task. This particular book focuses on those skills and competences you will need to acquire to show that you have met the requirements regarding Information and Communications Technology (ICT).

ICT is a powerful tool which can help you in your preparation, your planning and assessment of learning as well as in the actual teaching that you do. At this point we need to make an important distinction. This book is more about using ICT effectively as a tool for you as a teacher than it is about you teaching the ICT curriculum to your pupils (though this forms a part of the book). The emphasis in 'Qualifying to Teach' is on this broader use of ICT as a tool for use across the curriculum and to support you as a teacher more generally.

> Those awarded Qualified Teacher Status must demonstrate . . . they know how to use ICT effectively, both to teach their subject and to support their wider professional role.
>
> (TTA, 2002: 2.5 p. 7)

There is more to using ICT effectively in your teaching and in the teaching of ICT as a subject of the primary curriculum than simply having a good knowledge and understanding of ICT. One of the major tasks ahead of you is to develop the ability to transform what you know and understand about such technology to support your teaching and to provide worthwhile teaching and learning experiences for your pupils in all subjects of the curriculum. This means that you need to develop your *pedagogical skills, knowledge and understanding* of how ICT can contribute to effective teaching and learning. This is as important as your knowledge and understanding of the National Curriculum Orders for each of the subjects and how ICT contributes to each. The National Curriculum documentation provides you with an outline of *what* to teach in each of the subjects of the curriculum for primary pupils. It does not tell you *how* to teach it – how to plan, organise, manage and assess the learning of the thirty or so children in your class, each with varied and changing needs. The National Literacy and Numeracy Frameworks and the Schemes of Work produced by the Qualifications and Curriculum Authority (QCA) offer more detailed guidance. However, the details of how you organise, manage and teach your class is left to your own professionalism. This book is designed to help you to make a start on this task.

Overview of this book

Very few students on primary initial teacher training programmes begin their courses as experts in ICT. Even those with expertise are unlikely to have used such technology with pupils. While such experience and expertise does vary from person to person, you all have one thing in common – *potential*. You have successfully cleared the hurdles of the application form and the interview and have been offered a place on a primary initial teacher training course. Your tutors have decided that you have the necessary personal qualities which indicate that you are capable of acquiring the skills, knowledge and understanding needed to become effective primary teachers. In other words, you have shown evidence that you have the potential to *meet the standards*.

This book is designed to help you to do this, but it is only a part of the picture. It will be most useful to you if you read it in conjunction with the other experiences offered to you on your training programme. These will range from theoretical to practical in the following ways.

- *Directed reading:* reading might be handouts related to lectures, books and articles for assignments or professional newspapers and magazines simply to broaden your own professional knowledge;
- *Taught sessions:* these could take the form of formal lectures, informal practical workshops or combinations of either, whether in schools or in your training institution;
- *Talks/discussions:* again, these could be held in school or in the institution and can range from formal structured seminars with a group to more informal one-to-one discussion, usually with the aim of integrating theory and practice and developing your understanding;
- *Tutorial advice:* one-to-one sessions with a tutor, mentor or teacher to plan for and reflect upon your practical experiences;

- *Observations:* opportunities to watch your class teacher and other experienced primary teachers at work in their classrooms;
- *Restricted experience:* opportunities to try out, under the guidance of your teacher or mentor, limited teaching activities with a small group of children, perhaps building up to a whole class session;
- *Teaching practice:* a block placement where you take responsibility for the planning, teaching and assessment of a class of children, under the guidance of your class teacher, school mentor and tutor and usually within defined parameters to develop your teaching skills.

What is important about all of these is the amount of effort you put in to them. No-one else can do the work for you. Your tutors, your mentors in school and your class teachers can all offer you advice, guidance and even supportive criticism, but how you respond is up to you. This, once again, is a reflection of your professionalism.

Some of the skills and competences that you are expected to acquire are best done in the practical context of the schools in which you will be placed for your teaching experiences. To this end, there are a number of tasks and activities for you to complete while on these school placements. Obviously, these will have to be interpreted flexibly by you, as schools and access to children and ICT equipment will vary. Other tasks are suggested to encourage you to think about how theory and practice work together, in other words to begin the process of reflection.

Information and Communications Technology and the Standards

This particular book in the series of *Meeting the Standards* looks at the role and potential of Information and Communications Technology (ICT) in effective teaching and in developing pupils' learning. The UK government has invested considerable sums in ICT in education over the past decade through the 'National Grid for Learning', which aims to create an effective infrastructure, and through the £230 million investment of National Lottery money in ICT training for serving teachers. The outcomes for this training (TTA, 1999) emphasise the importance of teachers' understanding of ICT and its 'significant . . . potential for improving the quality of pupils' learning'.

ICT is both a subject in the National Curriculum (DfEE, 1999) for England and Wales and a complex tool which can be used by teachers and by pupils in teaching and learning. This makes the approach in this book different from the others in this series. Our intention is to look at ICT as a tool and the evidence for how it can contribute to the teaching and learning across the curriculum, rather than just the development of ICT as a subject within the curriculum.

The book is written with the aim of giving you a general introduction to using ICT effectively as a teacher in primary schools. However, this is an area which changes rapidly. The book can only offer you some basic guidance and principles about effective use. Throughout, whenever appropriate, there are references to recent research for further readings into topics and issues in the use of ICT in primary teaching. You will need to take up some of these opportunities and identify ways in which developing technologies can help you in your teaching.

Note

1   These tests are more commonly referred to as 'SATs'; however, this term is a registered trademark of the US College Board tests and they are therefore known officially as NC tests in UK government documents.

Further information and readings

If you would like to explore further some of the more general issues mentioned in this introduction, the following books and websites might be of interest to you.

Cashdan, A. and Overall, L. (eds) (1998) *Teaching in Primary Schools*. London: Cassell.
   In their book, Cashdan and Overall bring together a collection of views on a range of issues to do with primary education. It is an ideal text for the trainee in that it provides the background from the perspective of government's requirements on new entrants into teaching, in particular the generic skills, knowledge and understanding underpinning Annex A of Circular 4/98.

Edwards, A. and Collison, J. (1996) *Mentoring and Developing Practice in Primary Schools: Supporting student teacher learning in schools*. Milton Keynes: Open University Press.
   For trainees interested in the role of schools and teachers in the process of initial teacher training, this book provides a detailed discussion. Written primarily for the primary teacher taking on this role, it considers the different aspects of the role and how the trainee can best be supported and developed.

Moon, B. (2001) *A Guide to the National Curriculum*. Oxford: Oxford University Press.
   This fourth edition of Moon's book brings the discussion up to date in the light of the 2000 revisions and provides and excellent overview of the National Curriculum, its nature and evolution. It contains extra information on testing, special needs, and the role of parents, as well as information on national literacy and numeracy strategies.

http://www.tta.gov.uk/training/qtsstandards/
   You will need to become thoroughly familiar with the Professional Standards for Qualified Teacher Status available from the TTA's website.

PART I

Your ICT skills, knowledge and understanding

This book is divided into three parts:

Part I   Your ICT skills and knowledge;
Part II   ICT and teaching in the classroom;
Part III   ICT and your own professional learning.

It is designed to be dipped into as needed. You may choose to skim through some parts and work through others in more detail. Some of the information is repeated in the different sections of the book – this is intentional and is designed to support flexible use of the information, the ideas and tasks that it contains. However, this means that you will also need to think about how to get the best from the book. We suggest getting a quick overview of what it contains (the section introductions aim to help you do this) then read Chapter 1 and identify from the self-audit which sections can offer you the most support.

The first part provides an overview of the skills and knowledge you will need in order to undertake your professional responsibilities as a teacher, using ICT effectively in your work, as well as the skills and knowledge required to teach the National Curriculum requirements for ICT. This helps to address the requirements in the professional standards for qualified teacher status (TTA/DfES, 2002) to 'know how to use ICT effectively, both to teach their subject and to support their wider professional role' (2.5 p. 8).

As a teacher you will also need to know about how ICT applies to the subjects that you will be teaching. The specific aspects of the professional standards are 'have a secure knowledge and understanding of the subject(s) they are trained to teach' (2.1 p. 7). These requirements vary according to the age range that you will be teaching. For nursery and reception teachers you will need knowledge of the Foundation Stage curriculum guidance and the Literacy and Numeracy Frameworks as these apply to reception age children (2.1a p. 7). Each of these documents refers to ICT. For teachers in Key Stages 1 and 2 you need to 'know and understand the curriculum for each of the National Curriculum core subjects, and the frameworks, methods and expectations set out in the national Numeracy and Literacy Strategies' (2.1b p. 7) as well as 'sufficient understanding of a range of work' across the foundation subjects (which include ICT) and religious education.

The chapters in this section are organised as follows:

- Chapter 1 Auditing your own skills and understanding ICT capability – It is important that you assess the extent to which you will need to develop your skills, knowledge and understanding of ICT and how it relates to your chosen career. At the heart of this book is the idea that ICT is a tool for teachers to use. As you become experienced in using ICT and in developing your teaching skills you will be able to make decisions about when, where and how to use ICT more effectively.

- Chapter 2 Text, pictures and multimedia – Computers can manage information in different forms, particularly as text (including numbers), as pictures and sounds or combinations of these (multimedia). This chapter provides an overview of these aspects of ICT, the programs you can use to work with different media and what the National Curriculum requirements are.

- Chapter 3 Managing and understanding information – The 'information revolution' has changed the way that we deal with information. It is not just about data, but how we manage, relate and understand information that is bringing about significant changes in the ways that we work. This chapter looks at handling and managing information and software like spreadsheets and databases which are designed to help us deal with the increasing quantities of information.

- Chapter 4 Communicating with and through ICT – Communication is a key feature of ICT. This chapter considers the different ways in which computers and other forms of ICT can support communication in teaching and learning, both in terms of preparation, planning and your wider professional role as well as teaching in the classroom.

- Chapter 5 What does the research say? – Computers are often heralded as a way of raising standards in schools. This chapter looks at the evidence for this claim and sets out some guidelines from research about how ICT can help learning and teaching in schools.

This book cannot offer you more than guidance about what you could do and how you might develop your skills, knowledge and understanding. ICT capability is about being able to make complex professional choices as to how best to use a range of fast-developing technologies. There is not a simple solution. You can learn some of the principles and ideas from books and by carefully observing what happens in schools. This book attempts to provide part of this big picture. Most of the understanding will only come with experience and reflection. You need to try things out, experiment, practice and think about how to develop your skills to improve your teaching, and, most importantly, the learning of your pupils.

Further information and readings

DfEE/QCA (1999) *The National Curriculum: Handbook for Primary Teachers in England.* London: DfEE/QCA (http://www.nc.uk.net/).

QCA (1998/2000) *Information and Communications Technology: A scheme of work for Key Stages 1 and 2* (http://qca.org.uk/).

TTA (2002) *Qualifying to Teach: Professional standards for qualified teacher status* (http://www.tta.gov.uk/training/qtsstandards/).

1 Auditing your own skills and understanding ICT capability

In order to get the best from this book (and your course of initial teacher training) you need to understand the task ahead of you. In terms of Information and Communications Technology, this falls into three broad areas. First, there is your own knowledge, skills and understanding about using ICT. How confident are you in using a range of programs on a computer and other related technologies? This is to help you with your professional responsibilities as a teacher. ICT is a tool that can be a real support with a wide range of tasks that you need to undertake on a daily or weekly basis. Then there is the curriculum that you will be teaching. This is in terms both of ICT as a subject and how ICT can be used in teaching across the curriculum. What do you know about the specific entitlement of learners in the age groups that you will be teaching and what opportunities are there for using ICT to enhance teaching and learning? What educational equipment and software are you familiar with? Finally, there is the most important issue of all: ICT capability. How can you put together your knowledge and skills to use ICT effectively as a teacher?

Knowledge, skills and understanding of ICT

As a trainee teacher you should be confident to use a wide range of software:

- word-processing (such as Microsoft's Word);
- drawing, painting and image manipulation (Microsoft's Paint; Adobe Photoshop etc.);
- presentation software (such as Microsoft's PowerPoint or Apple's Keynote);
- spreadsheets and graphing programs (such as Microsoft's Excel);
- databases (e.g. Microsoft's Access; Claris' Filemaker);
- Internet software (e.g. e-mail programs and web browsers such as Internet Explorer, Netscape, Safari etc.).

You will also need to develop skills in using a range of equipment:

- computers (possibly with different operating systems – Windows, Macintosh, Acorn) and certainly with different versions of operating systems (Windows 2000, XP, skills in using tablet PCs etc.);
- input devices (e.g. wireless keyboards and mice; keyboards and switches for learners with special needs);
- getting images onto a computer (scanners, digital stills and video cameras);
- output devices (printers, speakers, presentation technologies – such as data projectors and electronic [or interactive] whiteboards);
- control technology (such as temperature sensors or switches controlled by a computer).

It is extremely unlikely that you will already be familiar with all of the equipment and software outlined here. It will also not be possible to develop all of this expertise during your course. There simply isn't enough time! You should therefore try to identify particular areas where you feel you need to concentrate as you undertake your training and build on opportunities as they become available (for example using an electronic whiteboard if you are in a school or classroom that has one available).

You should be able to undertake tasks for yourself (such as writing assignments or completing planning documents) AND to prepare materials for your actual teaching (such as templates for pupils to use on a computer). You will also need to become familiar with some of the common programs that are used in schools and how the features of these programs may differ from other versions of the software (see the next section).

ICT and the curriculum

You will need to develop your knowledge of the curriculum and what skills in using ICT are expected with different ages of pupils. This is mainly about learning what is in the National Curriculum for ICT and the associated QCA (Qualifications and Curriculum Authority) Scheme of Work for ICT. For early years professionals there is helpful information in the Foundation Stage guidance. The main difference is that the National Curriculum is a statutory document and therefore part of what schools are legally obliged to cover or part of a pupil's legal educational entitlement. The QCA Scheme of Work exemplifies how the National Curriculum entitlement can be covered. It is not compulsory, though for a trainee teacher it provides helpful guidance on how to tackle teaching the range of requirements with suggestions for lessons and activities. The Foundation Stage guidance indicates how ICT can con-tribute to the learning of young children. One of the issues that you will have to tackle is learning about software (and occasionally hardware) that it is appropriate for pupils of different ages to use. The types of applications that are found in schools are similar to those in the list above and used by adults, but many of them have been adapted and developed for use by younger learners:

- text handling (RM's TextEase or FirstWord; Microsoft Publisher etc.);
- drawing and painting (e.g. KidPix (The Learning Company); Dazzle (SEMERC); Colour Magic (RM));
- data handling (spreadsheets such as Number Magic (RM), graphing programs and databases such as Pictogram/Dataplot (Kudlian Soft), PickaPicture (Black Cat), Junior Pinpoint (Longman Logotron), FlexiTree (Flexible) etc.;
- specific curriculum software (programs to teach aspects of mathematics such as LOGO, or appropriate CD-ROMs for history for learners of different ages);
- specialist software for younger children, such as My World (Granada), or for special needs, such as Inclusive Writer (Inclusive Technologies);
- other ICT equipment (such as programmable robots, digital cameras etc.).

The challenge here is that different schools will be using different software (though you are likely to find that similar software is used in schools in the same Local Education Authority, for example). You cannot possibly be an expert in using them all (and even if you were, new software is continually being developed). You will need to develop strategies to help you learn how to use these different programs.

You will also need to become familiar with the opportunities for ICT in the other subjects of the curriculum. A number of these are specifically outlined in the National Curriculum documentation or the Frameworks for Literacy and Numeracy. The QCA Schemes of Work for other subjects also contain activities to apply and use particular ICT skills in order to develop subject-specific knowledge and understanding (such as using a CD-ROM about animals and their habitats in science for example).

Although these official publications are helpful (especially as you get to grips with what is required and what is possible) you should not rely on them. As a teacher it is ultimately up to you to decide how to use ICT in your teaching. You will have to make sure that the pupils that you teach develop their own skills, knowledge and understanding of ICT (as outlined in the National Curriculum for ICT) and that you provide opportunities for them to use these skills to further their own understanding. This is as much about your knowledge and skills as it is the pupils!

Understanding ICT capability

This term, ICT 'capability', was first applied to pupils as a way of evaluating how they were developing their understanding of IT in the early days of the National Curriculum. Skills and knowledge are not enough. Using ICT effectively is about developing your understanding of what technology has to offer.

For pupils this is about not just assessing what skills they have been taught but how they make use of those skills in another context. They may have been taught how to alter the size and font of a document, but do they make use of these skills appropriately when designing a poster, for example?

The same concept can be applied helpfully to your own understanding of how to use ICT in your professional life. It is not just about acquiring skills, but developing understanding and judgement about how to use those skills appropriately. Once you

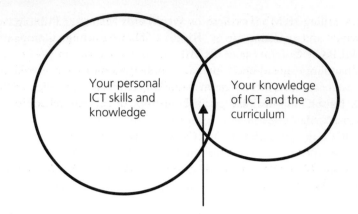

Figure 1.1   Your initial ICT capability

can use PowerPoint or other presentation software and have access to a data-projector in your classroom, you could create a presentation for every lesson that you teach. However, this would be rather to miss the point about what ICT is useful for. As a teacher you need to decide when such a presentation is an effective use of the technology (in terms of what possibilities PowerPoint offers and how you can present information with it), but also you need to make a judgement about the class or group of pupils that you are teaching. It may be that you have already used a similar presentation on the previous day. There is then a danger that the children will not find your presentation so compelling. It may be that you are teaching young children who may enjoy the spectacle, but not gain much from the content. You have to make a decision about *why* this would be better than other teaching techniques. At this stage in your training the overlap between what you know and can do with ICT and what you know about the curriculum and opportunities for using ICT may be limited. You may have used a word-processing software to write essays or letters, you will be able to see how such

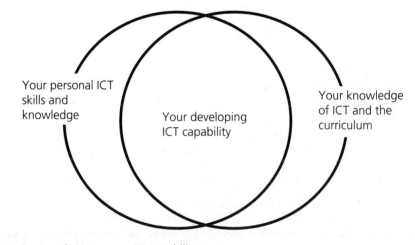

Figure 1.2   Developing your ICT capability

software could be used in schools to help children learn to write (particularly in redrafting and improving their writing) without laborious copying out by hand.

The aim of this book is to get you started in increasing the size of this overlap. As your skills and knowledge of ICT increases the opportunities you will identify for using ICT in your teaching will increase. Similarly as your knowledge of the curriculum and how to teach it develops, you will identify further opportunities to use ICT effectively in your teaching.

Tasks for you to provide evidence of effective use of ICT to meet the Standards

In order for you to review and assess your progress towards the Standards for QTS this book contains a number of tasks that you could undertake to provide evidence of your skills, knowledge, understanding and learning about ICT. The first task is therefore for you to consider what your main priorities are. If you are already a confident and experienced user of ICT, it may be that you will need to focus on developing your knowledge of the curriculum in order to apply and use what you already know and are confident to do. Alternatively if you have not had many opportunities to use ICT, you will need to prioritise developing your basic skills in order to ensure that you can teach what is expected in the National Curriculum.

Task 1.1 Skills, knowledge and understanding	Reflect on your skills, knowledge and understanding. What skills do you already have? What areas do you think you will need to focus on?

1 Developing your own skills?
2 Your knowledge of the ICT curriculum?
3 Your knowledge of the rest of the curriculum and how ICT applies?
4 Your experience in applying your exisiting knowledge and skills?

The diagrams above should help you to become more specific in thinking about where you are now. You should be able to think of examples that apply to each of the different areas of the Venn diagram.

Task 1.2 Your own ICT skills and applying them to your teaching	Have a look at Figure 1.1 and Figure 1.2 in this chapter. Identify an aspect of ICT that fits into each area of the diagram:

      1 something you can do with ICT, but are not sure how you would use it in your teaching;
2 something you can do with ICT and can see how you would use it in your teaching;
3 something you think you could teach now, but you do not know how ICT might support this.

You could also audit your skills and knowledge across the different kinds of information, software and equipment.

Table 1.1 An audit grid

Auditing your ICT skills		For yourself			In your teaching		
		Beginner	Confident	Expert	Beginner	Confident	Expert
Basic use	Basic operations (opening programs, shutting down)						
	Organising work (saving, managing files and folders)						
	Using a network (finding files, saving work)						
Software	Word processing						
	Drawing, painting						
	Spreadsheets and graphing programs						
	Databases						
	Internet software						
	Presentation software						
	Educational software						
Equipment	Desktop computer						
	Data projector						
	Printers						
	Digital camera/video						
	Scanner						
	Electronic whiteboard						
	Control technology						
Targets	1						
	2						
	3						

Task 1.3 Auditing your needs	First of all have a look at the grid (you could photocopy Table 1.1 above) and tick the boxes in each row as they apply in terms of your **personal** skills and confidence, then in terms of your skills and confidence in using them in your **teaching**.

Look back at your responses to the previous two tasks. What are the areas you need to focus on? You could colour or highlight your main priorities.

Next identify three priority areas for development. Be realistic! What do you really need to do? What opportunities are you going to have? Do you need to concentrate on basic skills in order to pass the QTS skills test (see the next section below). Don't be afraid to make changes as further opportunities arise. Record the areas you think you should concentrate on.

The QTS skills test

Everyone who wants to be a teacher needs to pass online tests in literacy, numeracy and ICT. These are little bit like the theory part of the driving test and you will need to book a time at a specified centre then complete the test on a computer. Your course tutor will be able to give you more information about where the local test centre is. This book does not aim to prepare you specifically to pass the QTS Skills test. However, if you tackle the issues covered in the tasks and activities you should develop the skills that you need to pass this test. The test is fairly basic. It only assesses your skills in using ICT (set in a professional context), rather than in using ICT to teach. If you are a confident user already you may need very little further practice, though you should be aware that the test assesses particular skills through specific tasks and you are likely to find these questions easier if you practise first. There are materials to help you practise on the Teacher Training Agency's website.

In order to pass the skills test you will need:

- **general** ICT skills such as:
  finding your way around the computer;
  opening programs and files;
  choosing appropriate applications;
  copying between files and applications;
  using the mouse (double clicking, highlighting);
  printing (and altering print settings);

- **specific** skills for handling or coping with information:
  researching and categorising information;
  using an e-mail program and address book;
  searching a database (including using precise queries);
  using a web browser effectively (navigating forwards and backwards and using hyperlinks);

finding your way around a spreadsheet;

developing and modelling information:

adding records to a database, finding and sorting;

using functions and tools in a word processor (inserting pictures, using styles);

using a spreadsheet (including basic formulas);

organising records or layouts or data and numbers in a spreadsheet;

filtering e-mails;

moving text, pictures and slides around different programs;

presenting and communicating information:

displaying and managing text (font, style, layout, margins etc.);

formatting data (including between spreadsheets and tables);

managing e-mails (copying, forwarding);

preparing a presentation (altering styles, adding buttons, and transitions).

Many of these skills will be those that you can already do or will be able to practise during your course. You should look to see which of these you feel confident about and which you may need to work on. You can arrange to take the test at any time. Make sure you use the practice materials before you sit the test. The test itself is timed and this can put an added pressure on you, even as a confident user. You may not be able to do things the way you are most familiar with (such as using particular keyboard shortcuts) or the test programs may not show things the way the program you use most often does. Get used to exploring menus and looking for other options when you use new software. This will help you to develop more flexible skills.

Summary

- In order to meet the requirements for Qualified Teacher Status you should be able to use ICT confidently and effectively. You will need to pass an online test in basic skills in using ICT.
- You should become familiar with a range of ICT equipment and software. This is to develop your own skills to help you with your professional responsibilities.
- You have to be able to teach ICT to your pupils as part of their curriculum entitlement. This is both in terms of ICT as a subject and in terms of opportunities for ICT across the curriculum.
- You also need to develop your understanding of ICT or develop your 'ICT capability'. This is so that you are able to be judicious in when, where and how you choose to use ICT to support the learning of your pupils.

Suggestions for further information and reading

Lyn Dawes and Marylin Leask's 'Undertaking an ICT Self Audit' in M. Leask and J. Meadows (2000) *Teaching and Learning with ICT in the Primary School*. London: Routledge Falmer. Has further, more detailed audit lists for different areas of ICT.

Passey, D. and Samways, B. (1997) *Information Technology: Supporting change through teacher education*. London: Chapman and Hall.
Contains international perspectives on the challenge that information and communications technology poses to teacher education and features views of trainee teacher experiences with computers as well as insights into the ways in which ICT can be used to link teachers and students.

www.qca.org.uk
Curriculum guidance for the Foundation Stage as well as the Schemes of Work (for ICT science, history, geography, music, PE) can be found on QCA's website.

Information about the skills test can be found on the Teacher Training Agency's website: http://www.tta.gov.uk/training/skillstests/.

Ferrigan, C. (2001) *The ICT Skills Test*. Exeter: Learning Matters.
Offers practical advice about the test.

2 Text, pictures and multimedia

Displaying and changing text is the most familiar form of information that most people undertake on computers. Word-processing programs are designed to make this task easy so that you can type (or even dictate) words and sentences into the computer, then make changes to alter the *content* of this information (by adding, deleting or redrafting) or its *form* (by changing the font, size or style). As computers have become more sophisticated it has become easier to add pictures to text, whether these are produced on a computer (such as clip art or drawn or painted in another program) or by other means (such as scanned-in drawings or digital photographs). Specific software helps you to work with pictures (images and graphics) more effectively, and you will need to understand the implications of the way computers work with pictures. Adding photographs, sound or video clips to a page of text is now relatively straightforward and most computers now offer full multimedia capabilities where such combinations are easy to achieve. This ranges from just putting together text and pictures to more sophisticated combinations of words, pictures, sound or video.

This chapter outlines the range of ways that ICT can be used to handle text, pictures and multimedia, and how these features can be used by you as a teacher as well as what the expectations are for how primary age pupils should be able to exploit such tools. As software has developed the distinctions between different types of programs has become blurred so that most so-called 'word processors' have drawing tools in them and can now handle pictures, sound and even video clips. Most basic software therefore has some of the features of 'desktop publishing' programs used to produce newspapers and magazines, though you may still come across references to particular programs as either 'word processing' or 'desktop publishing'. You will also need to be able to use drawing and painting programs (or at least the common drawing and painting tools that are found in programs frequently used in schools, such as Textease or Microsoft Word's drawing tools).

Expectations for you as a teacher

As a trainee teacher you should be confident to use this kind of software, which is designed to manage and manipulate text (such as Microsoft's Word in the Office suite). You should be able to undertake tasks for yourself (such as writing assignments) AND to prepare materials for your actual teaching. You will also need to become familiar with some of the common programs that are used in schools and how the features of these programs may differ from other versions of the software.

You will need to be aware of the potential of ICT for supporting your work in the preparation of teaching materials. This might be by using the same piece of text for different pupils in different ways by changing the font size, changing sentence length, adjusting the range of vocabulary, or supporting reading through highlighting or hot-linking key words or adding sound files. The same basic resource could then be adapted for use in different forms by teacher and pupils, e.g. as a printout, a transparency for an overhead projector, an electronic 'worksheet' for use by pupils on screen, or as an electronic presentation using a digital projector or electronic whiteboard.

It will always be important to recognise that your use of ICT will become more efficient as you become more familiar with the potential of ICT and as you develop a bank of resources which you can adapt in the future. One tremendous advantage of electronic media is that they can be exchanged and shared with colleagues either on your course or over the Internet.

You will need to be familiar with basic drawing and painting programs and ways to get hold of pictures on a computer (insert or import) and make changes to them (manipulate images). Pictures on a computer come in a wide variety of formats. Most of the time this does not matter as software is designed to work with this range (the Glossary contains information on most of the common file formats). There are two important differences which you will need to be aware of, however. The first of these is that some pictures, called bitmap images, cannot be enlarged without losing quality. The bigger you make the picture the more you will lose definition (edges of objects will become jagged and the colour 'blocky'). The computer records where each colour starts and finishes (including blank or empty areas). Each time it shows the picture it effectively has to paint it again. Other types of pictures, often referred to as vector graphics, can be enlarged without this happening. These object-oriented drawing programs produce pictures stored as a series of mathematical equations (vectors) which tell the computer where to start or place different colours or lines. No matter how large you make the picture it will retain smooth lines and even colours.

The second major difference is in the way that these different pictures can be changed or manipulated. With vector graphics that have been created with drawing tools the computer can separate the shapes and move them independently, so if you have created a worksheet for use in a mathematics lesson with pictures of different types of shapes, each of these is placed in a layer on the screen and you can make them overlap, then add more shapes or reorganise and resize them. With a painting program it is like working on a canvas: once you have painted a circle over a triangle you can't separate them again. You might be able to copy and paste parts of the painting, but it will literally be like cutting out a section of a painting and sticking it down on top of another part of the painting.

The details of these differences are not important, but some of the consequences are. One consequence in these different types of files is the amount of memory they take up. Vector graphics files are relatively small because the information is stored mathematically and the computer effectively calculates the picture on screen each time it displays it. Because a bitmap image is effectively painted, the computer has to use more memory to record where all the colours go. File size is an issue, as even a medium quality digital photograph stored as a bitmap file may well be too big for a floppy disk. If you want to work with such pictures and move them from computer to computer (such as at home or college and school) you will need to learn what to do to make this easier. The second main consequence is that, wherever possible, you should work with drawing tools to produce activities as you will be able to edit them more easily in the future.

A framework for thinking about ICT

It is helpful to consider why using ICT might be better than other approaches. What are the particular features or characteristics that make it such a powerful tool?

The Teacher Training Agency devised a framework to identify these features which was used to underpin the New Opportunities Fund programme of ICT training for serving teachers as well as the first version of the National Curriculum for ITT (4/98).

- **Interactivity**: what feedback can ICT provide that will help childen to learn?
- **Provisionality**: how can we make changes or develop ideas using ICT that focus attention on the key aspects of learning?
- **Capacity and range**: how can we use a wider range of information or what types of information can we use with ICT that would not be available (or available so easily) through other means?
- **Speed and automatic functions**: what can be done routinely or more quickly with ICT so that we can focus attention on the key aspects of learning?

Some specific features of word-processing software that you might want to exploit in your teaching could include some of the *automatic* functions for hiding or reordering text for pupils to uncover. Through such uses, your pupils can apply their understanding of spelling rules, grammatical structures and style in order to make reasonable predictions. Using the thesaurus function in word-processing software can enable pupils *quickly* to explore the effect of language choices on meaning, e.g. through substituting synonyms. *Automatic* spelling checkers can indicate possible spelling errors and suggest alternatives. Computerised speech is often available in word processors, particularly those used in schools. These talking word processors can both support pupils' learning in reading and writing by giving them direct spoken *feedback* or confirmation in response to their reading or writing. Similarly talking books can provide support by combining text, a spoken (or computer 'read') version of the text with additional pictures or animations on screen. However, there are implications for you to consider in order to achieve specific teaching objectives when using these automatic functions. For example, with word-processing software, grammar and spell checkers may help to improve the accuracy and presentation of pupils' writing. However, you will need to be aware that their use may not help to achieve teaching objectives related to spelling and handwriting, so these skills will have to be covered through other teaching activities. Similarly if you have added picture or spoken sound clues to a piece of writing to support more *interactive* and independent use of a text, you will not be able to assess the pupils' reading of the text alone.

One of the main advantages of ICT is the *range* of material that you can find in written form. The Internet offers a vast amount of written material that can be adapted for use in lessons (see also Chapter 4). As a result your pupils can have access to a wider range of texts and text types from a variety of sources, through CD-ROM and the Internet, than were previously available. Pupils can also communicate with other writers and have access to critical comment on their work through this inter-action. You can also easily choose from texts for a variety of purposes including, for example, historical documents written in the style of a previous generation or modern texts written as news reports. This not only helps to teach aspects of English (such as understanding different genres of writing), but helps you to ensure pupils stay motivated through the range and variety of materials that you can use.

Another feature you need to be aware of is how the *provisional* nature of informa-tion on computers can allow text to be updated quickly and easily in response to new information, for example when creating and updating a newspaper article. Pupils can redraft their writing to improve accuracy, to change the style or to address specific audiences, thus improving their communication skills and the quality of what they write. ICT helps to make this process more efficient as you can get pupils only to make changes where they are needed, rather than laboriously reworking a complete piece of writing.

This aspect of provisionality can be exploited as you can edit the same piece of text for different purposes. You could change the font and size to make writing easier to read for presentation on a large screen or you could adjust the sentence length, using synonyms for less familiar vocabulary or highlighting key words to support reading comprehension. You could similarly develop a range of activities with different levels of support for different levels of attainment in your class. In this way the easily changeable nature of information on a computer can help to make the time invested in learning how to use it extremely efficient.

ICT can enable pupils to adapt and present the same information in a range of different forms for different audiences. You could advertise a school event to parents, to the local secondary school, or to local community groups by different means, such as a taped advertisement for local radio; a leaflet; a poster; or a web page. All of these could start from the same piece of text about the event, but then the text could be adapted for these different purposes.

Some uses of ICT can make a unique contribution, such as using a video camera to record a class discussion. This can allow pupils to review and reflect on their own contributions, which can increase their confidence as speakers. Taking short video clips and annotating them with recorded speech or text could form the basis of a pupils' own assessment of their developing skills.

When creating text using word-processing software, teachers and pupils can review the development of their writing by saving documents at regular intervals or using automatic facilities to track changes in their writing.

As with all other resources, careful preparation and planning are needed when using ICT as part of your teaching. For example, it is better to teach pupils to refine searches and review and reflect on their strategies rather than allowing them to randomly roam on the Internet or explore a CD-ROM without clear objectives. The pupils may well appear to be gainfully occupied, but you have to be critically aware of what it is that they are learning.

Just like all teaching resources and equipment, ICT should only be used when it can effectively or efficiently support the teaching of clear learning objectives with the particular pupils you are teaching. So, for example, a word processor can help pupils to compose and redraft a text because it is easier to manipulate and change writing on screen than on a hand-written page. It is particularly efficient where pupils do not have to enter all of the text, as this tends to be a rather laborious process. This takes advantage of the provisional nature of the information stored on a computer. Altering a file which you have already created, perhaps personalising a narrative in the first person from a third person account which you have written, can be an excellent way to achieve this focus. The pupils only need to concentrate on what needs to be changed. In this example it would allow a clear focus on first and third person pronouns and verb forms. Preparing a file in a word processor in which pupils are asked to use a wider range of connectives than 'and' and create a more exciting text would be another possibility. Using a word processor more frequently has implications for the development of pupils' handwriting skills, and some aspects of writing could not be assessed if pupils have used other software tools on the computer such as spelling or grammar checkers!

Similar criteria apply for other subjects. In history, for instance, you might ask the pupils to compare a CD-ROM with books for the evaluation of sources of information. However, the task would need to be focused on the *content* of the different sources. If the pupils evaluated the *process* of finding the information then the task would become an ICT task, because pupils would be considering the advantages and disadvantages of electronic sources of information. The teaching of critical thinking strategies, such as how to identify the relevant information or to distinguish between bias and objectivity, becomes increasingly important when ICT is used because of the ease and availability of information on the Internet.

If you decide to use ICT for a writing activity it should always be because it is more efficient or more effective than doing it another way. For example, copy-typing a hand-written draft into a 'best' version on the computer is a waste of the computer's (and the pupils') time! Word-processing software is valuable because it is good for drafting and redrafting on screen, and not just because the text looks prettier. You should avoid ICT activities which do not develop and extend pupils' language skills. There is little value, therefore, in letting pupils spend a whole lesson experimenting with different fonts, sizes and colours, for example. Hence the need for clearly identified learning objectives which the pupils understand and know how to achieve.

Entitlements and expectations for primary age pupils in using ICT for text, pictures and multimedia

The expectations and entitlements for pupils regarding ICT are clearly set out in available documentation. This is in the Curriculum Guidance for the Foundation Stage (QCA, 2000) and in the National Curriculum (QCA, 2000). Additional information is contained in the Frameworks for Teaching Literacy and Mathematics (DfEE, 1998), for these subjects and in the more detailed guidance produced by the QCA in their Schemes of Work. All children have an entitlement to learn how to use ICT as part of their education and this is clearly set out in these documents. As their skills develop you will be able to include ICT as a teaching strategy to support their learning in other subjects. Once pupils can use a keyboard and basic word processor it is more effective to teach them about redrafting using ICT than to get them to correct and rewrite their work, particularly if they are producing several drafts.

In the **Foundation Stage** children are expected to show an interest in ICT and should be encouraged to add to their first-hand experience of the world through the use of ICT. Early years practitioners are expected to provide opportunities for the use of ICT to develop skills across the areas of learning, for example a talking word processor to develop language and communication, vocabulary and writing, talking books for early reading, a paint program to develop early mark making, a telephone for speaking and listening, CD-ROMs, video and television and musical tapes to find things out.

At **Key Stage 1** children will need to learn how to gather information from a variety of sources (ICT 1a) enter and store information (ICT 1b), to use text, tables, images and sounds to develop their ideas (ICT 2a) and to select from and add to existing information (ICT 2b). They should also be taught to share their ideas by presenting information and a variety of forms (ICT 3a) and to present their work effectively (ICT 3b). Opportunities to use these skills are identified in other subjects of the curriculum such as in history (Hist 4a) and geography in supporting their recording with digital photographs (Geog 4a) or accessing a range of texts (Geog 2d; 6b).

At **Key Stage 2** children should be taught to talk about the information that they need and how to prepare information (ICT 1b), how to organise and reorganise it (ICT 2a) how to share and exchange it (ICT 3a), as well as consider its suitability for its intended audience and its content and quality (ICT 3b). Again there are clear links across the curriculum such as in history (Hist 4a; 4b; 5c) geography (Geog 1e) and science (Sci 2h).

In both **Key Stages 1 and 2** children should be taught to review, modify and evaluate their work as it progresses (ICT 4a; 4b; 4c) as well as have the opportunity to work with a range of information (ICT 5a) and explore a variety of ICT tools (ICT 5b).

Tasks for you to provide evidence of effective use of ICT to meet the Standards

Task 2.1 Writing an assignment	Use ICT to submit a written assignment for your course and use the features of the word-processing software to ensure you meet the presentation requirements.

This task can provide evidence for the following skills:

- creating, opening, saving (and backing up!) files;
- changing font, size and style (e.g. for heading or for appropriate bold, under-lining and italic for references in the bibliography);
- altering page margins (to meet the submission requirements);
- adding page numbering;
- using other features appropriately (e.g. page breaks, bullet points, tabs and indents);
- using support tools or on-screen help (such as spellchecker or guides to take you through more complex tasks such as setting tabs or using styles).

Task 2.2 Preparing resources	Use ICT to prepare specific resources for teaching a lesson or an activity with a group or class of pupils.

This task could provide evidence for a wide range of skills from basic (such as combining text and pictures to make a printed worksheet) through developing hybrid resources (such as templates or writing frames that can be printed or completed on screen) to advanced (such as creating interactive forms for pupils to use on screen or a document with added sound or video). You should plan to make a series of resources during your training that will develop and extend your ICT skills. The following skills may provide a degree of challenge:

- using the 'Save as . . .' feature to create a new document efficiently;
- inserting text and pictures from other documents or a clip-art resource;
- adding digital photographs or scanned images;
- editing or manipulating pictures;
- protecting documents (such as by making them read-only);
- creating templates (so that your original document will not be changed);
- using styles (such as for headings so that you can set the font and size easily);
- using painting tools (that create bitmap images which lose quality when they are enlarged);

- using drawing tools (that create vector graphics which can be increased in size without losing quality);
- including sections (such as to produce a newspaper style with columns);
- exploiting the forms tools to create pick lists or drop-down menus for pupils to use;
- adding hyperlinks to take pupils to other resources or activities;
- incorporating sounds or short video-clips to enhance a learning activity.

Task 2.3 Planning for learning	Plan, use and evaluate the contribution of ICT in a series of teaching activities where: 1 you use aspects of ICT involving text, pictures and multimedia (such as to present a shared text or in a guided writing activity); 2 the pupils use aspects of ICT involving text, pictures and multimedia (such as completing a writing frame that you have created as a template).

This activity should be in an area of the curriculum *other* than ICT where you identify how ICT can contribute to teaching and learning of that subject (or subjects). Make sure you read Chapters 6–11, which will help you plan activities in different areas of the curriculum.

Task 2.4 Developing pupils' ICT skills	Plan and teach a lesson or an activity which develops pupils' ICT skills and understanding in the use of text, pictures and multimedia.

This activity should be based on the National Curriculum for ICT and should contribute to developing pupils' ICT skills, knowledge and understanding or the development of their ICT capability (see Chapter 12 for more details). You will find the QCA scheme for ICT helpful in thinking about the activities that the children could undertake and the specific skills, knowledge and understanding that they might develop.

Summary

- You will need to become familiar with a range of software that works with text, pictures and sounds.
- This is both for you to be able to teach ICT to your pupils as part of their curriculum entitlement as well as to help you do the job of teaching effectively and efficiently.
- There are a range of different ways that computers deal with pictures which have practical consequences for the way that you can work with them.

Suggestions for further information and reading

Leask, M. and Meadows, J. (2000) *Teaching and Learning with ICT in the Primary School.* London: Routledge Falmer.
This book provides a good overview of the issues in teaching and learning as well as practical examples and advice.

www.becta.org.uk/technology/infosheets/
The British Education Communications and Technology Association provide a wealth of information on ICT and teaching and learning in schools. They offer a range of helpsheets on using ICT in different topics (such as portable computers or keyboarding skills) and different subjects (such as using ICT in the core curriculum at Key Stage 2) as well as research summaries about the use of ICT for teaching and learning.

www.qca.org.uk
Curriculum guidance for the Foundation Stage as well as the schemes of work (for ICT science, history, geography, music, PE) can be found on QCA's website.

www.ncaction.net
Practical examples of children's work using ICT are available on this website; these will give you a clear picture of the expectations at each stage for pupils' achievement with ICT.

3 Managing and understanding information

Managing and understanding information is where computers offer real benefits to the way that we work. This is the I in ICT. Not only can information be presented in different forms as we looked at in the last chapter, it can also be related in different ways. The commonest programs in this area are databases, spreadsheets and graphing (or charting) software, though the Internet uses and manages data and information in increasingly sophisticated ways.

This chapter outlines the range of ways that ICT can be used to manage information and how these features can be used by you as a teacher, as well as what the expectations are for how primary age pupils should be able to exploit such tools in order to develop their understanding.

Expectations for you as a teacher

As a trainee teacher you should be confident to use the kinds of software which are designed to manage information (such as in a spreadsheet like Microsoft's Excel in the Office suite or Microsoft's database program Access). You should be able to undertake tasks for yourself (such as using a spreadsheet to calculate and model costs or add up test scores and calculate averages) AND to prepare materials for your actual teaching (such as preparing a database, entering sample records for pupils to add further records or producing a graph from a spreadsheet as a resource for a mathematics lesson). You will also need to become familiar with some of the common programs that are used in schools and how the features of these programs may differ from other versions of similar software. This is particularly challenging in the area of databases, where educational versions of the programs can be a little quirky or dedicated to one particular task. For example, you will need to be able to use a type of database which sorts and organises information in a branching tree structure (for classifying living things, for example). It is very unlikely that you have encountered this type of program before (or ever will outside of the requirements for teaching at Key Stage 2).

Spreadsheets, graphing software and databases

A spreadsheet is a grid of boxes or 'cells' each of which contains a piece of information. This can be as text, a number (a value, a percentage, or as currency). Each cell has a unique address (a bit like a map reference) usually a number and a letter (so A1 refers to the cell at the top left-hand corner of the 'sheet'). This data can usually be sorted, searched and rearranged as in a database. Additionally each cell can be given instructions or programmed like a calculator to work out a total or an average of the values in other cells (a 'range'). This is where spreadsheets become powerful. Each little box in the grid can contain data (such as the cost of an item in a shop) or it can contain a calculation (the total cost of 10 items in the shop by adding up the individual cost of 10 specified items). It can also contain formulae (such as working out the VAT costs at 17.5 per cent for each item, then the total amount for each item). As a teacher you will need to show pupils how to use spreadsheets as part of their ICT curriculum: you can then use them to investigate aspects of numerical information in mathematics or science or other subjects of the curriculum.

Most spreadsheet programs, such as Microsoft's Excel, have built-in charting features that let you create a graph of the information in the spreadsheet. When using software to create graphs and charts, the main issue is not the technology. Drawing a pie chart with a computer is considerably easier than using a protractor to measure the angles for each of the sectors of the circle (the 'slices' of the 'pie'). However, the issue is the knowledge of mathematics that is required to know when using a pie chart is appropriate; in this case when it is meaningful to talk about the relative proportions of what is being shown in the chart and when there are no categories included with a zero value. The purpose of using graphing programs is to develop a better understanding of the numerical data that is shown in the graph.

When thinking about numerical data you can distinguish between three main types. First, *categorical* data such as *kind of pets*, which can be classified into categories such as *dogs*, *cats*, *birds*, *fish*. These categories are distinct (do not overlap) and cannot be put in a particular order (or at least an order that is not purely arbitrary such as alphabetical, which bears no relationship to the concept of 'pets'). The classification in *discrete* data, by contrast, can be ordered. So, for example, the *number of goals* scored in a football match could be 1, 2, 3, 4, 5 etc. But it is not meaningful to talk about half a goal. The values have to be whole numbers or discrete chunks. The final category is *continuous* data, which cannot be easily chunked into clear amounts. A graph showing the *height of the children* in a class is measured on a continuous scale and each child's height is going to be slightly different from another child's. The type of numerical data affects how it is collected, recorded and presented.

Databases are similar to spreadsheets in that they relate information in boxes (this time called 'fields'), to other information in the database. Databases can usually contain a greater range of types of information, however, such as numbers, text, pictures, or even video clips and sounds. At a basic level these programs are similar to a card index file (like an old library catalogue) where each card or 'record' contains standardised information such as the title, the author, date of publication (the 'fields'). The structure of the database remains the same for each record, however: they all have a space for each type of information, but only the information specified. You could add another field to a library record for 'abstract', but then you would have to go back through the database and add an abstract to each entry. These kinds of databases are sometimes called 'flatfile' or 'tabular' databases. You can usually see the whole database in a 'view' where the information is organised in rows and columns, rather like a spreadsheet, but you may not be able to alter or edit the information in this form. More complex databases are called *relational* databases because the way that information can be related is more flexible: you can reorganise the way that you see the data – sometimes called 'layouts' or 'views'. Information is 'tagged' rather than entered into pre-specified fields, and you can usually alter or edit information in any of the ways that you can see it. In this way it is easy to create mailing labels from a database of addresses, as well as writing personalised letters using information from the same database, but at each stage you can edit the information that you see. The National Curriculum and the National Numeracy Strategy's Framework for Teaching Mathematics also mention 'branching tree' or 'binary' databases. These are designed to help identify items, rather like a scientific key or taxonomy, by asking questions to which the answer is 'yes' or 'no'. The visual structure of the 'tree' is an excellent support to help pupils understand aspects of classification, and the nature of the program(s) forces pupils to be precise in their use of language to identify the 'key' questions. It is highly unlikely that pupils will ever use such a program outside of primary school, though it is argued that the benefits outweigh the investment of time and skills development on the part of teacher and pupils (see Figure 3.1).

In practice the distinctions outlined above between these different ways of managing information are blurred in many programs these days. You can often use a spreadsheet as a database and chart the results in the same piece of software.

You will need to be aware of the potential of programs such as these for supporting your work in your planning, the preparation of teaching materials and your assessment and record keeping, as well as for delivering aspects of the National Curriculum appropriate for your pupils. Again, however, it is fair to say that databases are simply not used efficiently in schools. Whilst it would be possible to have a school database with information on pupils, integrated with termly and weekly planning so that you could check to see what aspects of the curriculum a child missed through an extended absence, or simply to add assessment data, this rarely happens. Management information (such as class lists and dates of birth) are kept separate from teaching information (such as records of planning). This means that routine tasks like creating book labels by simply choosing a database layout for your class cannot be done from the class list that is already on a computer (somewhere) in school.

This issue gets to the heart of managing and understanding information. Whilst it is possible for computers to handle many of the regular tasks that schooling requires (like working out attendance totals on the class register) it would need the data to be entered into the computer first. If the register is completed with a paper and pen then it is simply too time-consuming to re-enter the information so that totals can be calculated automatically. Similarly with the database example outlined above, it would require a significant investment of time and money to get such a system operating. Time and money are two of the vital things that schools lack! The key decision is

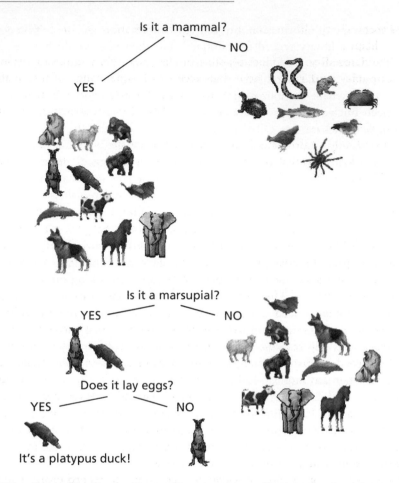

Figure 3.1   A branching tree with questions to sort a collection of animals

about efficiency and effectiveness. A computer can handle information extremely effectively. What you will need to decide is when it is an efficient use of your (or someone else's) time to enter information into a computer in order to manage that information. What makes this decision difficult is that the work usually needs to be done first. To get the benefit you will need to invest significant time and effort in setting up a system (or learning how to use a piece of software) and in keeping the information up to date.

Why is managing information with ICT important?

It is helpful to use the framework we introduced in the previous chapter to consider why using ICT might be more effective or more efficient than other approaches. What are the particular features or characteristics that make it such a powerful tool in terms of management of information?

- **Interactivity**: how does interacting with information or getting feedback help?
- **Provisionality**: how does adapting or changing information support learning?
- **Capacity and range**: how does access to a wider range of information (or types of information) benefit learning or what types of information can we use with ICT that would not be available (or available so easily) through other means?
- **Speed and automatic functions**: what can be done routinely or more quickly with ICT so that we can focus attention on the key aspects of learning?

Some specific features of information handling that you might want to exploit in your teaching might be some of the *automatic* functions for searching for relevant information on a CD-ROM or the Internet. This also provides *feedback* to pupils which can help them or require them to refine the key words or categories for their search. It is also *quicker* than using an index or manual search.

The *interactive* nature of ICT can help pupils to explore mathematical simulations or models. For example, pupils investigating fractions can watch a representation which shows the range of ways in which halves or thirds of different shapes can be constructed; pupils could also take advantage of the *provisional* nature of a spreadsheet model to explore the options available when planning a visit or a holiday on a fixed budget.

One of the main advantages of ICT is the *range* of material that you can find. You can access historical or geographical records and statistics and other mathematical information from CD-ROM or the Internet in order to provide pupils with real data with which they can work. The *capacity* of a database or spreadsheet to manage large quantities of information can also be a benefit. It is possible to manage larger quantities of information than with paper-based materials.

A temperature sensor can be connected to a computer to record changes over time *automatically*. The results can then also be analysed on computer to look at trends or to plot charts or graphs of results *quickly* and easily. This then increases the amount of time you have to discuss and interpret the results (rather than just drawing the graph).

As with all other resources, careful preparation and planning are needed when using ICT as part of your teaching. For example, it is better to teach pupils to refine searches and review and reflect on their strategies rather than allowing them to randomly roam on the Internet or explore a CD-ROM without clear objectives. The pupils may well appear to be gainfully occupied, but you have to be critically aware of what it is that they are learning.

Just like all teaching resources and equipment, ICT should only be used when it can effectively or efficiently support the teaching of clear learning objectives with the particular pupils you are teaching. So, for example, asking pupils to enter lots of records into a database is probably not a good use of their (or the computer's) time. It may be important for them to enter some data (and make occasional mistakes so that you can discuss the issue of the quality of information), but then they will need to work with the database, making queries and retrieving information, if they are to develop their understanding of how to handle information.

Entitlements and expectations for primary age pupils in using ICT for managing and understanding information

As with text pictures and multimedia, the expectations and entitlements for pupils regarding the management of information with ICT are clearly set out in available documentation. This is in the Curriculum Guidance for the Foundation Stage (QCA, 2000) and in the National Curriculum (QCA, 2000). Additional information is contained in the Frameworks for Teaching Literacy and Mathematics (DfEE, 1998), for these subjects and in the more detailed guidance produced by the QCA in their Schemes of Work. All children have an entitlement to learn how to use ICT as part of their education and this is clearly set out in these documents. As their skills develop you will be able to include ICT as a teaching strategy to support their learning in other subjects. Once pupils can use a spreadsheet or a database you can investigate data in a range of subjects to develop their understanding across the curriculum.

The Foundation Stage

Children are expected to show an interest in ICT and should be encouraged to add to their first-hand experience of the world through the use of ICT. Early years practitioners are expected to help children to become aware of technology around them in the setting, local environment and home, for example washing machines, street lights, telephones, cash registers and burglar alarms are all examples of handling and managing different types of information. It is the teacher's responsibility to stimulate all children's interest in ICT and other technology by providing opportunities for the use of ICT. This is also to develop skills across the areas of learning in order to help them to make sense of the world. This forms the foundation for later work in science, design and technology, history, geography, and information and communication technology (ICT) specifically. Examples might include talking about a computerised shop till which adds up the prices and tells you how much change to give, or a visit to a doctor's surgery where the computer records who needs to see the doctor or nurse. It is important to ensure that stereotypes are not reinforced and that both girls and boys are given equal opportunities to use and talk about ICT.

At Key Stage 1

In terms of the National Curriculum pupils in Key Stage 1 should develop their knowledge skills and understanding by (1a) gathering information from a variety of sources (such as from databases and CD-ROMs); (1b) entering and storing information in a variety of forms (including storing work in a prepared database); (1c) retrieving information that has been stored (such as from a CD-ROM). They should (2b) select from and add to information they have retrieved.

If you use the QCA scheme of work for ICT the children will learn how to recognise information in a variety of forms (ICT 1c), enter and store information (ICT 1b), to represent information graphically (as a pictogram) (ICT 1e), to give instructions (ICT 1f) and control a floor robot (ICT 2d) and to select from and add to existing information (ICT 2b). They will also be taught to find information on a CD-ROM (ICT 2c). Opportunities to use these skills are identified in other subjects of the curriculum such as using CD-ROMs in history (Unit 4) and geography, using a spreadsheet (Unit 2) or creating graphs (Geog Unit 1), handling and managing information in science (e.g. recording measurements in Unit 1B, Growing Plants, or Unit 2A, Health and Growth, or using a CD-ROM to investigate types of seeds in 2B, Plants and Animals in the Local Environment).

At Key Stage 2

In terms of the National Curriculum, pupils in Key Stage 2 should develop their knowledge, skills and understanding by (1a) talking about what information that they need and how they can find and use it (such as by searching the Internet or a CD-ROM). In addition they should (1b) prepare information and develop it using ICT (such as by creating a class database); and (1c) interpret information.

Following the QCA scheme the opportunities become more extensive as children are introduced to databases (QCA Unit 3c). Children should be taught to talk about the information that they need and how to prepare information (ICT 1b), how to organise and reorganise it (ICT 2a) how to share and exchange it (ICT 3a), as well as consider its suitability for its intended audience and its content and quality (ICT 3b). Again there are clear links across the curriculum such as in history (Hist 4a, 4b, 5c) geography (Geog 1e) and science (Sci 2h).

In both **Key Stages 1 and 2** children should be taught to review, modify and evaluate their work as it progresses (ICT 4a, 4b, 4c) as well as have the opportunity to work with a range of information (ICT 5a) and explore a variety of ICT tools (ICT 5b).

Tasks for you to provide evidence of effective use of ICT to meet the Standards

In order for you to review and assess your progress against the Standards for QTS, you will need to undertake a number of tasks that provide evidence that you can handle and manage information effectively. It is important to adapt these tasks appropriately for the context in which you are working.

| Task 3.1 Using a spreadsheet | Use a spreadsheet to create a simple recording grid for a class that you are teaching. |

This task can provide evidence for the following skills:

- creating, opening, saving (and backing up!) files;
- changing font, size and borders in cells to display the information effectively;
- printing a specific part of a spreadsheet to fill a page (such as by using the 'Set print area' and 'Page setup options');
- using formulae in spreadsheets (if you enter the data and calculate totals or averages).

Task 3.2 Using a spreadsheet or database for teaching	Use ICT to prepare resources for teaching:

EITHER by creating a graph or chart suitable for the age group you are teaching where you can ask questions about the information as part of the oral/mental starter of a mathematics lesson;

OR by preparing a database that your class can add some further information to and then retrieve information from and ask questions which the database can answer.

This task could provide evidence for a wide range of skills from basic – creating a graph from a spreadsheet through developing resources (such as spreadsheets of mathematical calculations that can be printed or completed on screen) – to advanced (such as creating interactive spreadsheets and databases for pupils to use on screen or where they get feedback about their responses) (see Figure 3.2).

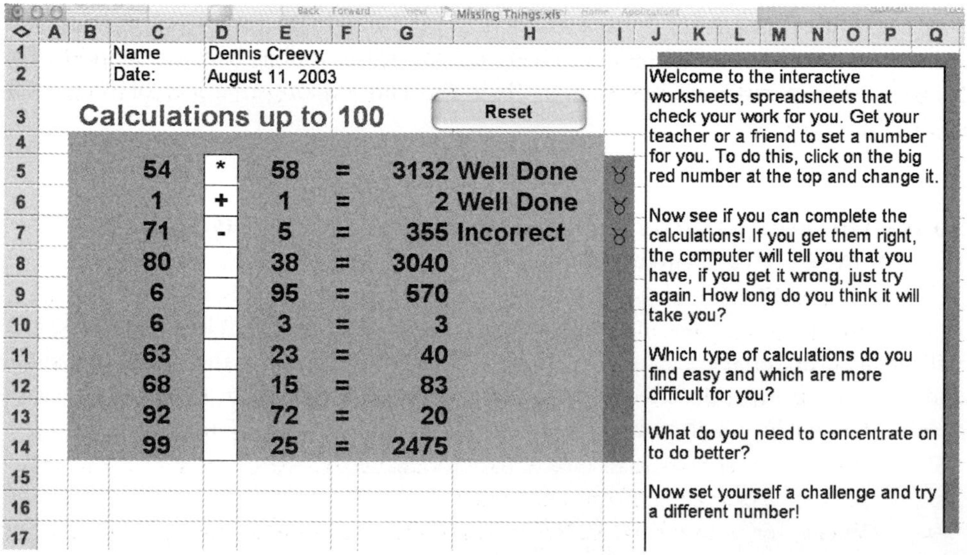

Figure 3.2 An example of an interactive spreadsheet created using Excel

Task 3.3 Developing pupils' information handling skills	Plan and teach a lesson or an activity which develops pupils' ICT skills and understanding in the handling of information.

This activity should be based on the National Curriculum for ICT and should contribute to developing pupils' ICT skills, knowledge and understanding or their ICT capability (see Chapter 12 for more details). You will find the QCA scheme for ICT helpful in thinking about the activities that the children could undertake and the specific skills, knowledge and understanding that they might develop.

You should plan to make a series of resources during your training that will develop and extend your ICT skills.

Task 3.4 Planning for learning with information	Plan, use and evaluate the contribution of ICT in a series of teaching activities where: 1 you use aspects of ICT involving handling information (such as presenting a spreadsheet or database as part of a teaching activity); 2 the pupils use aspects of ICT involving handling information (such as creating a graph from a table of data or searching for information on a CD-ROM) but where the learning objectives are in a subject other than ICT (such as geography or science).

These activities should be in an area of the curriculum *other* than ICT, where you identify how ICT can contribute to teaching and learning of that subject (or subjects). Make sure you read Chapters 6–11, which will help you plan activities in different areas of the curriculum.

Summary

- You will need to become familiar with a range of software that handles information, particularly spreadsheets and databases. Although this will be time-consuming, databases potentially offer much more efficient and effective ways to manage information than most schools currently use.
- You also need to be able to teach ICT to your pupils as part of their curriculum entitlement, and exploit opportunities to develop and use these skills in other areas of the curriculum.
- There are a range of different ways that computers manage information which have practical consequences for the way that you can work with them.

Suggestions for further information and reading

Fox, B., Montague-Smith, A. and Wilkes, S. (2000) *Using ICT in Primary Mathematics: Practice and possibilities*. London: David Fulton.
Contains specific ideas and advice on using databases and spreadsheets in mathematics.

Somekh, B. and Davis, N. (1997) *Using Information Technology Effectively in Teaching and Learning: Studies in pre-service and in-service teacher education*. London: Routledge.
Invaluable examples of the development of the use of ICT in schools. See Chapter 4 in particular.

Higgins, S. (2003) 'Does ICT make mathematics teaching more effective?', in I. Thompson (ed.) *Enhancing Primary Mathematics Teaching*. Milton Keynes: Open University Press.
Offers an overview of the way that ICT can support teaching and learning in primary mathematics.

4 Communicating with and through ICT

Communication is now literally at the centre of information technology. Since the Stephenson Report in 1996 and the national superhighways' initiative (DfEE, 1997a) communication was added to IT to make it ICT. The intention of the change was to reflect the revolution that has started in the way that we communicate and in the way that computers and other information technologies exchange information with each other. The pace of change is rapid in this area. We are starting to see more integration of different technologies such as mobile phones and computers, and it is difficult to predict how these changes will offer opportunities in schools to develop learning and teaching. ICT can be used as a medium of communication where it transmits and exchanges text, pictures and sound *through* the computer (such as e-mail or video-conferencing) or where the technology is used to enhance aspects of presentation such as displaying text on screen (or to be printed out) where you are communicating *with* ICT.

A further important distinction to bear in mind when thinking about communication and ICT is whether the exchange of information requires the other person to be there (such as a telephone call or video-conference) or whether the communication can take place by an exchange where each person can respond in their own time (such as e-mail). This distinction is based on the time of the exchange: synchronous communications are where both parties have to be together; asynchronous where they do not. These terms are not important, but the idea that they express is. It helps us to think about how ICT can support communication.

Expectations for you as a teacher

As a trainee teacher you should be confident to use software which helps you to communicate with and through ICT. You will need to be able to use the Internet to find and exchange information to help you with your professional responsibilities as

Table 4.1 Asynchronous and synchronous communication with and through ICT

	Through ICT	With ICT

Synchronous	ICT is used to transmit and exchange information to people who are not in the same location, but are using the technology at the same time
	e.g. video-conferencing
	    chat-rooms
		ICT is used to support communication to an audience that is present at the same time
		e.g. PowerPoint presentations
		    interactive whiteboards

Asynchronous	ICT is used to transmit and exchange information to people who are not in the same location, and who respond in their own time
	e.g. e-mail
	    discussion groups
		ICT is used to communicate information but there is no exchange needed
		e.g. web-pages
		    e-learning materials

well as develop skills in using ICT to present information to the pupils that you are teaching. For the purposes of this chapter we are including not only e-mail and web browsers, but also other specialist software for communication – presentation tools such as Microsoft's PowerPoint or Apple's Keynote or specialist programs which work on interactive whiteboards such as Promethean's Active Studio or RM's Easiteach. You will also need to ensure that you can teach the aspects of ICT that involve communication for the age groups that you are training to teach.

The Internet: e-mail and web browsers

The Internet is the general term used to describe the communication and exchange of information in all its forms between computers across the world. This includes e-mail, video-conferencing, file transfers and web pages.

Web browsers

The World Wide Web (WWW or just 'the web') is the network of 'pages' of information written in a specific code or language (hypertext mark-up language or html) that particular software called 'browsers' can read. The commonest of these programs is Microsoft's Internet Explorer, though some computers use other web browsers such as Netscape or Apple's Safari or Acorn's Fresco.

You can look at information that is on another computer by 'pointing' your browser to 'look' at information on another computer. It then makes a temporary copy of that information in a 'window' on your computer. To do this your computer needs to know where to look. It uses an address or URL (Uniform Resource Locator) which specifies a particular 'page' on a particular computer. On the web most addresses start with 'http://'. This stands for 'hypertext transport protocol' and lets your computer know how to interpret what it finds on the other computer: a sort of ICT Esperanto. You do not need to know the details of how all of this works (please see Appendix C if you would like a light-hearted introduction to the geek-speak of the technology world), but you do need to be aware of the implications.

In order to view web pages on computers around the world you need to be connected to the Internet. This has advantages and disadvantages. It means that you have access to a fantastic resource of information, materials, programs and ideas that you can use in your teaching. The downside is that you have to wade through commercial interests, irrelevant and inaccurate information and avoid pornography and other possible dangers. This is particularly the case where children have use of the Internet – don't forget that Internet access works in both directions – if you have access, the rest of the world (potentially) has access to you and the children in your class.

You therefore need to learn how to ensure that the Internet is *safe* if you intend pupils to use it (or parts of it). All schools should have an Internet policy or an acceptable use policy and will have some kind of restrictions on what you can access on the Internet. You will need to check what these are and what the parents of the children in the schools where you are working expect.

The next issue is with the *quantity* of information. There are literally millions (if not billions) of pages on the web. You have to find relevant information that will be useful. Imagine a huge second-hand bookshop where someone has mixed up all of the books on the shelves (or better still removed all the spines and thrown the books into a vast heap on the floor). You know that there is something useful in there, but you are not sure where. This is what the Internet is like. Fortunately there are ways to search and locate information, using search engines and indexes. No search engine or index covers more that a fraction of the content available on the web, but it means you should be able to find *something* valuable. Please see Appendix A for more specific information on searching the web.

The final issue is to do with the *quality* of information that is available on the Internet. It is not the same as published books where there have (usually) been some quality controls on what is produced. Anyone with a computer connected to the Internet can put up a web page. You will need to be much more critical of what you see and evaluate its quality and appropriateness (even on 'educational' websites). Please see Appendix B for a list of sources of information where the quality is usually sound.

E-mail programs

These programs enable you to send electronic 'letters' to another person who has an electronic address (an e-mail address). In addition you can attach other information to these messages, such as pictures or other computer files: a bit like sending electronic parcel post. Most programs are fairly easy to use, though there are some general distinctions between web-based e-mail such as Hotmail or Yahoo!Mail which work through web pages and separate e-mail programs, such as Microsoft's Outlook, Eudora (QUALCOMM) or Pegasus (David Harris). The key common features are the ability to send and receive messages and to manage or file your messages in an 'inbox' and 'outbox'. You will have an address book to save you typing in addresses each time and you can easily copy messages you send to other people and forward messages you have received. These features should be used with caution. Just because you find a message you have been sent hilarious that doesn't mean that everyone in your address book will; you *can* send your 96 digital holiday snaps to everyone you know who has an e-mail address but it does not mean that they will all appreciate them cluttering up their inbox.

As with the other types of software discussed in the previous two chapters, there is considerable convergence in the current development of software. Whereas in the past you needed a file transfer program, a web browser, a separate e-mail program, a text-chat program and a video-chat program if you wanted to use all of the features that the Internet offered, most of these functions can now be managed within a single program, a web browser such as Internet Explorer.

Presentation software

ICT offers a significant step forward in terms of presenting information to a group or class of pupils. With a blackboard, whiteboard or flipchart you are limited to your own writing and artistic skills. With an overhead projector you can project text and pictures which have been written, drawn or printed onto transparent acetates to project them onto a screen, but with a computer connected to a projector you can combine a range of types of information which include dynamic information (moving diagrams and pictures) as well as video and the more usual text and pictures. Showing a picture of a human body, then having labels appear for parts of the body, followed by a cutaway version showing where internal organs are located and then circulation of blood flow around the body provides a clear representation of how the body works in a way that it is difficult to achieve using other methods.

Anything you can see on a computer screen can be projected onto a large screen for a class to see. So you could edit a piece of text in a word-processing document and talk about how the meaning changes as you alter particular words; the class will all be able to see the text you are talking about. Similarly with a spreadsheet or graphing program, you could add data to a table of figures and see a graph of that information change on screen. Such dynamic uses of computers are powerful, helping children to focus on important aspects of information and make connections in their learning.

Specific programs are also available for presentation. Many of these have been developed for the business world, but with a little creativity the tools and features that they offer can be used to good effect in classrooms. These programs enable you to create slides or screens to which you can add text pictures and sound. In addition you can control the way these elements appear on the screen. A series of these slides can then be combined into a 'slideshow', so you could, for example, present a poem verse by verse in large text so that pupils can see and read the text with you. An obvious example is Microsoft's PowerPoint. Although it was designed for use in the business world it is now widely used in schools (and even by pupils in Key Stage 1).

Specialist educational software has also been designed for interactive or electronic whiteboards. These are large wall-mounted screens where you can control the computer (as you would with a mouse) by touching the screen with your finger or a special pen.

You can then stand in front of the class as you use the computers to present information. This is often more convenient than sitting at a laptop or desktop computer and talking to the class. It feels more natural to talk to the class from in front of the electronic whiteboard and can be easier to demonstrate things using the interactivity of the board. Any program that runs on a computer can be used on such technology. In addition most of the suppliers of the boards have proprietary programs for education which take advantage of the possibilities of interacting with the computer through the screen (it is hard to enter text, for example, so most of them have some kind of annotation tools to let you 'write' on the screen). Other specialist software is also available. For example, the National Numeracy Strategy have sponsored the development of 'inter-active teaching programs' (ITPs) with particular tools such as number grids, number lines or clocks which can be used by a teacher with access to an electronic whiteboard.

There are other technological possibilities. Tablet PCs let you control a computer using a wireless tablet or a slate, which the teacher can hold and use while pupils look at a large screen. You can also get wireless keyboards and mice so that you can pass these input devices to pupils who can then interact with what is being displayed to the class.

What is at the heart of these developments is the effective integration of techno-logy into the classroom. Once the technology does not get in the way of teaching (as a laptop, projector, large screen and metres and metres of connecting wires can) then the teacher and pupils can focus on the content of the learning that is taking place. New technological possibilities offer new teaching (or pedagogical) possibilities. Recent developments seem to be making this technology more transparent in the classroom. Effective communication is the essence of effective teaching. Communications techno-logy provides opportunities to develop more effective communication and more effective teaching.

Why is communicating with and through ICT important?

It is helpful to use the framework we looked at in the previous two chapters to consider why using ICT might be more effective or more efficient than other approaches. What are the particular features or characteristics that make it such a powerful tool in terms of communication of information?

- **Interactivity**: how does interacting with information or getting feedback help?
- **Provisionality**: how does being able to make changes in information make communication more effective?
- **Capacity and range**: how does access across distances or using different forms of communication (such as text, voice, a picture or live video) help?
- **Speed and automatic functions**: what can be done routinely or more quickly with ICT so that we can use communication as part of the learning process?

Some specific features of communication that you might want to exploit in your teaching may use some of the *capacity and range* functions of ICT, for example by sending e-mails or faxes to classes in other parts of the country (or around the world). This also offers *interactivity* to pupils in that responses are received by the computers. It is also *quicker* (and cheaper) than using postal services.

The *interactive* nature of other kinds of communication, such as text and video chat, are clear, though such opportunities are not often exploited in schools (and would require careful monitoring). However, it would be possible to arrange for an 'expert', an author perhaps, to communicate with the class or a group of pupils to capitalise on this aspect of technology.

The Internet is now a major medium of communication and pupils will need to learn how specific software that lets you interact with the content works. One of the main advantages of the web is the *range* of material that you can find, though when using a search engine it is the *speed* of the response and the *capacity* of the search engine to look through vast amounts of information *automatically* that offer such benefits.

As a teacher you can also exploit the benefits that ICT offers for communication within the classroom. These features are related to the advantages outlined in the two previous chapters, in terms of the type of information and the way that you can help pupils to make connections between ideas by relating content on screen (such as between tables and graphs) – using the aspects of *capacity* and *range*. Presentation software lets you do this *quickly* and *automatically* by allowing you to present information as a slide show. Once you have developed one presentation, it is easy to develop or re-work the content as the basis for another lesson or activity, taking advantage of the *provisional* nature of content when using ICT.

As with all other resources, careful preparation and planning are needed when using ICT as part of your teaching. Using the web and communicating with e-mail raises significant issues about children's safety and the appropriateness of the information that they can view. Is it also all too easy to overuse presentation software, because it is so convenient, with the result that the pupils become bored with bullet points flying in from the right, or they are more interested by the sound effects than the content.

Just like all teaching resources and equipment, ICT should only be used when it can effectively or efficiently support the teaching of clear learning objectives with the particular pupils you are teaching. The benefit of using e-mail to communicate is that it offers a means of exchanging information with other people (children and adults) who it would otherwise be difficult to contact. It is of little value if all that happens is a ritual exchange of messages with children in another class whose teacher you happen to know.

Entitlements and expectations for primary age pupils in using ICT for communicating information

As with the other areas of ICT, the expectations and entitlements for pupils regarding communication with ICT are clearly set out in available documentation. For the Foundation Stage and in Key Stage 1 there is, however, relatively little on using ICT to communicate *through* (with e-mail or video-conferencing). The emphasis is on using ICT to present information (using text, pictures and displays): to communicate *with*. As their skills develop you will be able to include ICT as a teaching strategy to support their learning in other subjects. Once pupils are familiar with web and e-mail programs there are a variety of ways that you can use them to develop their understanding across the curriculum.

The Foundation Stage

Children are expected to use ICT to develop skills across the areas of learning, for example a talking word processor to develop language and communication, vocabulary and writing, talking books for early reading, a paint program to develop early mark-making, a telephone for speaking and listening. It is the teacher's responsibility to stimulate all children's interest in ICT and other technology by providing opportunities for the use of ICT. This is also intended to develop skills across the areas of learning in order to help them to make sense of the world. Opportunities can also be found in the area of role play, where children could use ICT to pretend to send information to characters in stories or outside of the early years setting.

At Key Stage 1

In terms of the National Curriculum, pupils in Key Stage 1 should develop their knowledge skills and understanding by (3a) sharing their ideas by presenting information in a variety of forms and (3b) presenting their completed work effectively.

At Key Stage 2

In terms of the National Curriculum, pupils in Key Stage 2 should develop their knowledge, skills and understanding by (3a) sharing and exchanging information in a variety of forms, including e-mail and (3b) being sensitive to the needs of the audience and thinking carefully about the content and quality when communicating information (for example publishing on the Internet). The Internet is specifically covered in a number of the QCA units for ICT: e-mail (3e), analysing data and asking questions where complex searches are needed (5b) and multimedia presentation (6b). In addition, other units could be supported with online resources and information, such as information around us (1c) or exploring simulations (3c).

In both **Key Stages 1 and 2** children should be taught to evaluate their work and talk about the effectiveness of ICT (4a and 4b) as well as investigating and comparing the uses of ICT inside and outside school (5c).

Tasks for you to provide evidence of effective use of ICT to meet the Standards

In order for you to review and assess your progress against the Standards for QTS you will need to undertake a number of tasks that provide evidence that you can communicate using ICT effectively. It is important to adapt these tasks appropriately for the context in which you are working.

Task 4.1 Exchanging information	Exchange information (with another trainee or with a teacher or mentor) by e-mail to support your work in school.

This task can provide evidence for the following skills:

- composing and sending messages;
- replying to messages;
- attaching other files (such as digital photos or word-processing documents);
- using an address book;
- forwarding, copying and deleting messages.

Task 4.2 Finding resources on the web	Use the web to find and adapt resources for teaching:

EITHER finding materials that you can download and adapt for use with your class;
OR by identifying materials on the web for your pupils to use.

This task could provide evidence for a wide range of skills from searching for information, downloading files, bookmarking sites or even creating your own web page to support pupils' research into a specific topic.

Task 4.3 Developing pupils' communication skills	Plan and teach a lesson or an activity which develops pupils' ICT skills in communicating information.

This activity should be based on the National Curriculum for ICT and should contribute to develop pupils' ICT skills, knowledge and understanding or the development of their ICT capability (see Chapter 12 for more details). You will find the QCA scheme for ICT helpful in thinking about the activities that the children could undertake and the specific skills, knowledge and understanding that they might develop.

You should plan to make a series of resources during your training that will develop and extend your ICT skills.

Summary

- You will need to become familiar with a range of software that supports communication. These can not only help you directly in your teaching and interaction with pupils, but support your professional role more broadly.

- You also need to be able to teach the use of such technologies to your pupils as part of their curriculum entitlement, and exploit opportunities to develop and use these skills in other areas of the curriculum.

Suggestions for further information and reading

James, G. (2000) 'Talking to the world through video, sound and text', in M. Leask and J. Meadows, *Teaching and Learning with ICT in the Primary School*. London: Routledge Falmer.
Chapter 11 shows what can be done in primary schools with synchronous communications.

The BECTA website has a considerable amount of information about using the Internet in schools with briefings on acceptable use policies, Internet safety and other relevant issues http://www.becta.org.uk/technology/infosheets/.

Sharp, J., Potter, J., Allen, J. and Loveless, A. (2000) *Primary ICT: Knowledge, understanding and practice*, 2nd edn. Exeter: Learning Matters.
There is a good section dealing with the Internet and searching for information.

Somekh, B. and Davis, N. (1997) *Using Information Technology Effectively in Teaching and Learning: Studies in pre-service and in-service teacher education*. London: Routledge.
Invaluable examples of the development of the use of ICT in schools. See Chapter 4 in particular.

5   What does the research say?

In the UK we have invested heavily in information and communications technology (ICT) for use by teachers and by pupils in schools. Some of this investment has been directly by the government through multi-million pound initiatives such as the National Grid for Learning and the New Opportunities Fund ICT Training for Serving Teachers. Substantial sums have also been spent by Local Education Authorities, Education Action Zones and schools themselves on ICT equipment and resources, though this is harder to quantify. The purposes of this investment have not always been clear or made explicit. Two main themes are apparent in this drive to develop the use of technology in schools. Part of the motivation towards encouraging greater use of technology in education seems to be external and aimed at modernising schools and equipping the pupils of today with skills that will make them able to use such technology in the workplace once they leave school. Other stated goals have been about internal efficiency, such as to reduce teacher workload by making planning and resources available over the Internet or to reduce bureaucracy by providing and exchanging information in electronic form. Teachers in schools have become sceptical about the ability of ICT to deliver on these goals, and it is certainly necessary to cast a sceptical eye over the value of this expensive and extensive investment.

Perhaps the ultimate goal in promoting the use of ICT in schools has been to increase the effectiveness of teaching and improve pupils' learning. It is this goal that is the focus for the questions underpinning this chapter:

- What is the evidence that ICT can have a positive impact on pupils' learning in schools?
- How can ICT be used effectively in schools to improve pupils' learning?

A range of sources were consulted for this chapter and the key themes which emerged from the research identified.[1] A general overview of the impact of ICT on teaching and learning introduces the review and sets this research in a broader educational research context. Next, separate sections identify research evidence grouped under particular themes, namely: practice; feedback and interactivity; the presentation and representation of information in different forms; classroom talk and pupils' thinking; and the role of the teacher. A final section considers issues arising from the evidence base and some of the implications from what we do not know.

ICT can raise attainment

There is certainly some evidence from educational research that ICT can help pupils to learn and teachers to teach more effectively. However, there is not a simple message in such evidence. ICT will not make a difference simply by being used. The findings from this research suggest that although ICT can improve learning, there are a number of issues that need to be considered if such technology is going to make a difference. Some caution is therefore called for at this broad level of where and how ICT might have an impact. Two main issues can be identified. First is the modest effect of ICT compared with other researched interventions: other innovations have more impact. Second is the almost negligible effect of the provision and use of ICT when this is examined at a general level: schools which use computers a lot are not necessarily more effective.

There has been extensive research into computer-assisted instruction (CAI) and computer-based learning (CBL). Some major reviews of this extensive work have been undertaken. One study (Fletcher-Flynn and Gravatt, 1995) into the effectiveness of CAI limited the studies it examined to those that took place between 1987 and 1992 and identified almost 400 reports of research that met this criterion. The impact of the use of computers was then combined statistically to identify the overall impact. In this meta-analysis the mean effect size (the average impact) was relatively small (0.24) for the five years in question but increased for more recent studies analysed (0.33). This kind of improvement would move an 'average' class of pupils from fiftieth to about fortieth in a list of 100 classes ranked in order of attainment. This study therefore suggests two things: first, it is possible that the beneficial impact of computers may be increasing; second, ICT only produces relatively small improvement. Other forms of educational interventions, such as peer tutoring, reciprocal teaching and homework, for example, all produce greater average impact in terms of effect size (Hattie, 1987, 1992). In a study of the effect of different types of study skills interventions the average effect size was 0.57 (Hattie, Biggs and Purdie, 1996); this would move a class from fiftieth to the top 30. A study of the effect of thinking skills or metacognitive approaches (Marzano, 1998) indicates the average impact would move a class into the top 20 (an effect size of 0.72).

A study by the British Educational Technology Association (BECTA, 2000) found no link between level of resources for ICT and either reading or mathematics grades at Key Stage 1 in 1999. At Key Stage 2 there was a significant, but very weak, association between ICT resources and pupil attainment. This indicated that the provision of ICT resources was at least 99.5 per cent independent of pupil performance at Key Stage 2 (no correlation coefficient exceeded 0.07). Information about computer use from a longitudinal study in the USA was analysed (Weaver, 2000). This study also found a very small link between computer use in the curriculum in school and improvement in pupils' test scores, though again the link was very weak (no correlation coefficient was higher than 0.035 for mathematics, science and reading) which again indicates that at this general level computer use makes very little difference to pupils' achievement.

A similar weak link between high computer use and pupil attainment was reported in a Teacher Training Agency study in England (Moseley et al., 1999: 82) though the authors did not interpret this as a causal link, but rather that more effective teachers (and more effective schools) tended to use more innovative approaches, or tended to use the resources that they had more effectively.

The same study also reported dramatic impact on pupil attainment in its 16 development projects in primary schools. The average gain on standardised tests was 2.8 months' progress per month of the project in mathematics and 5.1 months' progress per month in literacy. The report states, however, that these gains do not prove that ICT *will* raise attainment, but that 'teachers *can* raise levels of pupils attainment when they use ICT to support their teaching in literacy and numeracy' (Moseley et al., 1999: 6). In these projects the use of ICT was planned to have an impact on particular areas of pupils' learning using research evidence from literacy and mathematics as well as the effective use of ICT. The development work involved working closely with the class teachers over an intensive period using a range of different equipment and software. These projects did not use control groups, but the consistent and significant increase in the attainment of pupils in mathematics and English suggests that where ICT is targeted at specific areas of learning, with a clear rationale for its use from a broad research base (about ICT, about pedagogy and about professional development) it can have a positive effect.

There are a number of ways that using ICT can have an impact on teaching and learning in schools. The subsequent sections in this chapter look at the effect of using computers under different headings, so that the possible mechanisms that might make a difference can be considered. Computers on their own won't be of much help: as a teacher you will need to know how and why they might be helpful.

Practice makes perfect

One key factor in why pupils' attainment in different subjects improves when using ICT is because they simply spend more time working at or practising the skills being studied and tested. Many pupils enjoy using computers and one benefit of computers may also therefore be the combination of such motivation and the increased practice at particular tasks. Computers can therefore help by increasing the amount of time pupils spend on particular activities, by increasing pupils' motivation and engagement when doing these activities and by providing practice at an appropriate level.

There is evidence of the impact of ICT on practising skills from a wide range of studies, including simple programs with a particular focus such as learning about negative numbers in mathematics (Hativa and Cohen, 1995) or early reading (Mioduser, Tur-Kaspa and Leitner, 2000) as well as more complex Integrated Learning Systems (ILS) which have all improved pupil attainment. Some researchers have suggested that pupil practice is a crucial factor in any improvement in pupils' attainment (Van Dusen and Worthen, 1995; Underwood and Brown, 1997). Software can ensure that learners are given tasks at an appropriate level that can be matched to their prior attainment or their Individual Education Plans (Lynch, Fawcett and Nicolson, 2000).

Use of ICT can clearly be effective in improving pupils' performance in this way. However, such positive results do not help a teacher decide if the use of ICT is efficient, as other methods or approaches (e.g. reciprocal teaching) may similarly increase the amount of time pupils spend actually engaged in learning particular skills.

Feedback: Interaction with computers

There is research evidence to show that feedback from a computer can improve pupils' learning. Computer 'marking' of work in simple practice tasks across the curriculum and more sophisticated ILS programs have all produced evidence of improved pupil attainment. Feedback can, however, take very different forms. It can also be at a more general level of interaction, such as a list of websites returned from a search engine, or underlining text in a word processor where a word is spelled incorrectly or from a computer 'talking' in response to what a pupil does.

Text-to-speech feedback in a word processor or interactive storybook can improve early reading (Olson and Wise, 1992; Lewin, 2000). Voice input and text feedback (Miles *et al.*, 1998) can also improve pupils' reading and writing. These studies also indicate the importance of matching the tasks on a computer to pupils' current attainment. The quality of this feedback is important as, for example, second language learners may need higher quality feedback than text-to-speech generally offers (Lynch, Fawcett and Nicolson, 2000). The quality of response is also important in a tutoring or ILS program because pupils can be learning merely how to get the best help from the system (Balacheff and Kaput, 1996). This research indicates that effective use of computer feedback in mathematics needs monitoring to ensure the pupils are learning what they are supposed to learn. In mathematics tutoring programs, for example, feedback is usually only of the number of correct responses or the total scores of performance. This type of feedback does not help pupils to correct their errors, other than by trying again. Most software does not offer formative feedback that might help pupils to identify how they could improve (Higgins, 2001). It therefore assumes that they are motivated to learn and that they know what they are supposed to be learning. This is often not the case, as pupils simply want to complete the task or 'win' the game on the computer. Children may not see the purposes of tasks in the same way as teachers.

Multimedia: Presenting and representing information in different forms

ICT is powerful in presenting or representing information in different ways. This can be through different forms (text and pictures or tables and graphs) or by enabling changes to be shown dynamically, such as in mathematical modelling, or by helping visualisation of complex processes in science.

Information can be manipulated easily on a computer so that a pupil can make changes and evaluate the effect of those changes. This can be where the information is of the same type, such as text in word processing (Snyder, 1993; Breese *et al.*, 1996) or numbers in spreadsheets (Mann and Tall, 1992); or where it is in different forms (Ainsworth *et al.*, 1997). Observing changes in a graph when changes are made to the table of numerical information on which the graph is based, or by manipulating an algebraic formula and observing how a graph of that function changes on a computer or graphical calculator, can develop pupils' understanding of mathematical relationships. Computer tools can help students or teachers manipulate complex data sets which provides a context for discussion to develop mathematical understanding (Cobb, 2002). 'Visualisation tools' can help learners to picture scientific ideas (Jonassen, 2000) or to develop conceptual understanding.

Classroom organisation, pupils' thinking and computers

Computers can be used individually, in small or large groups or by the teacher with the whole class. Each approach has been shown to be effective, though there are some differences in approach and upon outcomes.

Individuals perform better than groups when carrying out drill and practice activities (Jackson and Kutnick, 1996). However, computers can be used effectively to support pupils' talk when they work in small groups on collaborative tasks (Wegerif and Scrimshaw, 1997) and even 'directive' software can support discussion and reasoning. Teachers may need to teach pupils how to interact with each other when using the computer collaboratively (Eraut, 1995; Dawes *et al.*, 2000). When ICT is used to promote discussion in small groups and in whole class settings this can help to develop pupils' thinking and understanding across the curriculum in a variety of subjects and with a range of outcomes. This includes learners' mathematical thinking (McClain and Cobb, 2001), their individual reasoning (Dawes *et al.*, 2000); their higher-order thinking through ICT as a subject (Kirkwood, 2000); conceptual change in science (Eidson and Simmons, 1998); and creativity through LOGO programming (Subhi, 1999).

The challenge for the teacher

Information and Communications Technologies present a range of tools that can be used by teachers to present and demonstrate or model ideas in front of the whole class as well as a tool for pupils to use as part of an activity as individuals or in groups. These technological tools can be explicitly designed for use in educational contexts, such as a mathematics teaching program or an overhead projecting calculator, or they can be equipment and software also used in other contexts, such as word processors and spreadsheets. The choice of when and how to use such technologies in teaching and learning is complex. The evidence above all clearly indicates that it is *how* ICT is used that makes the difference.

Knowledge of, and experience with, computers is not enough to enable teachers to make the best use of ICT in the classroom. Effective adoption of computers within the classroom takes time (Somekh and Davis, 1997), even up to a year with the support of an experienced team or through collaborative working (Sandholtz, 2001). In addition, the way in which teachers' skills, beliefs and practices are related is complex (Wild, 1996) and this affects the way teachers choose to use ICT and how effective they are at using it (Higgins and Moseley, 2001). As a teacher you are likely to use computers in ways that fit with your underlying beliefs and approaches to education. For example, if you like whole class teaching, you will probably enjoy using an interactive or electronic whiteboard. On the other hand, if you feel that learning is only effective when pupils have a chance to talk and discuss their learning, you will probably prefer small-group or collaborative activities with computers. Of course, both types of activities can be effective: it is just that you are likely to develop activities with ICT that you feel confident and familiar with.

The final issue is that ICT changes rapidly and new innovations offer new possibilities for teaching and learning. These not only open up new techniques to influence the existing curriculum more effectively or more efficiently but change the nature of that curriculum by altering the content of what needs to be taught, such as in the area of digital literacy with use of electronic texts or the progression of how a topic like algebra can best be taught in mathematics. However, the curriculum and its assessment act as a brake on this process of change (Torrance, 1997). As a teacher you will not be able to ignore the requirements of national testing, which will influence both the time available to use ICT and the way in which it is used. As pupils' use of computers is not formally assessed, it will always have a lesser role than other aspects of the curriculum that are tested.

What we don't know

There are a number of issues about the research and evidence on the effective use of ICT in teaching in schools. These are related to the nature of this research and pace of innovation. There are also some key things that it does not tell us. Research is rarely comparative in nature and so cannot help us to identify whether ICT is better than other approaches, and this makes it difficult to decide whether the use of ICT is cost-effective. Research also rarely reports on technical issues or problems with equipment, yet these are what teachers report as barriers to increasing the use of technology in classrooms (Moseley *et al.*, 1999).

The delay between research field-work and its publication in peer-reviewed journals is, on average, about two years (in some cases even longer). Reports in newspapers or on the Internet appear more quickly. However, the findings from research are usually more cautious or may even contradict the initial reporting. For example, the Internet is often heralded as a valuable teaching resource. One published study (Kramarski and Feldman, 2000) indicates that although the use on web pages may help motivate pupils, the approach is less effective than traditional instruction at improving reading comprehension and pupils' use of learning strategies. Similarly, the eager adoption of Integrated Learning Systems has been tempered by more conservative research findings (Wood, 1998). Caution is therefore indicated in interpreting preliminary findings relating to new or emerging technologies such as the use of interactive whiteboards and managed learning environments (MLEs).

There is little research with evidence of impact on pupil attainment. Observations in schools show that ICT is typically used for drill and practice and typing up of 'a best copy' (Chalkey and Nicholas, 1997). This may help to explain the generally low impact of ICT on attainment reported in the Impact 2 study (Harrison *et al.*, 2002). The aim of particular research is also important. Researchers often investigate computer-assisted instruction, where specific content is presented to pupils. This is often from a psychological or sociocultural perspective, which offers valuable insights into learning processes and theories. However, the findings may not translate into clear messages for more effective teaching in a classroom. By contrast, when teachers carry out action research, the preferred choice is more open-ended or generic software, but the investigations are usually small-scale and qualitative, making it hard to draw generalisable conclusions.

Summary

- ICT offers a wealth of possibilities to support teaching and learning, but effective use depends upon the choices that a teacher makes about how to use ICT as part of their teaching.
- Technology changes rapidly and each change opens up new possibilities for teachers and learners.
- It takes time to develop the skills necessary to use ICT effectively in teaching.
- Research indicates that ICT *can* make a difference to pupils' learning.
- In large studies there is a positive link between the provision or use of ICT resources and pupil attainment, but this link is weak.
- Analysis of targeted interventions using ICT shows a more positive picture, but not as effective as other educational innovations.
- More substantial gains in pupil attainment are achievable where the use of ICT is planned, structured and integrated effectively.
- Increased practice is a key feature of how ICT can help to improve learning, and computers can motivate pupils to undertake such practice and to help ensure they are practising at an appropriate level of challenge.
- Feedback from a computer can help pupils to learn in a range of different ways.
- Information on computers can usually be adapted or changed quickly and easily and this makes it possible to evaluate these changes.
- The type or medium of information can be changed or two types of information related to help pupils see connections between forms.
- Computers can be used effectively in a range of different ways to improve teaching and learning: by individual pupils, by groups and by the teacher to focus discussion.

- ICT can help to develop pupils' thinking in a range of different ways including reasoning, understanding and creativity.
- The rapid pace of change makes it difficult to evaluate technological innovations effectively and disseminate this information quickly.
- ICT can be shown to be effective in specific areas of teaching and learning, but it is difficult to tell if it is practical or efficient.

Implications

- There is no single or simple solution to the use of ICT in teaching and learning.
- Teachers need support to develop both new technical and pedagogical skills.
- The curriculum and its assessment need flexibility to accommodate technological change.
- Providing ICT equipment to schools or teachers will not necessarily make a difference.
- The way that this equipment and these resources are then used by pupils and by teachers is what makes the difference.
- Other options to improve pupils' attainment should also be considered.
- Target pupils who will benefit from increased practice.
- Identify aspects of the curriculum where it is difficult to get pupils to practise and use ICT to support this.
- It is important to monitor how feedback is being interpreted by pupils to ensure that it improves their learning.
- Computers should be used to enhance aspects of teaching through the presentation of information in different ways and in different forms.
- Pupils should manipulate and make changes to information on computers, so that they can develop understanding of the relationship between different types of information or through the process of changing that information dynamically.
- Grouping pupils when using computers requires a deliberate choice according to the aims of an activity.
- ICT can support the development of understanding across the curriculum.
- Teachers should be cautious of early adoption of new technologies.
- Comparative research is needed to evaluate the cost-effectiveness of ICT.

| Task 5.1 Finding relevant ICT research | Use the library at your college or university (or academic research published on the Internet) to find an account of some recent research into the use of ICT in primary schools |

that has implications for classroom practice. Summarise the research for your colleagues by answering the following questions:
- What does the research describe?
- What were the findings?
- What are the implications for your teaching?

Note

1   This chapter is based on the research undertaken to complete a Professional User Review, *Does ICT Improve Learning and Teaching in Schools?* for the British Educational Research Association (Higgins, 2003).

Further information and readings

The studies cited in the chapter can be found in the references section at the end of the book if you wish to follow up details of the particular research cited. Further information about the evidence of the impact of ICT on learning and teaching can be found on BECTA's website in their Research bibliographies (http://www.becta.org.uk/research).

There are a number of research journals that publish research about ICT and teaching and learning such as the *British Journal of Educational Technology* (published by BECTA), *Education and Information Technologies* (published by Kluwer) or *Computers and Education* (Elsevier). It is challenging to keep up to date with current research in ICT, but if you are looking for information, then journals like these can be a good place to start.

PART II

ICT and teaching in the classroom

The aim of this section is broadly to help new teachers to address the requirements in the professional standards for qualified teacher status (TTA/DfES, 2002) to 'know how to use ICT effectively, both to teach their subject and to support their wider professional role' (2.5 p. 8) and to 'use ICT effectively in their teaching' (3.3.10 p. 12).

As a teacher you will also need to know about how ICT applies to the subjects that you will be teaching. The specific aspects of the professional standards are to 'have a secure knowledge and understanding of the subject(s) they are trained to teach' (2.1 p. 7). These requirements vary according to the age range that you will be teaching. For nursery and reception teachers you will need knowledge of the Foundation Stage curriculum guidance and the Literacy and Numeracy Frameworks as these apply to reception age children (2.1a p. 7). Each of these documents specifically refers to ICT. For teachers in Key Stages 1 and 2 you need to 'know and understand the curriculum for each of the National Curriculum core subjects, and the frameworks, methods and expectations set out in the national Numeracy and Literacy Strategies' (2.1b p. 7) as well as 'sufficient understanding of a range of work' across the foundation subjects (which include ICT) and religious education.

ICT poses some interesting challenges for all teachers. It is a subject in that it has a dedicated time set aside for its teaching in most schools and in the sense that it has its own discrete curriculum documentation. ICT is also a tool to be used across the curriculum to support pupils' learning, and each National Curriculum Programme of Study includes a pupil entitlement statement to this effect. ICT is also a teaching tool and as such is the focus of huge investment of money, time and effort – through teacher training, development of resources and infrastructure – in the UK at the moment. ICT is also a relatively new phenomenon and is constantly developing and changing in a way that no other area of the curriculum does.

The point is that ICT isn't easily labelled. Like literacy it affects and is affected by everything that goes on in a school. It has the potential to be part of every lesson, every piece of planning, every piece of record keeping and assessment. It has the potential to completely alter the structure of the educational establishment. Most people just use it to type letters. . . .

That observation is perhaps unfair, but it addresses the real issue. Since ICT is relatively new, we are still trying to find out what we are supposed to use it for. This applies to experienced and effective teachers every bit as much as it applies to those just embarking on their teaching careers. When we are unsure what to do with something, we tend to stick to what is easy and safe, hence the observation that many people use computers as very expensive typewriters.

It is important to address the issue of what ICT is for in order to make sure teachers and students derive maximum benefit from using it. Each teacher needs to make informed decisions about when to use ICT, but importantly they also need to be able to make informed decisions about when ICT is an inappropriate tool to use. ICT can be very motivating for both teachers and pupils. New ideas and new technologies come along and their developers will have us believe that every school, every teacher needs one of these new gizmos to ensure that they are providing the best possible opportunities for their pupils. This isn't necessarily the case! In all the excitement of getting a new toy, teachers have to consider the implications of investing money that could be used elsewhere and, more importantly, investing time in learning how to use it effectively.

Undoubtedly some modern innovations have helped make the case for ICT even more compelling and many of these innovations are bringing real benefits to teachers and learners. What teachers need to do is consider what the potential benefits to the pupils in their class may be and act accordingly. Put bluntly, if there is no clear educational benefit, don't do it. (Here we would include the idea that tools that help the teacher prepare, deliver, record and report upon the work of their pupils and either make these processes more effective or more efficient, or both, could be considered as educationally beneficial).

A good lesson using ICT is the same as a good lesson under any other circumstances. A good lesson using ICT has clear learning objectives that the children understand and has clear and appropriate tasks to assist children in developing the desired knowledge, skills and understanding. ICT should enhance and support this process and not interfere with it. For this reason, when using ICT in teaching literacy, for instance, the skills and understanding required by the pupils to undertake the tasks and participate fully in the lesson should already be in place. If a teacher has to spend time explaining or supporting the use of ICT, then it is possible that the use of ICT is detracting from the impact of the lesson.

Of course, you need some experience of ICT and what it can do in order to help you make such decisions and this section provides a range of ideas, case studies and tasks. These will help you in gathering the necessary experience to achieve Qualified Teacher Status, but more importantly to start making informed decisions about when, and when not, to use ICT with your pupils.

Task Part II.1 ICT in schools	Whilst working in school you will have come across many instances of the use of ICT, good and not so good. Try to recall instances of the use of ICT within the curriculum in

the following:
- production of classroom resources;
- classroom management and/or display;
- use by the teacher in whole class teaching;
- use by children in small group or independent work;
- use by children in self-initiated tasks.

The majority of the examples and tasks in the following chapters are focused on the use of ICT in teaching and learning, rather than on ICT as a subject (though ICT as a subject is considered in Chapter 12). The main purpose of teaching ICT as a subject is to develop what is referred to as 'ICT capability' in pupils, to enable them to exploit the potential of ICT in supporting their learning. Teaching ICT is a relatively static and easily understood process, even if it still presents many teachers with significant challenges. Teaching *through* ICT is more complex, because it covers a wider range of issues but is essential to help teachers develop their own ICT capability.

The chapters in this section focus on the curriculum and how ICT can support teaching and learning in different subjects. Each chapter could have been a book in itself. What we have tried to do is provide some examples across a range of situations where ICT offers some potential to support teaching and learning.

- Chapter 6 ICT for literacy and the teaching of English – Teaching of literacy in primary schools is strongly influenced by the National Literacy Strategy Framework which provides a clear structure to support the development of children's reading and writing. Many opportunities to use ICT consistent with the NLS Framework are outlined in this chapter.
- Chapter 7 ICT for numeracy and mathematics – This chapter suggests ways that ICT can support the teaching of mathematics. Opportunities to embed the use of ICT in mathematics lessons are described, along with some key ideas to support the teaching and learning of mathematics.
- Chapter 8 ICT in primary science – Although somewhat the poor relation in terms of the core curriculum, ICT is an excellent tool to support the teaching of science. Sections focus on measuring and recording, on demonstration and visualisation, consolidating learning and using ICT to look for information and research ideas and themes in science.
- Chapter 9 ICT across the curriculum – ICT is a powerful tool which can support learning across the curriculum. This chapter presents some suggestions and examples which should help you get started. The ideas and examples are consistent with the QCA schemes of work, but also indicate some general principles which should help you develop your skills.
- Chapter 10 ICT in the Foundation Stage – Even very young children's learning can be supported and enhanced with ICT. This chapter looks at how

ICT can support teachers in the foundation stage by providing a focus for interaction and discussion, by supporting the development of fine motor skills as well as children's creativity. A section also looks at how ICT can help a busy teacher by supporting aspects of classroom organisation and management.

- Chapter 11 ICT and thinking skills – ICT is a powerful tool which can help children develop their thinking, reasoning and understanding. This chapter looks at practical strategies to develop thinking skills through ICT.

As with the first section above, this book cannot offer you more than guidance about what you could do and how you might develop your use of ICT in your teaching. Effective use of ICT is about being able to make complex professional choices as how best to use a range of changing technologies. There is no simple solution. We aim to suggest some principles and ideas which we hope will encourage you to observe closely what happens when you and your pupils use ICT. You still need to try things out, experiment, practise and think about how ICT might improve the learning of your pupils.

Further information and readings

DfEE/QCA (1999) *The National Curriculum: Handbook for primary teachers in England*. London: DfEE/QCA (http://www.nc.uk.net/).

QCA (2003) *A Scheme of Work for Key Stages 1 and 2 Information and Communications Technology: A teacher's guide*. London: QCA; also available from http://www.standards.dfes.gov.uk/schemes3/.

6 ICT for literacy and the teaching of English

As mentioned in the introduction to this part of the book, ICT has the potential to support effective teaching and learning throughout the curriculum. It is essential, however, to ensure that when ICT is to be used in support of teaching and learning in literacy, it is the literacy learning objective that remains the prime focus of the lesson. In this chapter we will look at how ICT can be used to support the teacher in preparing and delivering effective literacy lessons and on how ICT can be used to help pupils develop their English skills, knowledge and understanding more generally.

One of the most important contributions that ICT can make in supporting learning in literacy is that of helping teachers provide pupils with resources that allow them to focus on the specific learning objective or objectives for a lesson and avoid getting bogged down in other issues. A typical example would be using a word-processing package that includes a word bank tool. A word bank usually provides pupils with a simple way of getting prepared vocabulary into their written work without worrying about how to spell, or for that matter write, each word. Many such packages would also include a text-to-speech facility which 'reads' the text back to the pupil, helping them focus on the meaning of the writing by giving them instant feedback and without having to prompt them to re-read what they have written (see Figure 6.1). Literacy work done this way may help pupils concentrate on the flow of text and the meaning of what they are writing and reduce the relevance of issues relating to handwriting, spelling, editing and re-reading.

ICT in whole-class teaching in literacy

When considering the use of ICT in the teaching of literacy and the National Literacy Strategy (NLS), there is a range of opportunities to consider. Given access to the right equipment, using ICT in the whole-class teaching elements of the strategy can be very powerful. If you are lucky enough to have access to a digital projector in the

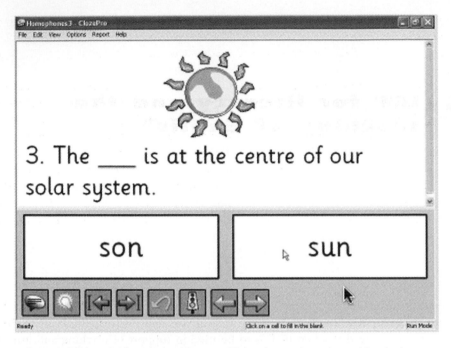

Figure 6.1   A Clicker Grid on homophones. Clicker is a universal word bank that can work with other word processors and contains text-to-speech functions (www.cricksoft.com)

classroom where you teach literacy this can dramatically enhance the opportunities you have for whole-class teaching. With a digital projector, sharing texts, activities and presentations is not only possible, but can be a real advantage.

Presenting sections of texts on a projector screen for shared text work is possible, though using extended texts may involve rather a lot of scrolling up and down pages or flicking through slides, which can be something of a distraction. The real power lies in being able to interact with the text in different ways. With text presented in a word processor, such as Microsoft's Word, it is possible to discuss features of text and highlight those features as necessary, perhaps by changing the colour of the section of text or by using the purpose-made editing features built into the application. A simple search for the adjectives in a piece of text is now a very visual and engaging whole-class task. It provides pupils with strong visual clues that can help them develop their understanding of the concept being discussed. This not only helps pupils engage with the concept, but also provides a degree of support when offering suggestions of their own. They can use the evidence of other people's answers to help them work out whether the answer they want to offer seems to fit. A degree of comfort about the accuracy or appropriateness of your answer tends to make you much more willing to contribute to the discussion!

A digital projector will also enable you to demonstrate how to use worksheets or other prepared resources if they were originally developed on a computer. If you create a worksheet or activity on a computer then you can use the original file to show pupils how they should use the paper-based version of the resource. Even more powerful is the ability to use this file again in the plenary session, where it is possible to discuss pupils' ideas and answers and share those ideas instantly with the whole class.

A digital projector also gives you the opportunity to use presentation software, such as Microsoft's PowerPoint, Textease Presenter or Apple's Keynote, to present ideas and concepts in more engaging ways (see Figure 6.2). This type of software allows teachers to build presentations that incorporate animations, sound effects and transitions and add time delays and so on. It is possible that a presentation used within a whole-class session could also be used by pupils in small-group or individual work sessions. This provides a good introduction to the task and is also an excellent platform for pupils to present their work and their ideas. All they have to do is run the presentation from the PC connected to the projector, and describe what they have done.

Figure 6.2 PowerPoint presentation used to help children develop early phonic skills

Whole-class presentation technology also gives you easy ways to bring stimulating materials into the class; you could project current news items from the World Wide Web as a way of discussing report genre or idioms; you could show short video clips or play real news radio footage to discuss features of spoken news reporting; you could study the features of scripts for radio plays or adverts; you could use live web pages to look for information about specific topics or different points of view when discussing argument; you could conduct searches of CD-ROMs to find text relevant to the subjects you are discussing and so on. It would even be possible to have a piece of text and a video clip from the same story to play side by side in order to discuss the changes and differences between the two formats. None of these ideas requires the use of an interactive whiteboard, but consideration of the opportunities that that might offer should be made.

Not all schools have digital projectors and fewer have them available for use in every classroom, though this picture is changing rapidly.

Case study part 1: Editing a playscript

The following section describes how a teacher might use ICT in whole-class teaching consistent with the NLS. The teacher of a Year 3 class has access to the ICT suite twice a week. Usually she uses the suite once in order to cover the requirements of the ICT curriculum and once for using ICT within the curriculum. This lesson is a literacy lesson. The suite is set up with 16 computers on benches around the suite and has some tables set up in the middle of the room for work away from the computers. There is a digital projector and screen at the front of the classroom.

The teacher has brought photocopies of a play script to use as the shared text. The script was printed using a word processor having been downloaded from the Internet, and the original file is projected onto the main screen for all to see. At first, the teacher reads the script, using different voices for each character in the play. The class discuss the structure of the script and the clues to characterisation within it. The teacher uses the highlight function in the word processor to show the selections of text that the children think give clues to the nature of each character in turn. The class make some decisions about the nature of each character and the teacher makes notes on the whiteboard to the side of the projector screen. The teacher then shares out the roles to some of the class and they re-read the script, trying to use some of the ideas modelled and discussed previously. The annotated script is left projected on the screen in the ICT room as the pupils move on to the individual- and group-level work.

Task 6.1 Using ICT in whole-class literacy teaching	Find out if there is a digital projector available at your next or current school placement and, if it is not sited in a teaching area you have access to, find out what the procedures for booking and using it are.

Using the ideas above as a starting point, design a whole-class activity that fits with your literacy planning and try this out with the class. If you need to build your confidence, try the idea in a group-work session instead. This could be done around a single monitor rather than using a digital projector, and could be a good way of trying the idea out if you are working in a school that does not have projection facilities.

ICT in group or individual work in literacy

ICT can also provide valuable opportunities for pupil learning through group or individual work. Many teachers will use ICT to assist in the preparation of worksheets and learning resources for use within the classroom. This section, however, covers the use of activities that are designed to be carried out on a computer. Some of the ideas and activities are applicable for use with group activities, in which case it may be possible to use a single PC or laptop in the classroom; others really require individual access for pupils. Some schools have access to several computers in classrooms, especially where access to a suite of wireless laptops has been provided. It is more likely that you will have access to a computer suite and it should be possible for a literacy lesson to be delivered in this setting, or that groups can access the suite during the lesson.

Access to resources and activities on the computer can provide pupils with similar support, as outlined in the previous section, at an individual level too. Working with raw or prepared texts on a computer can help pupils focus on specific objectives and identify relevant features, record observations and ideas and amend relevant sections quickly and easily. Identifying parts of text for further work, discussion or analysis can be done very easily with ICT. You can simply highlight text (if your word processor offers this feature) or change its colour or embolden it to make it stand out. Once relevant features have been identified, they can easily be reworked, without the need for laborious rewriting.

Many word processors also provide pupils with access to 'writing tools', which might help them review or refine their work. Access to spellcheckers can obviously help pupils to identify and correct spelling or typing errors, though whether this is beneficial in improving a child's ability to spell accurately is debatable. Spellchecking tools can be used proactively, however, by getting pupils to keep a record of spelling errors that are regularly identified by the checker. These words can be entered (or copied and pasted) into a personal spelling log or word web which can then be used as a technique to focus on developing more effective spelling strategies later. Many word processors also have grammar checkers, which can be used to help pupils focus on the sense and structure of their writing. Both these services can also be turned off if they interfere with the composition process. Sometimes it can be more appropriate to turn writing tools off so that little red wiggly lines don't distract pupils from the actual writing process or interrupt the flow of their work. These tools can then be turned back on during the editing and reviewing stages of the writing process.

One of the things primary age pupils find most frustrating about the editing process is the tedious rewriting of the text that it often involves. Editing on-screen can help address some of these issues. Indeed, it also enables you to break the editing process into a series of separate processes. Editing involves several individual elements, such as checking for meaning, clarity, good use of language, aspects of grammar, punctuation, spelling, and finally presenting the text. These can all be tackled separately as discrete steps on a computer. It may also provide wider opportunities for developing and working with texts. Since electronic versions of texts are easy to copy and distribute (either using printed copies or duplicating files across networks or even as e-mail attachments), texts may be shared for use in peer-review sessions. This is especially effective if you are using a word processor that can 'track changes'. This feature lets you see what has changed between drafts (and who has changed it) and can be the basis for a discussion about re-drafting. ICT can also provide authors with an audience. Through e-mail or use of the web, children can start to write for real and varied audiences and purposes.

Individual work can be effectively supported through use of specialist software, such as the word banks and speech feedback facilities mentioned earlier. Such facilities can be very effective in providing full access to learning opportunities for less able pupils and, indeed, even more specialised equipment can also help provide greater access to a mainstream curriculum for pupils with even severe and complex special educational needs.

It is the flexible nature of ICT resources that is the most important factor here. First, there is the opportunity for effective differentiation that ICT provides. If a teacher sets up a specific activity for higher achieving pupils, say, a prepared text for studying idiomatic language, then it can be a simple process to adapt that resource for others within the class. Here, high achieving pupils may be asked to identify and explain the idioms within the text, others may have the idioms highlighted for them and all they have to do is explain what they mean. Others might be given explanations and they have to identify the idioms from those explanations, some might even have a text-to-speech function enabled so that they can 'read along' with the computer to help them follow the meaning of the text.

Flexibility is also provided through the range of sources of information pupils may have access to. The Internet may provide pupils with opportunities to explore sources of information, especially up-to-date information, that can be hard to provide through other media. The Internet can also provide a wide range of opportunities for studying differing points of view by looking at differences in reported information from different organisations. This can provide a valuable insight into the importance of taking everything you read on the Internet with an enormous pinch of salt and is extremely important in helping children to become 'critical users' of the Internet, indeed, critical users of any source of information.

Work at any level can be provided using software for different purposes. For instance, a computer-based activity at word level identifying and sorting verbs perhaps, using software that is really designed for desktop publishing, can be very effective. Desktop publishing software (you may come across packages such as Microsoft's Publisher or Textease Studio (Softease) in schools) is designed to make manipulation and placing of separate elements easy. In the above activity, the words are the separate elements and being able to simply drag them around the screen makes for a simple sorting device. The page would be set up with elements such as instructions and spaces into which words can be sorted first (see Figure 6.3). These elements can often be 'locked' in place so that only the words to be sorted, which are added later, can be moved. Sorting in this way allows for review and a change of mind in ways that cut-and-stick or transcribing words from a given list do not.

On the other hand, providing prepared texts for pupils to use in a presentation package such as Microsoft's PowerPoint can offer access to the same range of writing

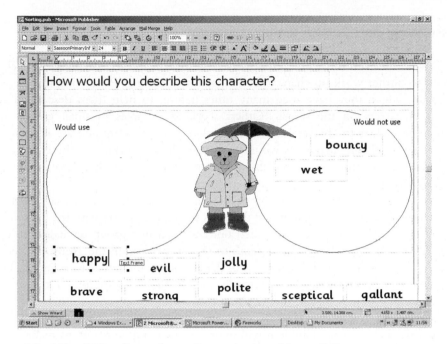

Figure 6.3   Using DTP software for sorting and categorising activities

tools that you might find in a good word processor, but has the advantage of having presentation features built in. Work done with presentation software is ready to present back to the class at the end of the activity. Not only will this provide effective material for use in the plenary to a lesson, it also provides opportunities for pupils to develop speaking and listening skills as well, allowing children to reflect upon their performance and their understanding. An example may be a prepared file with a sequence of instructions for a simple task. In PowerPoint, with the instructions presented in the wrong order, each instruction can be 'dragged' into the right place to construct the correct sequence in the 'slide sorter' view. This can be especially effective if the sequence is potentially ambiguous: does it matter if you fill the kettle first or wash your hands first when making a Cup-a-Soup? This opens up debate and encourages children to justify their ideas.

It may also be worth considering using different software tools for different stages in the writing process. For instance, mind-mapping or concept-mapping software could be very useful in the planning stages of the writing process. This kind of software is designed to help children clarify their thinking by allowing them to discuss and reflect upon the relevant issues in a task. Everything you know about making a model in technology could be written down as separate elements in the software and then sorted, categorised and linked together to provide a 'map' of your ideas, for instance.

It is important that the software tools you choose to use with pupils are appropriate for their skill level, of course. It is also essential that they are familiar with the use of these pieces of software before you use them in a literacy lesson to ensure learning is specifically focused on the literacy learning objective.

Case study part 2: Developing characterisation

Following on from the whole-class work described in the section above, the class go on to further work on characterisation, some working at PCs, using word bank software, which they have used many times before, to help them describe illustrated characters on the screen. Others working at tables in small groups are highlighting clues to characterisation in another piece of script and are illustrating what they think the characters would look like. Pupils working at the computers save their work onto the shared drive on the schools network so that it can be retrieved later.

In the plenary, the teacher shows a couple of examples of descriptions of characters done at the computer and discusses the choices made with the class. The work done at the computers is printed out and used in a group discussion in the next literacy lesson. The teacher intends to review work with the group and see if everyone agrees about the descriptions of the characters the pupils were given. The children will be encouraged to make changes to their descriptions if they have changed their minds about the characters after the discussion. Others will be encouraged to 'polish' their language and try to find more effective adjectives to use within their writing. Children will return to the computer suite to make these changes in the following lesson. The final versions of the printed text will be used in a 'Rogues' Gallery' display in the classroom.

Task 6.2   Using ICT in group or individual work in literacy

Plan a specific task where the pupils you are teaching will use ICT as part of a literacy lesson. You will need to assess their skills and may need to discuss aspects of the activity with their class teacher. Remember the focus of the task is on achieving literacy objectives – you should not be spending time teaching ICT skills!

Before trying to use any of the ideas above with the class, learn how to protect the files you prepare. On most computers this involves 'write-protecting' the file by right-clicking on the file, selecting 'Properties' from the menu and making sure the 'read-only' box towards the bottom of the properties window is checked. This has two effects. First, it means that the file can be shared by several computers at once (essential if you are going to use shared work areas) but second and more importantly it means that any changes made by the pupils will not change your original file. When they come to save their work they will be asked to give the file a name as if it was a brand-new piece of work and they won't be able to over-write your original file.

It is also essential that you know how to access shared areas on the computer network. Ask the school's ICT coordinator or technical support person to show you how to use the network.

ICT in planning and preparation for teaching literacy

ICT offers teachers many ways in which to handle their professional responsibilities in terms of planning, preparing and delivering effective lessons as well as in managing their classrooms and their pupils. Many teachers use word processors or databases to compile termly or yearly reports, to keep work records and pupil profiles up-to-date and so on. When it comes to the teaching of literacy, ICT is especially useful in terms of preparation and delivery of learning opportunities, as discussed above. ICT also provides teachers with access to resources that help them manage this process.

The government is keen to promote the use of ICT, and particularly communications technologies, to help teachers develop their professional practice and for this reason the DfES put a great deal of effort into its online strategy. All planning documentation used in schools, including the National Curriculum for English and the Literacy Strategy, are available online through the Standards site. To back up this planning the Literacy Strategy also publish a significant amount of support material, from lists of recommended texts to support for the use of the Literacy Strategy for pupils with special needs. Through the NC Action website (www.ncaction.org.uk), the DfES are also providing materials to help teachers assess their pupils' work and government-sponsored sites such as Teacher Net (www.teachernet.org) or Gridclub (www.gridclub.org) have materials that directly support teaching in literacy. Through the e-Learning Credits scheme (together with Curriculum Online) the government are effectively sponsoring the adoption of e-learning materials in British schools.

Individual schools also have access to specific learning materials, possibly purchased through government schemes and delivered through ICT. Banks of digital learning materials including video clips that act as stimuli for lessons or interactive activities that are designed to help pupils consolidate basic skills. It is worth finding out what is available in the schools you encounter.

As mentioned earlier, many teachers prepare resources for their lessons using computers. A digital version of a worksheet is easy to adapt and therefore helps to provide more effective differentiation. Preparing and storing work on a computer provides starting points for new work. Many teachers who use ICT regularly to develop teaching resources and classroom aids will tell you that they never open an empty file and start work; they almost always open an existing file that is similar and work over the top of that. This approach is usually much quicker as there is less formatting and planning to be done.

If you try preparing resources that pupils will use on computers (as discussed in the section above) then an awareness of the level of support and control the pupils get when using the resource is important. For instance, checking a piece of text (perhaps originally written by the pupil) for spelling errors is extremely valuable. There is a reasonable amount of evidence that suggests that pupils find it easier to spot errors in printed or on-screen text because it is more clearly presented. However, leaving the spellcheck function in a word processor switched on may undermine the process somewhat. Finding out how to switch writing tools on and off can be extremely useful. In a similar vein, knowing how to add or remove tool palettes in different pieces of software can be useful. If you want pupils to use text formatting menus that allow them to select fonts, styles and sizes easily then these tools need to be present before you start. On the other hand, having tools that allow them to turn text into data-entry forms may be a distraction, so removing them before you start might be useful, too. Again, find out how you do this with the software you are using with your pupils; in many cases it is simply a matter of looking under the 'View' menu and investigating 'toolbars'.

When preparing files for use on the computer, it is also worth considering whether the format is appropriate for your pupils. Clearly, selecting the right sorts of fonts (probably those that match the school's handwriting policy as closely as possible are best) is important, but it is also important to consider whether they are an appropriate size, are they clearly legible? Does the presentation (style, colour etc.) help to clarify meaning or does it make it difficult to read? Can the page be set up to support specific needs? (For visually impaired pupils, increasing font size may work, but it might make little difference; children with conditions such as dysphasia may find that changing the background colour of the page from white to, say, blue, enhances their ability to read text and so on.) Is the presentation supporting independent work? The idea of locking parts of a page down so that they can't be moved is discussed in the previous section, but think also about how you could add instructions and prompts on screen in text boxes which might be helpful. If you have a talking word processor or computer with text-to-speech facilities, these instructions could even be 'read' by the computer!

Preparing a series of templates for pupils to use for written work might be appropriate. These templates could contain standard structures to help organise text, and the idea of writing frames works extremely well on computers. However, simply setting a blank template with the font and size of text already selected so that the pupils can get on with the task of producing the writing and the formatting is taken care of can be very useful, too.

It is also worth considering how the resources you create will be distributed. If you have access to a networked suite, it is likely that there will be a 'shared' storage area on a server. Storing files here gives access to anyone with appropriate rights and could give every pupil access to the work you want them to use without the need to copy the files to each machine (see the task above before trying this!).

Case study part 3: Developing descriptive language

In a follow-up lesson to the one on characterisation described above, the teacher prepares a piece of text describing a character from a book the class shared recently. The character was peripheral to the story so the pupils' ideas about the character are fairly limited. The shared text for the lesson is a passage from the book where the character is involved and the class discuss the clues as to the character's motivation and appearance. The prepared text is shared with the class and it is noted that the descriptive language does not help bring the character to life.

As an individual task, pupils are asked to consider how this description of the character could be improved, and consider whether the new description is compatible with what they already know about him from the book. The teacher has planned three similar tasks around the same idea with different levels of support for different groups of pupils. Higher attaining pupils get a printed version of the text and, in pairs, are identifying sections of the text that they think could be improved, making notes about their ideas and using thesauruses to find better descriptive words. For the pupils in the middle range of attainment, the text is presented on computer screen and in pairs the pupils are reworking the text, including using the online thesaurus built into the word processor (they have used this several times before). The lower attaining pupils again work in pairs but they have a version of the text that uses 'drop-down forms'. Here, the pupils click on a descriptive word or section of the text and select a 'better' word or phrase from the list that appears. They are all encouraged to talk about the reasons for their choices in order to develop their understanding of descriptive vocabulary.

In the plenary, the teacher shares a couple of examples of how the text has been developed, and can compare work from across the range of attainment in the class by focusing on the reasons for their choices without having to draw attention to the difference in the actual levels of attainment of the pupils.

Task 6.3 Using ICT to prepare resources for literacy

Use ICT to develop an appropriate activity for use in teaching literacy for your next placement. Using this activity, create two further activities, one providing a greater challenge, the other additional support. These activities can be for use on or off screen, depending on your confidence and the access to ICT within the school.

Try out the activity with your class and keep a careful eye on how effective the differentiation of the activities was.

Summary

- ICT offers powerful support for teaching literacy and English.
- This can be where the teacher alone uses ICT, such as presenting texts or modelling writing with the whole class.
- Pupils can also benefit from the specific features of particular software, such as effective use of the tools in a word-processing program to develop re-drafting skills.
- It is vitally important to focus on literacy objectives, however, to ensure that the task does not become an ICT skills activity.
- ICT also provides teachers with access to useful resources for teaching aspects of literacy and English, particularly through the ability to adapt and share those resources easily.

Suggestions for further information and reading

Monteith, M. (2002) *Teaching Primary Literacy with ICT*. Buckingham: Open University Press. This book is a valuable resource for more detailed information about teaching literacy and English with ICT. It has a number of chapters written by different authors looking at particular aspects of literacy teaching.

The Teacher Training Agency commissioned research into the effective use of ICT for literacy and numeracy which was published in 1999. It includes a number of case studies of how teachers used ICT to develop aspects of literacy teaching:
Moseley, D., Higgins, S., Bramald, R., Hardman, F., Miller, J., Mroz, M., Tse, H., Newton, D., Thompson, I., Williamson, J., Halligan, J., Bramald, S., Newton, L., Tymms, P., Henderson, B. and Stout, J. (1999) *Ways Forward with ICT: Effective pedagogy using information and communications technology in literacy and numeracy in primary schools*. Newcastle upon Tyne: University of Newcastle upon Tyne. It is available on the web at: http://www.ncl.ac.uk/education/ttaict.

The Standards site has a literacy section (http://www.standards.dfes.gov.uk/literacy/) which you should get used to checking from time to time so that you can keep informed about developments nationally.

7 ICT for numeracy and mathematics

The issues facing teachers in using ICT to support teaching and learning in mathematics are similar to those discussed both within the previous chapter and within the introduction to this section of the book. ICT is an effective support only where its use is transparent to the process; where it helps teachers demonstrate and explain mathematical ideas and where it helps pupils develop their mathematical knowledge, skills and understanding. In order to achieve this, any skills necessary for the use of ICT must be well understood and almost second nature to the user before using the skills within a mathematics lesson.

ICT can provide teachers and learners with resources that help them concentrate on the learning objectives within the National Numeracy Strategy (NNS) and avoid getting bogged down with other issues. For instance, a computer program that produces different types of charts from numerical data is an excellent way to study the interpretation of graphical information. Many such packages will automatically update charts as the numerical data is changed or added, and most will also produce different types of graph or chart at the press of a button or click of the mouse. In this way, pupils can consider the impact of changes in the data, begin to predict likely outcomes based on emerging patterns in data or consider which sort of charts are useful for representing different sorts of information without the need for producing endless new graphs by hand. Being able to plot numerical data onto graphs by hand is a useful and important skill, particularly when it comes to developing an understanding of scale, but being able to understand what it is that charts and graphs tell you and why they are useful is probably even more important. Here, ICT provides access to directly relevant experiences and helps maintain focus on the central issues.

The above example indicates one of the most important contributions that ICT can make to teaching and learning in mathematics. It is widely recognised that helping pupils to visualise mathematical ideas is extremely powerful. ICT provides teachers with opportunities to capitalise on this idea, especially in the areas of:

- visualising numerical patterns through number grids or number lines;
- relationships between shapes through activities that allow direct comparison of shapes and manipulation of their attributes;
- understanding of effects on shapes such as rotation, reflection and division;
- impact of changes in or patterns within data sets; and
- providing a range of ways of presenting the same idea in order to consolidate understanding.

ICT can also provide methods for helping pupils review and consolidate mathematical skills through what are termed 'drill and practice' programs. Mathematics perhaps lends itself to such programs rather better than literacy, since answers can be accurately calculated – which computers tend to be good at. It is not so easy to write an algorithm to evaluate a sentence as a piece of effective persuasive text! However, just because computers can do this, that does not necessarily make it a good thing. Such software has its place, but it should be used carefully as the quality of packages varies considerably. Many appear to be extremely motivating and children often find them engaging, but motivation alone can't justify their use. There are a few Advanced Learning Systems (ALS) that some would claim 'teach' pupils mathematical concepts and there is a fair amount of interest in such programs. We would argue that ALS present similar issues to ordinary 'drill and practice programs' and need to be used carefully. There are legitimate reasons to use programs like these, particularly if they allow a teacher to work more intensively with other pupils (in a smaller group perhaps) or they enable some children to develop quicker responses (which will help them calculate mentally more effectively). It is challenging, however, to ensure that pupils get sufficient practice at an appropriate level, even with the level of sophistication that software currently allows. Both approaches are discussed in more detail in the group and independent work section of this chapter.

ICT for whole-class teaching in mathematics

The National Numeracy Strategy has made its plans for the use of ICT in whole-class teaching through the Numeracy Strategy very clear with the development and distribution of a series of Interactive Teaching Programs (ITPs). ITPs are simple programs designed to help teachers demonstrate a specific learning objective using a digital projector or large (very large!) monitor to the whole class. ITPs cover a range of learning objectives, from demonstrating how to use a protractor to number grids that help you explore patterns and relationships between numbers. All ITPs can be downloaded from the Standards website (www.standards.dfes.gov.uk/numeracy/).

Looking at two of the ITPs in detail may be useful. TellTime is one of the programs available and has much in common with a set of ITPs that you might consider to be 'virtual mathematical resources'. TellTime is a clock face and could be used to do on screen what a more traditional classroom clock face would be used for. Other virtual resources include measuring cylinders, measuring jugs, rulers, scales and so on. As with the clock face, they are all virtual representations of standard classroom equipment. The benefits of using such virtual resources can be in terms of ease of use (such as with the measuring cylinders) and in being able to present lots of related examples (such as in both digital and analogue forms with TellTime) (see Figure 7.1).

Figure 7.1   A screen from the ITP 'TellTime'

A clock face projected onto a large screen at the front of the class can be clearly seen by every pupil, not always easy with a real clock. The program also provides a digital display. Each can be switched on or off to allow consideration of one clock or comparisons between the two. The digital clock can be used in 12- or 24-hour mode and both clocks tell the same time. When opened, clocks are set to real time, but it is simple to set them to whatever time you want. The program also provides a way to study intervals of time by allowing the teacher to advance or turn back the time in steps from 1 minute to 1 hour. Clarity and legibility will certainly help pupils as they are learning to tell the time, but more importantly, steps can be made with extreme accuracy (again, not always as easy as it might be with traditional resources) and comparisons are easy to make, too.

Another style of resource is exemplified by the 'Number Grid' program. Initially the number grid is an on-screen 10 × 10 grid on which numbers can be highlighted simply by a click on the squares. Different colours can be selected to use for highlighting numbers so that the teacher can easily draw attention to specific numbers or patterns. Other features include the ability to mask certain numbers (to see if pupils can apply their knowledge of number patterns to identify missing numbers etc.), increase or decrease the number of columns in the grid, alter the starting number and quickly pick out prime numbers or multiples. Again, the emphasis is on helping pupils visualise structures, patterns and relationships, but this sort of resource is more open-ended and flexible than the 'virtual resource' programs that demonstrate clocks or angles. In this particular program you can also alter the number of columns in the grid. This enables you to investigate how the number patterns for particular multiples are related to the row length (for example, odd and even numbers line up in columns with an even number of squares in a row, but make a chequer-board arrangement with an odd number of squares in a row). Getting the best out of a flexible and open-ended resource such as Number Grid (see Figure 7.2) will take some time and thought, but guidance is provided through the Numeracy Strategy Unit Plans (again, available through the Standards site at www.standards.dfes.gov.uk/numeracy/).

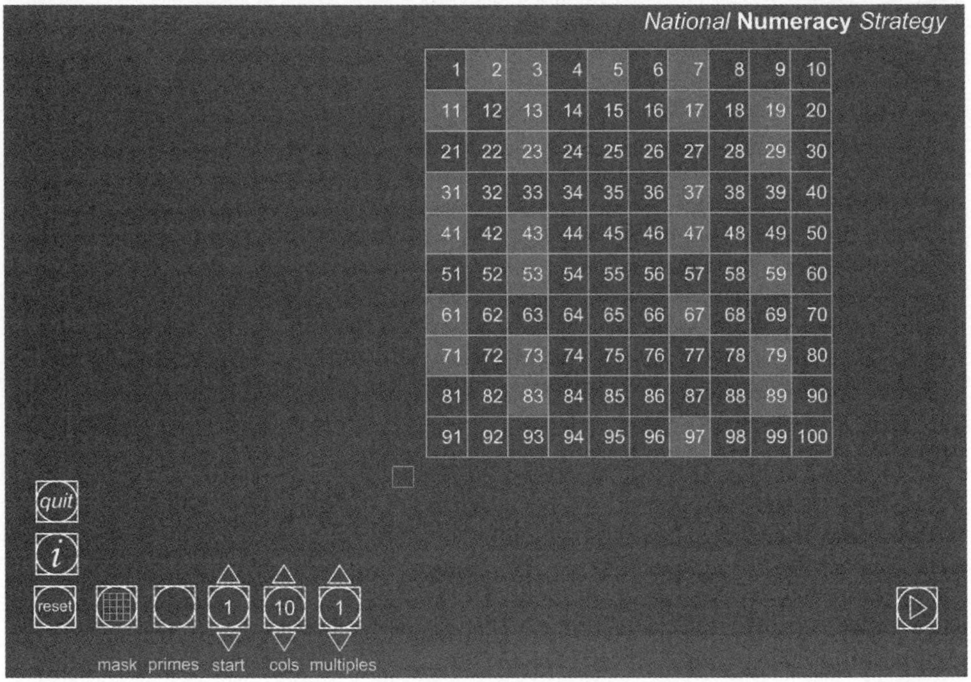

Figure 7.2 A screen from the ITP 'Number Grid'

Some of these programs are rather like one-trick ponies. They are designed in order to provide teachers with opportunities for effective demonstration for specific learning objectives in whole-class sessions. However, with a little creative imagination some of the more open-ended resources could be used very effectively for investigative work within a mathematics lesson, particularly where you want the pupils to be able to present what they have found out.

The ITPs are particularly interesting and relevant, partly because of what they say about the National Numeracy Strategy's idea of effective teaching of aspects of mathematics. In addition the programs have the advantage that they are freely downloadable from the web and are constantly being updated and reviewed. They have been developed to support particular aspects of the National Numeracy Strategy and have accompanying lesson plans and activities. However, whilst useful, they can be a little limited and you will have to spend some time becoming sufficiently familiar with the program to use it confidently in front of the class.

Other providers are working hard to build upon these ideas, and are producing whole suites of software and ready-made resources to support teachers in the use of ICT in whole-class teaching in mathematics. Notable packages would be Easiteach Maths (Research Machines) and Abacus Maths (Heinemann/Harcourt). Both provide teachers with a suite of virtual resources and ready-made lesson starters and also have the opportunity for putting together pupil activities related to the lesson starters. These resources are quite expensive, so not many schools will have them, but it is worth finding out if the schools you are working in do. As these programs are more complex, a little more time and effort will need to be invested in learning how to use them effectively. If you want to have a go, ask which member of staff might be able to help you get started. These packages also make a point of claiming that they are best used with interactive whiteboards as well as projectors. Whilst not essential, an electronic whiteboard will enhance the use of these packages.

Of course, access to a digital projector in the classroom can be a real boon when teaching mathematics, whether you are using ITPs, published mathematics software packages or not. Standard pieces of software can still be used very effectively. A spreadsheet application can be used to gather numerical information and present that information as graphs and charts (see Chapter 3 for further information). Most will also automatically update graphs and charts as numerical information is added or changed, allowing pupils to consider the impact of those changes. Most will also allow you to change the type of charts displayed so that different ways of presenting data can be compared.

Spreadsheets are really designed to help you work with numbers and can be used by pupils to do this too. Spreadsheets can, for instance, be set up as number machines – they can repeat calculation processes quickly and easily so that when putting a range of numbers into a spreadsheet each will be treated in exactly the same way. Can pupils work out what calculation is being carried out? How could this idea be used in oral and mental starter activities? Similarly, spreadsheets can be used to help solve problems where repeating calculations can help find the answer. If you are asked to find a sequence of numbers, for instance, a spreadsheet can produce ranges or sequences of numbers quickly (using what is called the 'fill-down' function) and then perform calculations on those sequences to help you solve the problem. Again, can these ideas be used with the whole class to get them thinking about patterns and applying their ideas to extend patterns?

Desktop publishing software is designed to help users create and manipulate objects on screen. As a result they can be very useful for studying properties of two-dimensional shapes. All DTP packages allow you to create simple shapes quickly and easily and most have built-in functions to rotate and reflect these shapes once created. Since shapes can be easily duplicated (copy and paste) and the reflection and rotation functions can easily be repeated on a computer, a series of similar shapes can be rotated (possibly in steps of, say, 90° at a time) to help pupils visualise the effect of rotation upon them. Similarly, reflection of shapes can be clearly demonstrated.

Once these ideas have been established, reflecting and rotating shapes can make for interesting activities developing patterns and investigating tessellation.

Working with shapes can also help pupils visualise other concepts, such as fractions. Dividing a square into halves provides a clear visual reinforcement of the numerical idea, but dividing a square into halves in different ways (horizontally, vertically, diagonally as well as obliquely) can help pupils understand the idea more completely. Of course, the idea can easily be extended to other fractions and to compare fractions (where one half clearly covers the same area of the square as two quarters etc.).

For more direct forms of teacher-led demonstration, presentation software can be used effectively and can provide nice ways of building up sequences or steps through animations. For instance, a presentation of numbers emerging one by one on a number grid might allow pupils a little time to consider the patterns that are emerging and predict what will appear next. Can they calculate quickly enough to beat the computer?

Case study part 1: Teaching percentages

The following describes how a teacher might use ICT in whole-class teaching within a mathematics lesson. The teacher has a digital projector and interactive whiteboard installed in the classroom. She has had initial training on the use of the whiteboard but does not consider herself to be especially competent in using it, or in using ICT in general. The school also has six laptop computers available for use in classrooms. These laptops are not networked and have basic generic software installed on them.

The teacher uses the classroom PC and the digital projector for an oral and mental starter session. The teacher had prepared a series of simple but incomplete number grids. The numbers in the grids followed increasingly complex patterns. Each grid was displayed for a short time on the screen and pupils had to identify a pattern and use their recollection of that pattern to fill in the numbers they had seen, and then the missing numbers on blank photocopied grids. The review of their answers includes discussion of strategies and patterns that were used to help complete the empty grids.

The teacher then went to the whiteboard to begin work on extending the children's understanding of percentages using a prepared number line in a DTP package (Microsoft's Publisher). The number line (more accurately described as an on-screen ruler made from a long narrow rectangle) was divided into 100 steps and marked in steps of 10. She began the lesson with an explanation of the meaning of the term 'per cent' and then used visual representations of percentages on the number line to show a percentage as a number of parts of 100. She created rectangles that were as long as a given percentage and used this to indicate that the position of the rectangle was unimportant, it still represented the same proportion of the total.

As a class they then began to consider different percentages of the total and made links to previous knowledge (relating to fractions). The teacher noted these observations and annotated the number line accordingly.

Task 7.1 Using ICT in whole-class teaching for mathematics Find an interactive teaching program (ITP) that is suitable for the age-group you are working with.

Practise using it and plan a whole-class activity as part of an oral/mental starter activity or as part of the main teaching activity for a lesson.

The ITPs are available on the Standards site (www.standards.dfes.gov.uk/numeracy). You will probably want to download them anyway as resources for your teaching of mathematics. If any of them are appropriate for work you are planning during your next placement, download the program and plan a lesson around it. Obviously, whether you can use the program effectively depends on whether you have the opportunity to use a projector or large screen in the classroom where you teach mathematics. If such technology is available, try it out as the whole-class teaching element of a mathematics lesson. As an alternative, you might be able to work with a small group in front of a computer with a large screen. If not, consider how you might replicate the ideas without the technology.

ICT in group or individual work in mathematics

ICT is particularly useful when preparing resources for small-group or individual work in mathematics because it allows teachers to make changes to the content of activities (even if it's just the challenge of the numbers used in particular calculations) without a great deal of additional effort. Once one activity is prepared it is a simple matter to change the numbers used to provide for differentiation, but also to provide a range of activities covering similar issues so that pupils have their own set of questions to answer – completing work is no longer a matter of copying what the child next to you has written!

ICT can be extremely useful for presenting and recording individual work in mathematics. Obviously, reusing some of the ideas discussed in the section above could be considered. Many of the ITPs discussed could be adopted for use as individual pupil activities, though they do not offer feedback so are better suited to open-ended investigation than practising skills to achieve specific learning objectives.

Work involving study of properties of two-dimensional shapes, for instance, can be as useful at whole-class level as it can at an individual level, though the purpose will be different. When studying properties of shapes at a class level, the use of ICT is about visualisation and accuracy (exact measurements of size, rotation etc.) but at an individual level, it is more about reinforcement and demonstration of understanding. With clearly worded questions from the teacher, children can demonstrate their understanding through their use of ICT. For instance, giving pupils an image of a scalene triangle and asking them to represent that triangle if it is rotated through 90° as a freehand activity with paper and pencil will either elicit an inaccurate answer or an extremely time-consuming one (while the children measure sides, angles and redraw the shape and then work out that rotating through 90° could be interpreted two ways and have to repeat the performance rotating in the other direction).

With ICT, speed and accuracy are easily provided and it also indicates a level of understanding of the concept that could be masked in other situations. Use of rotation and reflection tools within a desktop publishing package demonstrates an explicit understanding of the idea and cannot really be fudged in the way it might if you provide children with two-dimensional shapes for manipulation on the table-top. It also requires explicit use of appropriate mathematical terminology (selecting 'Rotate' from the appropriate menu shows that the pupil knows the difference between rotation and reflection, for instance). Another advantage of using ICT is that it is much easier to correct your mistake, if you spot it. This can be especially useful when trying to persuade pupils to check their own work (if correcting the mistake is easier it tends to be done with better grace!).

Of course, an on-screen activity for working with shapes or pattern sequences needs to be set up in a different way to activities done through whole-class teaching. First there needs to be more structure to the activity to keep pupils focused on the learning objective; second, the ICT skills required must be well within the capabilities of the pupils to ensure that there is no need to teach those skills at the same time as tackling challenging mathematical concepts.

Continuing with the idea of using DTP software, preparing an activity for use by individual pupils might need to include clear instructions and organisational mechanisms that support pupils in working independently. For instance, considering an activity on sorting two-dimensional shapes according to their properties might include a simple instruction on what to do, but also a sorting grid, similar to a Carroll diagram. Pupils could then sort shapes on screen according to number of sides and regularity. The sorting grid diagram would therefore have columns for three or four sides and rows for regular and irregular shapes. A collection of prepared rectangles and triangles that pupils can simply drag around the screen to sort appropriately would be provided. Most DTP packages would handle this sort of idea happily, but many will have the added functionality of being able to 'lock' some elements of the page so that they cannot be moved by mistake. This is incredibly useful – without it you will quickly find that in trying to sort shapes the children have mistakenly resized the chart and deleted all the instructions!

Sometimes 'locking' shapes involves moving them to different layers, and this should also be investigated. For instance, Microsoft's Publisher has two layers, the background and the foreground. Placing instructions and organisational devices in the background of the file, and the shapes into the foreground, means that pupils can play all day with the individual shapes and never run the risk of altering anything in the background.

ICT can also provide some nice opportunities for investigation. Developing individual tasks along the lines of group activities discussed above is fairly straightforward, but there are other pieces of software and that can be used very effectively. For instance, a child-friendly paint package will often have a 'stamper' tool, which allows young children to produce pictures with repeating elements (a row of recognisable houses along a street). This same tool can be a nice way for pupils to start making repeating patterns or collections of objects. These may be collections of things that are red, things that make nice patterns, groups of (five) things exactly the same, or pictures with three birds, three houses, three cars and three dogs and so on. The nice thing about this idea is that it works both ways. Setting a child the open-ended task of producing a 'counting' picture with three of everything gives them a challenge (both creatively and mathematically) but also provides a resource for activities with other children. Are there really three of *everything* in this picture?

In the above section we briefly considered published software for helping teachers prepare and deliver effective whole-class teaching in mathematics. Several software publishers are also developing software for use at an individual pupil level. These types of software are sometimes called Advanced Learning Systems (ALS) and claim to assess pupils' ability and present them with individually tailored activities that fit their attainment level and the Numeracy Strategy Framework. RM Maths (from Research Machines) is probably the most widely adopted ALS for Primary Maths. Certainly, used carefully, these sorts of packages do appear to offer significant opportunities for improving pupil attainment. However, it isn't as simple as plonking pupils in front of a computer with ALS software and letting them get on with it, despite what manufacturers might claim. In reality, learning gains can be quite short-lived and are only ever effectively maintained when used to supplement more traditional approaches to teaching and learning (see Chapter 5). They do provide excellent sources of assessment information to teachers, however. Many will provide question-by-question summaries for each individual pupil and will group these summaries according to learning areas, to help teachers focus their teaching on ideas and concepts that are comparatively less well understood. Some packages even support the use of individualised teaching (by the teacher, not the computer) to tackle specific misunderstandings.

Of course, 'drill and practice' programs, software that poses calculation problems as part of a virtual scenario, work at an individual child level too. As discussed above, their use needs to be carefully considered in the school setting. They can be very engaging and motivating for pupils, especially boys, if our observations are anything to go by. However, they often place emphasis on the wrong part of the learning task and rarely offer useful feedback to children. For instance, the purpose of performing the calculations may be to complete the course in the shortest possible time, or get the highest score. As a result, pupils are more interested in their score than they are in improving their strategies and techniques for solving problems or learning to tackle different problems. From a child's point of view, getting a score of 520,000 on Number Nuke-em!™ is more important than addressing the problem you might have had with the division question[1] . . . which brings us to another point. Few of these programs provide pupils with the sort of feedback that might help improve performance. Knowing that you got all the addition and subtraction questions right but struggled with the multiplication questions might be useful. Even more useful would be knowing that the multiplication questions that you particularly struggled with were from the seven- and eight-times tables.

Calculators have been deliberately left off this list. Clearly they are useful at both whole-class and individual work levels, but their use and usefulness is more widely acknowledged outside of education than computers. Debate drags on about calculators' role within schools and we don't intend to tackle these issues here. It seems obvious to us that they should be used to develop mathematical skills and understanding and not as a replacement for mathematical thinking. They are also cheap and convenient to use. However, it is difficult to have a sensible debate about such issues in the current climate.

Case study part 2: Developing resources

Following on from the introduction to percentages as a whole-class activity, one group of pupils is to investigate these ideas further. The teacher has prepared an activity for the group using the same DTP package as she used for the whole-class demonstration. The activity includes the same number line used previously, locked to the page so that it cannot be moved. There are a number of different length blocks on the screen and pupils have to identify what percentage of the whole number line each block represents. Once identified, pupils are asked to investigate how many combinations of blocks could be used to rebuild the full line and are encouraged to find likely answers through mental calculation and then test their ideas through experimentation.

Task 7.2   Using ICT in group or individual work for mathematics

Take one of the above ideas and try to recreate a similar activity, appropriate for your pupils, studying something relevant either in number work or shape, space and pattern. Using either a paint package or DTP package, either set a brief for an open-ended investigation or set up a structured activity. Before you start, make sure that you will have access to the necessary computers to make the task worthwhile.

ICT in planning and preparation for teaching mathematics

At this level, advice about the effective use of ICT in teacher preparation will be broadly similar, no matter which subject area is being considered. Therefore, the following advice is the same as offered for teacher preparation for teaching and learning in literacy, but with a numerical twist!

ICT offers teachers many ways in which to handle their professional responsibilities in terms of planning, preparing and delivering effective lessons as well as in managing their classrooms and their pupils. The government is keen to promote the use of ICT, and particularly communications technologies, to help teachers develop their professional practice, and for this reason the DfES put a great deal of effort into its online strategy. All planning documentation used in schools, including the National Curriculum for Mathematics and the Numeracy Strategy Framework, are available online through the Standards site. To back up the Strategy, the DfES also publish a significant amount of support material, including Unit Plans, that actually give teachers weekly planning and lesson plans for every week of the year. At the time of writing, plans are available for

Years 4, 5 and 6 but plans for Years 1, 2 and 3 are under development. In directing you towards the Unit Plans for the Numeracy Strategy, we would also suggest that you use these plans critically. Many teachers are finding that the plans provide a sound structure but some of the individual activities can be a bit dull. Be prepared to put time and effort into making the Unit Plans a little more interesting and engaging for your class!

Individual schools will also have a range of particular resources that they have purchased through various government schemes which can be delivered through ICT. These banks of digital learning materials may be Internet- or CD-based and are likely to including video clips that can act as stimulus for lessons, or they may be interactive activities that are designed to help pupils consolidate basic skills. Check what is available and find out how the school acquired them.

As mentioned earlier, many teachers prepare resources for their lessons using computers. A digital version of a worksheet is easy to adapt and therefore provide effective differentiation, or simply several similar versions to prevent pupils copying answers. Preparing and storing work on a computer provides starting points for new work, many teachers who use ICT regularly to develop teaching resources tell you that they never open an empty file and start work; they almost always open an existing file that is similar and work over the top of that. This approach is usually much quicker as there is less formatting and planning to be done.

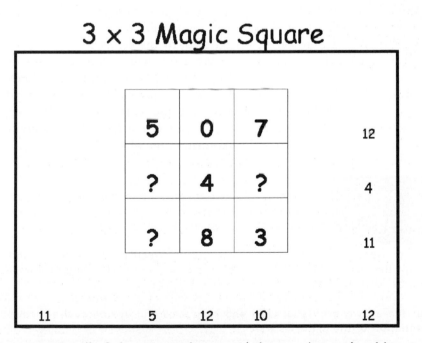

3 x 3 Magic Square

Can you make all of the rows, columns and the two diagonals add up to the same total ? Change the numbers in the square and see if you can make all the smaller numbers around the outside all the same.

Figure 7.3 A magic square activity based on a spreadsheet

When preparing resources for use on screen it is essential that you make sure that pupils will be presented with the tools they need to get the job done. For instance, many programs allow you to choose which tools appear in the toolbars at the top of the screen. If you are investigating patterns it may be important that pupils can easily access copy, paste and rotate functions, for instance. In which case, as part of your preparation for such activities, you need to make sure that the copy, paste and rotate buttons are available on the toolbar. However, it might be a distraction to have text formatting tools or flip tools available. Make sure that the way the tools are presented is as helpful to the purpose of the task as possible.

When preparing files for use on the computer, it is also worth considering whether the format is appropriate for your pupils. Clearly, selecting the right sorts of fonts is important (probably those that match the school's handwriting policy as closely as possible are best), but it is also important to consider whether they are an appropriate size, are they clearly legible? Does the presentation (style, colour etc.) help to clarify meaning or does it make it difficult to read? Can the page be set up to support specific needs? For visually impaired pupils, increasing font size may work, but it might make little difference depending on a child's particular needs. Children with specific visual learning difficulties may find that changing the background colour of the page from white to, say, blue, enhances their ability to read text and so on. Is the presentation supporting independent work? The idea of locking parts of a page down so that they cannot be moved is discussed in the previous section, but also consideration of instructions and prompts on screen might be helpful. If you have a talking word processor, these instructions could even be 'read' by the computer!

Make sure you know how the resources you create will be distributed. If you have access to a networked suite, it is likely that there will be a 'shared' storage area on a server. Storing files here gives access to anyone with appropriate rights and could give every pupil access to the work you want them to use without the need to copy the files to each machine. It is essential that you protect the resources you create and distribute in this way: see Task 6.2 for information on why and how!

Task 7.3 Using ICT to prepare resources for mathematics	Find the Unit Plans from the NNS for the year group you will be working with next. If they aren't available in school, download them from the Standards site.

Identify an aspect of the Unit Plans that could be effectively delivered through ICT and adapt the plan to make the activities interesting and challenging for the pupils you will be working with.

Try out the activity with your class and keep a careful eye on how effective the differentiation of the activities was.

Before undertaking this task, make sure that using the NNS Unit Plan is consistent with the approach or scheme of work within the school where you are placed. You will also need to find out what sort of access to ICT equipment you will have. You may have to adapt your planning accordingly to ensure that it fits with these possible constraints.

Summary

- ICT offers powerful support for teaching numeracy and mathematics.
- This can be where the teacher alone uses ICT, such as using specially designed software like ITPs or by demonstrating and modelling aspects of mathematics to the whole class.
- Pupils can also benefit from the specific features of particular software, such as software that lets them practise particular skills or apply their mathematical knowledge in a software environment.
- It is vitally important to focus on mathematics objectives, however, to ensure that the task does not become an ICT skills activity.
- ICT also provides teachers with access to useful resources for teaching aspects of numeracy and mathematics, particularly through the ability to adapt and share those resources easily.

Note

1   Not a real program (so far as we know!).

Suggestions for further information and reading

The Teacher Training Agency commissioned research into the effective use of ICT for literacy and numeracy which was published in 1999. It includes a number of case studies of how teachers used ICT to develop aspects of mathematics teaching:

Moseley, D., Higgins, S., Bramald, R., Hardman, F., Miller, J., Mroz, M., Tse, H., Newton, D., Thompson, I., Williamson, J., Halligan, J., Bramald, S., Newton, L., Tymms, P., Henderson, B. and Stout, J. (1999) *Ways Forward with ICT: Effective pedagogy using information and communications technology in literacy and numeracy in primary schools*. Newcastle upon Tyne: University of Newcastle upon Tyne. It is available on the web at: http://www.ncl.ac.uk/education/ttaict.

Higgins, S. and Mujis, D. (1999) 'ICT and numeracy in primary schools', in I. Thompson (ed.) *Issues in Teaching Numeracy in Primary Schools*, pp. 103–116. Buckingham: Open University Press.
Gives an overview of the potential contribution of ICT to the teaching of mathematics.

Higgins, S. (2003) 'Does ICT make mathematics teaching more effective?', in I. Thompson (ed.) *Enhancing Primary Mathematics Teaching*. Milton Keynes: Open University Press.
A review of the evidence about the impact of ICT on the teaching of mathematics.

Fox, B., Montague-Smith, A. and Wilkes, S. (2000) *Using ICT in Primary Mathematics: Practice and possibilities*. London: David Fulton.
For more information about developing the use of ICT in primary mathematics.

The Standards site has a specific numeracy section which you will need to look at from time to time to keep up to date with national developments (http://www.standards.dfes.gov.uk/ numeracy/).

The NCAction website (www.ncaction.org.uk) provides materials to help teachers assess their pupils' work; other government-sponsored or recognised sites such as Teacher Net (www.teachernet.org) or GridClub (www.gridclub.org) have materials that directly support teaching in mathematics. Through the e-Learning Credits scheme (together with Curriculum Online) the government are also effectively sponsoring the adoption of e-learning materials in British schools. Try and find out what the school you are placed in has purchased through this scheme.

8 ICT in primary science

Science currently has no National Strategy to support teachers in delivering the National Curriculum for Science, but the QCA (Qualifications and Curriculum Authority) has produced a Scheme of Work for Science in Key Stages 1 and 2 that exemplifies how the National Curriculum could be delivered. Many schools adopt the scheme, though most adapt the individual units of work to fit their school, their pupils and their resources. As a result, the majority of the content of this chapter focuses on the use of ICT in supporting the process of teaching and learning through the QCA Scheme of Work.

As with all National Curriculum subjects, there is a statement of pupil entitlement indicating that all children in primary school should have the opportunity to learn with or through ICT when studying science. The Scheme of Work indicates a few opportunities for the use of ICT but these are often fairly generic. For instance, in Unit 1A – Ourselves, in the list of resources a 'CD-ROM or video of animals moving' is included as is a 'tape of familiar sounds', but these are not elaborated upon. Research through ICT is often suggested too, but there is little guidance on how this should be done or how it relates to the activities described in the unit.

Of course, ICT can make a far more significant contribution to teaching and learning in science than these brief remarks might imply, and it is up to the teacher to decide how and when to exploit the opportunities ICT offers. Chapters 6 and 7 in this book were both arranged around three areas of the use of ICT: whole-class teaching, group and individual work, and teacher preparation. The structure of the QCA scheme means that these three discrete areas are perhaps not so relevant. Instead, areas for discussion in this section are based around the contribution that ICT might make to specific areas of scientific study; measuring and recording, data presentation and analysis, demonstration and visualisation, consolidating learning and research. Of course, within these themes there will still be opportunities for whole-class, group and individual work and teacher preparation and these are covered within each section.

Measuring and recording using ICT

A very important aspect of science is making accurate measurements and observations, and recording those measurements or observations in a useful and meaningful way. ICT tends to be extremely good at helping both to take measurements and record observations. In terms of measurement, computers can be used to gather certain forms of data automatically, accurately and whenever and however necessary. This process is referred to as either 'monitoring' or 'data-logging', and usually requires an interface that is plugged into a computer along with a series of sensors designed to collect different forms of information. In terms of recording, databases and spreadsheets can both be extremely useful in helping you to collect relevant information, to search through and sort that information and then to help you display that information in different ways. Recent innovations in digital technologies mean that schools now have access to digital cameras and digital video cameras. Both open up a range of opportunities to help children make accurate observations and provide an incredibly detailed record at the same time.

Monitoring

Monitoring can provide methods for collecting data that cannot be gathered in other ways. Typically, data monitoring hardware provides you with an interface (a little box of tricks) to connect to the PC and a range of sensors that can be used to record information such as temperature, sound and light levels. Other forms of sensor are available for measuring time, pressure, movement (like PIRs on an alarm system) and so on, but these sensors are not commonly used in primary schools.

Most sets of hardware are accompanied by software that allows you to configure the interface, design a data collection procedure and view the data recorded. You may have to tell the computer which sorts of sensor you have plugged into the interface, you then need to tell it when you want to take a measurement using each sensor (this can be a single 'snapshot' measurement when you click a button or it can be a series of 'snapshot' measurements, say every five minutes over the period of an hour, or continuous measurements over a whole day).

The advantages of collecting numerical data through such a system are many and varied. To start with, setting up a data collection procedure means that the computer can be left to get on with making measurements that would otherwise have to be done by hand. The computer won't forget to take a reading during PE or over lunchtime, no restrictions on taking measurements overnight and so on. You get consistent and accurate data pretty much every time. The accuracy of the reading is valuable, though perhaps not overtly so (until you compare them to the readings taken by hand!) but the way data is presented is also useful. Many pieces of data monitoring software will present the measurements collected as a chart, similar to a spreadsheet, and as a 'live' line or bar graph. The ability to graph data immediately can make looking for trends and making predictions as the experiment is taking place a real possibility. This means that interpreting the data is much more immediate, as compared with paper and pencil methods where charting or graphing results has to be done as a separate task.

Data monitoring is taught through a unit of work from the ICT Scheme of Work in Year 5 (Unit 5f – Monitoring environmental conditions and changes) but there are opportunities to use data logging software in the science Scheme of Work, even though the unit plans may not mention it specifically. For instance, Unit 3f – Light and shadows suggests that ICT may be used to provide information – 'secondary sources *e.g. reference books, CD-ROMs*'. Part of the Unit includes studying the patterns of the sun each day for two weeks and suggests pupils make observations and measurements each day at the same time. Monitoring light levels in the classroom every day for a week would not replace the original activity but could be a valuable supplement to it. Children in Year 3 may not be up to setting up the PC to gather the required data, but they are more than capable of understanding the graphs and charts that will be produced.

Monitoring can be used effectively in the study of light intensity (Unit 3f), temperature (Units 4c and 5d) volume of sound (Unit 5f) and could be used for timing some experiments with appropriate switches.

Recording using digital images

An important feature of primary science is that children learn to make observations and record what they see. These are important skills: however, it has to be noted that sometimes the process of recording observations can reduce the value of the observations themselves. Asking children to record what their seedling looks like each day, for instance, may produce a series of drawings or notes that do not bear any relation to one another so comparing them at the end of the study will not help. By using a digital camera to record what the seedling looks like each day you provide a quick and accurate record of the changes. (If you remember to plant a measuring stick of some sort alongside the seedling, you also have a perfect record of how much it grows each day.) Downloading these images into the PC and dropping them into, say, a prepared PowerPoint template will also make sure that the changes over time can be viewed easily as you flick through the slides.

Many scientific experiments could exploit the power and immediacy of digital stills pictures. Teachers need to consider how images taken are stored and managed once on the computer, but the fact that the recording itself takes such a short amount of time with a camera means that there is usually enough time to deal with the management side of it all, too. Units of work that might benefit from the use of digital cameras include:

Unit 1b – Growing plants;
Unit 2b – Plants and animals in the local environment;
Unit 2c – Variation;
Unit 3b – Helping plants grow well;
Unit 3c – Characteristics of materials;
Unit 4b – Habitats;
Unit 6a – Interdependence and adaptation.

Whilst many teachers are already using digital still cameras day in and day out, the use of digital video in classrooms is only just emerging. There is now a range of inexpensive devices that can be used to capture reasonable quality digital video that cost significantly less than £100 and are especially child friendly. Using video in the classroom is not only a possibility, but a very powerful opportunity. Attainment Target 1 in science is all about the process of carrying out an effective experiment and drawing conclusions from your observations, and digital video could be an extremely effective way of gathering evidence about pupils' abilities in AT1. Traditionally, AT1 has been hard to assess or keep records about because it is concerned with the discussions and thinking that go in to a scientific investigation.

In addition, evidence collected through digital video can be an integral part of the investigation, and can provide forms of recording and evidence that cannot normally be collected in the classroom. For instance, studying the effects of gravity and air resistance (Unit 6e – Forces in action – effects of gravity) children may drop pieces of paper from a set height. Each piece of paper would be exactly the same size but might be crumpled or shaped in different ways. Children will observe that each piece of paper moves differently as it falls, but exactly what difference do those variations make? Normally, recording how long it takes a piece of paper to fall a set height accurately would be extremely difficult. If, however, you take a piece of video of the experiments and then watch the video back it is possible to view the footage frame by frame. You can make direct comparisons between the different tests and calculate very precisely how long it takes for each piece to reach the ground. You can also study the path taken by the different pieces in great detail, providing useful evidence for discussion and review.

Making effective records

Perhaps rather less glamorous, but just as useful, is ICT's ability to help you record data in organised and efficient ways. Recording numerical data can be done effectively with a spreadsheet application, as the table format they use tends to be easy to work with. Also, once the data is in the spreadsheet it is easy to work with. This will be discussed in more detail in the following section but in terms of organising your data, spreadsheets can be set up to help children make accurate records because units of measurement can be listed in column headers, the table structure makes for clear records and the spreadsheets' ability to present numerical data as charts and graphs at the click of a button can be extremely useful.

The distinction between databases and spreadsheets can become blurred, but generally speaking, spreadsheets are good for recording numerical data and databases are good for collecting more general information. Databases are often referred to within the Scheme of Work and usually in the context of recording the findings of open-ended research. Collecting together relevant pieces of information about things children are studying so that findings from a range of different activities can be gathered together and reviewed can be very useful. For instance, if you were studying Unit 3C – Characteristics of materials, you might use various forms of investigation in a collection of materials, put all the data from the different investigations into one database and then use that data to help you make choices about the most appropriate materials for a given job. You may have collected information about materials in terms of buoyancy, rigidity, translucence, strength, relative weight and absorbency. Once all that information is put into the database you can ask questions and use the information to select the best material. The real trick is to look for different uses, so you could look for the best material for making a tree house (combining strength, lightness and weatherproofing) and then the best material for making a raft (rigidity, buoyancy and absorbency) and so on. Analysing this information also comes under the following heading, but the process of recording information effectively is relevant here.

Task 8.1 Using ICT for recording in science	During your next teaching practice, find out if the school (or your college or university) has digital cameras for pupil use. If so, borrow one for a short while and have a play to find out how it works. Consider how a digital camera might be used in

the science work you are covering with the class. If cameras don't easily fit into the activity the pupils may be undertaking, consider how you might be able to use it for developing understanding about AT1. Digital images of the process of the experiment the children undertook can be a useful stimulus for discussing what they did and why they did it that way. They also make great material for displays and evidence for your own portfolio!

Data presentation and analysis

As mentioned above, recording information using ICT can provide useful opportunities for helping pupils to analyse, interpret and present findings from their experiments. Spreadsheets are especially good for dealing with numerical data and can be used to sort, search through and present data quickly and effectively. It should be noted that ICT isn't just providing a simple way to make an effective record, however. Used well, collecting and analysing data from experiments helps pupils with a range of scientific skills, from spotting possible errors in the data to identifying patterns and predicting outcomes. For instance, data collected over a period of time and by hand may well contain mistakes. If pupils are recording temperatures over a period of time it is possible that one or two readings may not be accurate (either misread from the thermometer or written down inaccurately). When the data is presented as a list of numbers it is possible to spot errors, but it is often much easier to spot when the data is presented as a line graph (where a sudden spike up or down might seem to go against a general trend in the data).

Spreadsheets can be used to turn numerical data into graphs and charts instantly. When using monitoring hardware the numerical data is immediately turned into a line graph or bar chart: as the experiment continues it is possible to spot patterns as they emerge. Discussing the data as it emerges on screen allows children to refine their thinking and their predictions about the experiment. This immediacy can be much more powerful than recording a prediction at the beginning of an experiment and returning to that prediction at the end of the test. By discussing and reviewing their ideas as they go, children begin to work out their misconceptions for themselves, often helping them to understand the issues better.

If used simply to record data as it is collected by hand, having the spreadsheet turn measurements into a graph immediately can have a similar effect. It can provide opportunities for children to discuss what they have found, and it can also allow them to identify issues whilst the experiment is ongoing, making re-measurement much easier.

Of course, having a computer draw all your graphs for you not only helps children to spot patterns and make predictions, it also makes the process of producing charts much easier. Children do need to be taught how to draw and construct graphs, but it may not be necessary for them to do it after every experiment. The important issue is being able to understand what the graphs tell you, not that you repeat the process over and over until you can do it in your sleep. Here, ICT is a good way to get children to focus on the important issues and the science involved, rather than the skills involved in drawing the charts.

Indeed, having the ability to construct and change charts and graphs can help you understand the purpose of the different charts themselves. Presenting the same data as a bar chart, a line graph, a scatter graph and a pie chart can take a few seconds using a spreadsheet. Once constructed, children can consider what it is that each chart actually shows and whether or not they are helpful. Doing this by hand would be an extremely tedious process.

Task 8.2 Using spreadsheets in science	If you aren't especially familiar with using spreadsheets to create graphs and charts or to sort data, find out what sort of spreadsheet program your school has and familiarise yourself with it. Some spreadsheets, especially ones designed for use with children, produce charts quickly and easily, often at the click of a button. Sometimes spreadsheets don't do what you expect them to do with data, but playing around with different made-up sets of numbers will help you understand why they do what they do when drawing charts. This isn't something you want to discover in front of the children!

Demonstration and visualisation

Whole-class demonstration through ICT is as valuable in science as it is in literacy and numeracy, though the whole-class element of teaching science is perhaps not so heavily promoted as within the strategies. With access to digital projectors or large monitors many of the ideas discussed above can be effectively shared with the whole class. Undoubtedly the ability to present and discuss what graphs, charts, series of digital pictures or video clips can tell us will help pupils to understand both the scientific idea and the benefit of ICT.

By sharing this sort of information with groups of pupils not only do you stimulate more detailed discussion but you also provide visual clues to help pupils to see patterns and support recall of relevant information. There is a growing range of software and resources that allow pupils to 'see' things that previously they could only hear or read about in the classroom. For instance, access to the Internet through a PC linked to a projector gives teachers the opportunity to show pupils footage from the surface of Mars as recorded by NASA missions shortly after those images first hit the news (www.nasa.gov). Alternatively, satellite footage of weather systems moving, building and dissipating can be viewed from the Meteorological Office (www.metoffice.gov.uk/). Digital dissections can be shown to indicate similarities and differences between species and so on (for example, www.digitalfrog.com/).

The Digital Frog International website carries some excellent examples of how ICT can bring otherwise inaccessible scientific evidence into the classroom, and while the site's primary intention is to get you to buy Digital Frog software on CD-ROM there is a wide range of demonstration software that provides information and resources for anatomy and studying different habitats. These kinds of software are certainly worth a look if they meet the planning for your school placement and can be downloaded from www.digitalfrog.com/demo/dwnld_demo.html (see Figure 8.1), though don't try to download them unless you have broadband access as they are big files! The website also has a range of other resources such as digital field trips to the

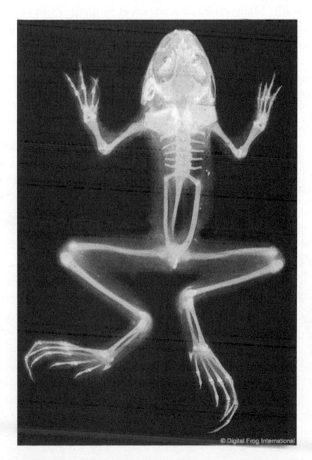

Figure 8.1 A screenshot from the Digital Frog resources. Reproduced by permission of Digital Frog International

rainforest or the desert as well as digital images, diagrams and links to other related sites that can be freely used in schools.

Concept Cartoons (http://www.conceptcartoons.com/) are an excellent way to discuss aspects of the science curriculum to assess pupils' understanding of key ideas and concepts. These resources are available on a CD-ROM and are designed to be used on an interactive whiteboard. A key scientific idea is presented in cartoon (or animated cartoon) format with an explanation from one of the characters. Pupils have to think up their own reasons and explanations for the particular events or scientific phenomena. The cartoons also come with background information for the teacher!

Whilst Internet access can provide you with a growing and changing set of resources that could be used effectively within the classroom, using the Internet for such work has its downside. The speed and reliability of your Internet connection can turn a simple demonstration into a frustrating experience for everyone if either or both decide to play up. Then there is the fact that sites often change, so finding the resources you saw even just a few weeks ago could be a problem (always check before delivering the lesson!). Many interactive sites require plug-ins in order to access some services, so you need to make sure that the PC you are using to demonstrate the site can display all the features you have planned to use.

Of course, using CD-ROMs can be a safer bet. Many CD-ROM encyclopedias have useful content in the form of diagrams, animations and film footage (such as time-lapse video) that can help you explain and discuss scientific ideas. You will

Figure 8.2 A concept cartoon: 'I'll go fastest down the hill because I'm the heaviest'

almost certainly find a stack of reference CD-ROMs in any school you are visiting and as likely as not, many will be unused or underexploited. Using CDs effectively requires a degree of familiarity with the content that takes a little time to develop. Without access to a projector, using a single reference CD in the class takes a long time for each pupil to have a turn and can therefore be unrewarding, but by sharing the process of locating and viewing the resources on the CD you get instant results and real benefits. Actually locating relevant information on CDs or on the Internet is an important skill to develop, too, but this will be dealt with later.

Other pieces of software that you might come across may include what is termed 'modelling' software. Models are used in science to try to gauge the effect of changing something and can be useful ways of showing how things might be related to one another. A classic scientific model is the relationship between plants, herbivores and carnivores in a food chain. A simple (perhaps over-simple) model would show that if the numbers of herbivores went up their food supply would diminish (due to more of them eating the vegetation) whilst at the same time (given a greater food supply) the number of carnivores would start to increase, both of which would mark a downturn in the population of herbivores (less food and more predators for them) and so on. Such models can be created using spreadsheets but more normally, teachers would buy the software from education suppliers or download it from the Internet.

One example of extremely simple but useful modelling software is Crocodile Clips Elementary. Crocodile Clips can be downloaded from its website (www.crocodile-clips.com) and performs a single task. It provides a set of simple electronic tools that allow children to create circuits that incorporate batteries, bulbs, buzzers, variable resistors, light-emitting diodes and different forms of switch. Elements of the circuit are simply dragged onto and around the screen and are connected to one another by drawing lines between the elements. The really nice thing about this software is that when a switch is thrown and the circuit completes, the bulb lights or the buzzer sounds. If the number of batteries in a simple circuit is doubled then the bulb will appear to glow more brightly and differences between series and parallel circuits can be investigated and so on. The point is that children can 'play' with the elements of the circuit and how it is connected and discover things for themselves. Should they make a hypothesis, they can then test out their idea on screen and easily compare two solutions or ideas side by side. It is the ability to freely experiment with their ideas and spot patterns or habits for themselves that makes using modelling software with children so powerful.

In 2001 the DfES struck a deal with the Intel Corporation and provided every primary school in the country with an Intel Microscope. These microscopes connect to a PC, but otherwise function just like traditional microscopes. They have different magnification levels and can handle sample slides. They can also be used to view solid objects (alive or dead) in small sample boxes. The real advantage is that, with a projector, a whole class can view the same sample at once. They might be studying the movement of an insect or the surface of different leaves, but comparisons can be made and discussed easily. Moreover, still images or short clips of video can be captured with the microscope, so evidence can be stored and reviewed later. In terms of providing first-hand evidence that helps you demonstrate your point and helps children visualise what these ideas mean, this can be an extremely powerful piece of equipment. You should find one in the school you are placed in.

Units of work that might be enhanced by using ICT-based sources to help children visualise scientific ideas include:

- Unit 2c Variation – Similarities and differences between animals (including humans) and plants;
- Unit 4a – Moving and growing (time-lapse footage of plants and animals growing);
- Unit 4d – Solids, liquids and how they can be separated (showing molten materials and change of state quickly and easily);
- Unit 5b – Life cycles (looking at parts of a flower, perhaps with the microscope);
- Unit 5e – Earth, Sun and Moon (demonstrations or pictures of Earth from space and movement of planets and moons etc.);
- Unit 6b – Micro-organisms (action of bacteria in time-lapse footage or under the microscope);
- Unit 6g – Changing circuits (modelling).

Task 8.3 Using ICT to demonstrate in science	If your school has a data projector that can be used in classrooms, find out how you get hold of it for a lesson and ask someone to demonstrate its use to you.

Taking one of the ideas above (see also below), familiarise yourself with a resource, web-based or CD-based, that could be used to demonstrate the scientific concept you will be studying with your class. Prepare a group demonstration or discussion around this resource.

Consolidating learning

There are many pieces of software that might help pupils to consolidate their scientific learning. Many such packages are 'scenario-based' in that they usually adopt a kind of puzzle as a context or scenario from within which to test or try out scientific ideas. The scenario might be set in a spaceship with a broken communication system and the pupils might be asked to help fix the ship by solving a series of puzzles. Some such software might actually guide pupils through discoveries, others simply test scientific knowledge. These sorts of software should be used with some caution, however. They can be engaging and entertaining but few have the capacity to actually teach children much. Instead they tend to be far more like a series of hoops to jump through, simply repeating the activity can help you achieve the goal – getting the communication system up and running – but you may have missed the point, which is to learn more about science! Children may like them but they are often better suited to home use than classroom use.

However, using modelling software as discussed above may have far more relevance when getting children to test out their ideas and demonstrate their understanding. There is a wide range of software, prepared files and activities that can be downloaded for free from the Curriculum Online website (http://www.curriculumonline.gov.uk/). Some, though by no means all, of these materials are available to teachers for free.

Task 8.4 Evaluating software and resources for primary science	Ask if you can have a look at the science software titles available within school that are appropriate to your class (age and curriculum). Spend some time investigating each one so that you are aware of what is available and how

each one works. Consider whether these would be appropriate for use during your teaching practice and, if so, plan to use the software. Consider how it will be used and if used at an individual pupil level, consider how you will manage the process of ensuring each child has an equal opportunity to use and benefit from the software. Most especially, plan group or class discussions around the software to ensure that what is going on, on the screen, is relevant to what is going on in the science work in the class.

Alternatively, if such resources are not available, see if you can find an appropriate free resource on Curriculum Online (www.curriculumonline.gov.uk) or the National Grid for Learning (http://www.ngfl.gov.uk/) website or using a search engine on the WWW.

Research

Many of the Units of Work within the science scheme include references to using ICT as secondary sources of information or for the purposes of research. The use of ICT is suggested from Unit 1a – Ourselves, right through to Unit 6e – Forces in action, but exactly which sources you are supposed to use and how you are supposed to use them is not discussed in detail (though the section on demonstration above should provide some ideas).

There are two issues with encouraging children to carry out research. The first is the ability to search effectively for information and the second is to know what to do with it. Both are quite challenging for young children and it is unlikely that many children can carry out both parts with any degree of independence until the very top of Key Stage 2. By providing access to appropriate software, you can begin to help younger children understand the principles of using non-fiction texts and ICT resources to help answer questions, however.

Software publishers such as Granada Learning and Sherston produce software designed for young children as 'talking books'. Exactly how these are presented varies from title to title, but many use standard reference book conventions such as contents pages and indexes to access relevant information. This information is presented in text form, but all the text can be 'spoken' by the computer to support children who have trouble reading fluently. Spoken text is often accompanied by images or animations to help clarify meaning and such software can certainly be used independently by young children.

However, effective research needs a clear and relevant purpose, and making information accessible to young children does not necessarily make it useful. The hard part about finding relevant information is asking the right question in the first place, and that requires experience of using reference texts. When using software that supports young children's independent use, it is a good idea to provide them with relevant and answerable questions that may be about general features and structure of the text as well as its content and, of course, there should be a great deal of discussion about what they find and how useful it is. As children gain experience of non-fiction texts they need to be supported in asking appropriate and relevant questions but then also supported in developing appropriate searches for the information they require.

Many CD-ROM encyclopaedias and Internet search engines use index-based or keyword searches and trying out searches as a class to see what information is offered is a useful experience. Children also need to be able to review search returns and select likely sources. For instance, a simple search on an Internet search engine will return potentially hundreds of thousands of possible matches and pupils need to have strategies for coping with this. There are two issues: the first is to skim and scan search results and identify which sources appear to be most appropriate, and the second is to refine searches to get better results.

Learning to skim and scan for likely material is a process that needs to be modelled for children, but real progress only comes with practice. Learning to carry out and refine searches also needs to be modelled but there are a few things you can do to help children practice and consolidate their searching skills. Many teachers use Internet scavenger hunts to introduce the idea of using a search engine and this can be a useful place to start but, once again, the discussion that follows this process is the important bit! Children need the opportunity to compare results and consider what works best and why. You can introduce children in upper Key Stage 2 to the idea of using advanced searches, where words or phrases can be included and excluded (so if you want information on Penguins you might include 'penguins', 'habitat' and 'antarctic' but exclude 'chocolate' and 'biscuit') to help cut down on the number of irrelevant returns.

Task 8.5 Using ICT for research and information in science	During a teaching practice you will have relatively little time to develop pupils' research skills, but if the opportunity arises, make sure you are prepared. The only way to learn how to teach children how to conduct research is to

be able to do it yourself, so try to use resources in school (CD- and Internet-based) for your own preparation and keep an eye on whether (and how) these resources could be used by pupils. You can use what you find in your preparation or teaching but you might also be able to plan an activity for the children which would be even more valuable.

Further information and readings

For more details about aspects of teaching primary science with ICT see John Williams and Nick Easingwold's (2003) *ICT and Primary Science*, London: Routledge Falmer, or Jenny Byrne and Jane Sharp's (2002) *Using ICT in Primary Science Teaching*, Exeter: Learning Matters.

The Association for Science Education (http://www.ase.org.uk/) is a valuable source of information, particularly about the use of ICT in science teaching. They are involved in a joint project with BECTA offering advice about aspects of science teaching and current events (http://www.ictadvice.org.uk/).

A number of museums offer resources and information to support the teaching of science. Have a look at http://www.nmsi.ac.uk/ which offers a gateway to a number of websites including the Science Museum in London, the National Railway Museum in York and the National Museum of Photography, Film and Television in Bradford, as well as other resources such as the Science and Society Picture Library.

SCIcentre (National Centre for Initial Teacher Training in Primary School Science) at Leicester University offers self-study materials with units of work for trainee teachers designed to support knowledge and understanding of the science required to teach the primary curriculum (http://www.le.ac.uk/se/centres/sci/selfstudy/selfstudy.html).

NESTA Futurelab has published a review of primary science and ICT by Collette Murphy. It is available from: http://www.nestafuturelab.org/research/lit_reviews.htm.

9 ICT across the curriculum

Identifying opportunities for ICT across all the foundation subjects is a challenging task, as the wealth of different opportunities that ICT offers are appropriate to different subjects in different ways. In order to try to make sense of the similarities and differences in the ways ICT can relate to foundation subjects, this chapter is presented in two parts. The first is a brief overview of the range of opportunities that ICT might be considered to offer the Primary curriculum, including but going beyond the opportunities outlined in the National Curriculum and QCA Schemes of Work. The second section takes each foundation subject in turn and looks at the opportunities for ICT as suggested in each Scheme of Work, with further suggestions for development and investigation.

The openings for ICT described in the first section are fairly general and include the ideas and opportunities outlined and discussed in previous chapters. The intention is that general descriptions in the first section will be exemplified and discussed in more detail within the second section by applying the opportunities to specific curriculum issues. It is hoped that this approach will help both teachers in training and recently qualified teachers to develop a wider understanding of the role that ICT has within the curriculum and help them to develop their own ICT capability. (ICT capability is to do with knowledge about, and skills and understanding of, how ICT can be used effectively. It is discussed at length in Part 1 of this book.)

We should make it clear at this point that each QCA Scheme considers the use of ICT within the subject in different ways. Some schemes consider broad applications of ICT within the subject and go into detail about how ICT can be used to enhance teaching and learning within the subject. Others, in our opinion, appear to pay little more than lip-service to the issue. It should also be noted that the QCA ICT Scheme itself is not considered in the same way as the others. The Scheme for ICT is concerned with developing ICT capability for pupils and as such is described in the first section of this book.

Opportunities for ICT

Describing the opportunities that ICT offers succinctly is a challenge. This is partly due to the fact that information and communications technology is a very broad field and partly because finding headings under which aspects of the use of ICT can be neatly categorised is complex. Each element of ICT shares features, techniques, skills, concepts and technologies with other elements. The following is offered as a brief overview and guide. Wherever possible we have tried to keep the boundaries between the different aspects of ICT distinct, but there is still some duplication of ideas.

Word processing

Word processing is the form of ICT most commonly used by teachers and pupils. At a fundamental level it is the easiest to understand because the concept has been with us for a very long time, in the shape of the printed word and typewriters. However, word processing has a lot more to offer than the neat presentation of text. Most modern word processors allow users to incorporate images, photos and charts with their text, providing quick and easy ways to get children to think about what they write and how they communicate their meaning effectively. The use of images and charts substantially changes the writing process, and children need opportunities to consider how and why this happens.

As well as being an obvious tool to use to explore the writing process, word processors also offer tools that can develop more specific language skills across the curriculum. Since pieces of text in a word processor can be edited easily, teachers can provide opportunities for children to study specific features of text in relevant and detailed ways. Simply highlighting adjectives to describe landscapes in a piece of text can be done on paper, but if it is done on screen, pupils can also consider whether (and how) the geographical vocabulary they have used can be improved upon and make changes just to the relevant parts of the text without the need for substantial rewriting. This would work at other subjects when developing specific aspects of the vocabulary and language of different subjects (for example, words to describe pictures or paintings in art then being classified according to whether they are about line, form or colour).

Spelling and grammar checkers can be used to help children to focus on common mistakes and improve the quality of the language they use. Many word processors incorporate further writing tools such as interactive thesauruses or specialist dictionaries to help older pupils refine their written work. The use of styles and headings can be used to develop understanding of the structure of a piece of writing and the key points or underlying concepts structuring writing in different subjects. At the other end of the spectrum many also incorporate text-to-speech facilities. This can help children who are just learning to read and write in working independently. Text-to-speech facilities can enable children to access more complex texts independently and can help them to check the sense of their own written work. Used even more carefully they can also support reading activities that target specific reading difficulties.

Many word processors also provide ways for interacting with and displaying data. Incorporating charts and graphs into text may be one way of using data, but word processors can often merge data into documents, allowing users to adapt text according to the requirements of the reader. At a simple level this could be taking the name and address of a list of recipients in a spreadsheet and adding them to the head of a standard letter to save time addressing envelopes (mail merge), but this feature may be used more creatively. For instance, a mail merge may be used to select different statements for different users or to help users select the parts of a set of information that are most appropriate for them. Such data-handling capabilities have limited relevance within the primary curriculum, though many teachers will use such features to help with class management, but an awareness of the ability for text to be manipulated automatically with such tools to address differing audiences is part of the National Curriculum.

Word processors can support pupils who have special needs with a variety of specialised keyboards. These have usually been designed to allow pupils with severe and complex special needs to produce written work more independently (such keyboards are often used alongside specialist software that can use symbols to produce text, such as Writing with Symbols by Inclusive Technologies, www.inclusive.co.uk). Other additions may include software-based solutions which provide pupils with adaptable text-input systems so text can be inserted by whole words or partial sentences at the click of a button and selection can be supported by appropriate images (Clicker 4 by Crick Software is an excellent example, www.cricksoft.com). These tools are often under-used: developing a word bank in Clicker for use in history can be an excellent way to support writing of even high attaining pupils by encouraging them to extend the vocabulary that they use.

Desktop publishing

Desktop publishing (DTP) software is used by many teachers to produce worksheets and classroom resources because it makes setting out graphical elements and images on a page rather easier than a word-processing package might. Such software is also used regularly by pupils for producing things like posters and leaflets as part of their work across the curriculum. There are many similarities between desktop publishing and word processing and as word processors become more and more sophisticated in the way they handle images and charts, this boundary becomes increasingly blurred. It is important, however, that capable ICT users understand the difference between the two types of package, as each is designed for a different purpose and each has advantages and disadvantages for specific tasks.

DTP software lends itself to tasks that do not require the use of extended pieces of text. Short, specific messages are communicated through short pieces of text and images, which encourages a style of writing that can be more complex and long-winded if presented using more traditional methods. Individual words or short phrases can be used in DTP applications in the same way that shapes and pictures can be used. They can be edited for size as well as for font, style and so on but they can also be dragged around the screen easily, as can numbers, statements, icons and parts of illustrations. This feature means that DTP software can be used extremely effectively in activities that require children to sort words, phrases or objects according to specific criteria. Tasks exploring word order, Venn or Carroll diagrams, sequencing (narrative or report), ordering or matching activities can all exploit DTP software's ability to handle pieces of information as separate elements.

DTP software is usually flexible and accessible and is well suited to arranging and altering the layout of several separate elements on screen.

Graphics

Graphics packages span a wide price and functionality range, from the free applications bundled with most computers or downloadable from the Internet to state-of-the-art packages such as Adobe PhotoShop costing several hundred pounds. However, they all do the same fundamental job – they allow users to create or modify images on screen using digital equivalents of traditional artists tools, from paint brushes and spray cans to scalpels, oil paints and palette knives. In general the more you pay, the more sophisticated the tools and the greater the control over layout and placement of pictures and text.

There are essentially two types of graphics package, though the boundaries between the two are also becoming increasingly blurred (see also Chapter 2 for the implications of some of these differences). The first is bitmapped-graphics software. Bitmapped graphics are the digital equivalent of paper and pencil (or paintbrush). Marks made on the screen behave in the same way as marks on paper would, in the sense that they have to be rubbed out or painted over to change them. Bitmapped images are literally made up of a series of coloured dots on the page and each dot is independent of the one next to it. The other type of graphics package is what is called vector-based. Vector-based graphics are described mathematically, so each line or shape or colour is actually a calculation that determines how long the line should be, what direction it should go in and when and where it should bend or twist. Vector graphics tend to have smaller file sizes but the real advantage is that as each element in an image is a separate calculation, they can be edited and moved independently of the rest of the image (in the same way that parts of a DTP page can be edited independently, see above). Pupils in Key Stage 2 will need to understand the limitations of the different types of pictures that they can use in their work. The terminology is not essential, but understanding the implications of these differences is. If you try enlarging different pictures on a computer you will soon see the difference. A bitmapped image will become grainy or jagged, a vector image can be made bigger without loss of quality.

Graphics packages are used across the curriculum for producing images that may help illustrate ideas, designs and events. The use of graphics packages to create and edit images is only specifically described in the Scheme of Work for Art (especially when investigating patterns) and in the scheme for design technology. However, it is appropriate for children to use and develop these skills in other subjects by choosing or creating illustrations for their writing.

Working with data (databases and spreadsheets)

Databases and spreadsheets are often considered to be very similar types of software. In some respects this is true, but they are designed for different purposes and as such should be considered to be good at different things. Spreadsheets are primarily designed for number-crunching, for organising numerical data, performing calculations and producing charts automatically. Databases are primarily designed to help you to gather, organise and locate other types (text and images) of information. As such, they provide different opportunities.

Spreadsheets will mainly be used in teaching mathematics (collecting and presenting survey information or exploring relationships between numbers, like function machines), and then using numerical data in other subjects. This might be in science or geography (for collecting and presenting information gathered through investigations and for spotting patterns in data), though they can also be very useful for helping teachers with classroom management (record sheets for activities and attainment etc.). The use of spreadsheets is also suggested in the QCA Schemes of Work for Citizenship and Design Technology, both for looking at and analysing survey information, though this could equally apply to census data in history too.

Databases, on the other hand, are used much more widely across the curriculum, mainly due to the fact that databases are used in two different ways. Designing and creating database structures is exclusively the domain of ICT lessons (though the context for the activity may be taken from another curriculum area). Databases to help you locate or summarise and interpret information can be used right across the curriculum. Any Internet-based search will use a database, as will any reference CD. Whilst creating a database gives children an insight into the nature and structure of usable data, learning effective search techniques and developing the literacy skills that enable you to identify relevant pieces of information (skim, scan etc.) is the way most people will exploit the power of databases. They provide opportunities for independent and self-initiated learning by giving children access to a huge range of information and wide variety of learning opportunities. Using a database effectively is challenging. It is all too easy for children to browse through information without any real purpose, so they need to be set challenges in finding or summarising information about a particular theme or issue that they have the ICT skills to manage successfully.

The use of databases is specifically mentioned with the Schemes of Work for geography and design technology, where they are used primarily for research. In the Schemes for history, art and citizenship the use of sources of information is often mentioned and this will, inherently, involve the use of databases, too.

Modelling and control

Modelling and control are also often grouped together and, though there are similarities between the two, there are also significant and important differences. Modelling is about using computers to try out ideas or conduct 'virtual' experiments. Models can be tested in spreadsheets by creating numerical relationships between variables and then testing what happens when one variable is set to a higher or lower number. For instance, if you could try to show a relationship between hours of sunshine, amount of water and growth of a plant and program this into a spreadsheet, you could conduct a virtual experiment into what might happen if you increase the amount of sunshine a seedling has, or decrease the amount of water, or both! In practice, few teachers would want to develop such a spreadsheet, but there are several pre-prepared activities that use similar ideas available in many schools.

Slightly less complex models might include number-function machines where changing an input number for the machine produces an output that is determined by the number function that the machine performs. The idea is to try to find out what that function is. (For more information try, http://www.kented.org.uk/ngfl/ssheet/function.html.)

ICT lends itself to much less complex forms of modelling, too, as it is very good at letting users make changes without investing considerable amounts of time or effort in the process. For instance, experimenting with changing the colour of text in a poster by highlighting it and picking colours from the text colour palette to see which one looks best is simple modelling. Many of the activities outlined above in the section regarding DTP are forms of modelling, too. Again, however, it is important that you set a specific task with a clear purpose that is relevant to skills, knowledge or understanding in the subject you are teaching. It is all too easy for such tasks to be undertaken with enthusiasm and considerable experimentation by pupils, but with little or no actual learning due to a lack of clear purpose or review of what they have done.

Control is primarily about using a computer to control on-screen or off-screen events and often involves the use of some sort of programming language. Where it overlaps considerably with modelling is that developing ideas, testing them and refining those ideas is part and parcel of the use of control technology – essentially carrying out virtual experiments.

Control technology can also be used to control events on screen, such as in a LOGO program where children have to describe movement in terms of properties of shapes (direction, distance and rotation), or off-screen, usually through the use of some sort of interface that allows you to use the computer to switch devices such as motors and lights on or off at set times or following specified inputs (like flicking a switch).

Other than in ICT, the use of control technology is only mentioned within the Scheme of Work for Design Technology, though some aspects of developing sequences and repeats on an electronic keyboard in music actually use similar skills.

Simulation

Simulations are similar to models in the sense that they are designed to exploit computers' abilities to let you experiment freely without worrying about the consequences. Simulation software will often use real or imaginary scenarios to provide a context for investigation or revision. For instance, a simulation of a visit to a fairground may provide a context for handling money to pay for the rides you want to go on, or it might provide a context for allowing children to consider the complexities of running a business (installing the right rides at the right prices in your fairground will encourage customers to visit, but if there aren't enough places to eat they may not stay long and so on).

Simulations are designed to allow children to experience events, or consider the issues behind systems and processes that they could not normally access. They are specifically mentioned in the Schemes for ICT but can also play a significant part in teaching and learning in history, geography, science and citizenship.

Digital media

Digital media, such as projected images, digital photographs, digital video and digital audio, are becoming increasingly accessible in schools. Opportunities for using digital media are primarily only considered within the schemes for ICT under the rather general banner of 'multimedia'. However, digital media has developed rapidly in the last few years so that current guidance and existing professional practice often do not exploit the potential of such technologies fully.

Digital photographs can be used in many ways, from classroom organisation and management (such as taking digital photographs to show how to store equipment on shelves instead of text labels or hand-drawn 'shadows'), using digital photographs or even video clips as a record of visits (and then being reused to make big books, reports, multimedia presentations and displays). Taking a series of digital pictures to record findings in scientific experiments or the different stages of design technology projects, or capturing evidence in art or PE quickly and for easy storage are all opportunities that are easy to exploit with currently available digital cameras.

Digital audio can be used to help young children record their ideas about all manner of things, from retelling of stories to recording their ideas about what they have discovered in the sand tray today, without the need for what can become the long-drawn-out process of writing it down. It can also be used by older children to record ideas quickly when their hands are occupied with other things, such as in scientific experiments.

Digital video can combine many of the benefits suggested for digital photos and audio and combine them into powerful presentations. Older children can learn about the complexities of communicating using highly sophisticated modern techniques, while teachers can use digital video to capture evidence about pupils' attainment and understanding that has been impossible or unusable until recently.

Digital projection has brought a wealth of new teaching opportunities into the classroom. Digital projectors are available in the ICT suites of most schools and are invaluable for demonstrating skills and techniques in ICT. They are also moving into classrooms where teachers are learning to exploit their potential in whole-class teaching, demonstration, for sharing ideas and work and for introducing the use of the Internet or digital video into the teaching across the curriculum.

Communication

The 'C' in ICT has been added relatively recently as the issues of communicating through new technology have become more and more significant. DTP and presentation software, the Internet, e-mail, SMS and associated technologies (streamed video, picture messaging, video-conference, mp3 audio files and so on) are having a major impact on the way people communicate on a personal or more formal level (the difference between sending an e-mail and posting a message on a website). They are changing everything from what and how we communicate, even down to spelling in text messages. Children need to learn the significance of these different forms of communication, what they are effective for and how the different modes or genres have their own conventions. All areas of the curriculum provide opportunities for the use of communicating through ICT, and all schemes of work contain something about using ICT to organise and present ideas.

Research

One of the major benefits of ICT for modern society is the ability to track down information about almost any subject relatively quickly and easily. The Internet is a vast repository of useful ideas, information, images, video, illustrations, music, sounds and like-minded people. It is also a vast repository of useless (dangerous and discriminatory) ideas, disinformation and some of the worst kinds of images and video, so it needs to be used with caution. The fact that the Internet gives teachers access to such a wealth of source material is clearly of benefit in helping them to prepare effectively for their lessons. Teachers use the Internet to find appropriate images and source material to act as stimuli for lessons but they also use it for professional development, sharing and exchanging ideas and prepared activities, accessing relevant documentation from the government or Local Education Authority and so on. This isn't to suggest that accessing such useful information is always quick and easy, but given the time to carry out the research, teachers can find something relevant to any idea they wish to tackle in class.

Pupils' use of sources of information is also especially relevant and is discussed briefly in the section above on working with data. Some of the wider issues about the use of the Internet in schools are outlined in Appendix D.

Task 9.1 Using ICT in teaching the whole-class across the curriculum	Find out if there is a digital projector available at your next or current school placement and, if it is not sited in a teaching area you have access to, find out what the procedures for booking and using it are.

Using the ideas in this chapter as a starting point, design a whole-class activity that fits with your planning in one of the foundation subjects (or RE) and try it out with the class. If you need to build your confidence, try the idea in a group work session instead. This could be done around a single monitor instead of using a digital projector, and could be a good way of trying the idea out if you are working in a school that does not have projection facilities.

Opportunities for the use of ICT in the QCA Schemes of Work

Art

ICT can support teaching and learning in art in many different ways, from helping children to develop their ideas about line, tone, colour and form to providing source material for discussion or new subject matter (see Figure 9.1). It can also provide opportunities for presenting and sharing artwork more quickly and to a wider audience than the traditional classroom display. ICT can also be the medium used in art. A large proportion of contemporary art is produced on or using computers, and whether pupils are using the simplest of graphics packages to 'paint' a picture on the PC or are using digital video montage to illustrate an event or feeling, they should have the opportunity to explore what ICT can do for their study of art.

Figure 9.1 The National Portrait Gallery archives. Reproduced by permission of the National Portrait Gallery, London

Research (source material): Many of the units within the Scheme of Work for art suggest that source material is studied and discussed in preparation for creating art using similar techniques or themes. ICT provides many excellent opportunities for gathering, viewing and finding out more about works of art. There are a significant number of art galleries that have digitised their collections and display most of them on their websites. In addition to being able to search collections for work by specific artists you can often search by style, subject matter or technique, allowing you to study related works easily.

Whilst few galleries allow you to print and distribute images or artwork, most allow images to be used in schools. Check copyright information on each site before you do, though. Displaying such source material on a digital projector or large screen will make for good group discussions.

Almost all of the units of work suggest that studying work by other artists would be beneficial, and while some suggest that a trip to a local gallery or sculpture park would be appropriate, where this is not possible a little research on the Internet may provide the next best thing. Some units, such as Unit 4C – Journeys, where aerial photos may be used, become far more interesting and accessible with access to the Internet (try www.multimap.co.uk and look for aerial photos of schools, local shops, streets and so on).

Digital media (digital cameras): Digital images provide instant access to source material in art. For instance, in Unit 1A – Self-portrait, children are encouraged to make a self-portrait to communicate ideas about themselves. Having a digital photo of each child in a class may provide an excellent starting point and an opportunity to discuss in detail the features of their faces and what makes them look different to their classmates. The unit is not specifically about reproducing a life-like portrait, but this sort of discussion will help children focus on specific details.

It is possible to insert digital images into graphics packages and work over the top of the image on the computer. Again, considering Unit 1A, children could use a photo of themselves as the base for their work, and use paint tools and clipart over the top of the image to add ideas to develop a representation of themselves or other images from clipart collections (you may think that they should just add horns and a pointy tail, but it is interesting to see how children view themselves or interpret other pictures). This would be a substantial challenge for many Year 1 pupils, but most would tackle the idea with some enthusiasm.

Using digital cameras on field trips, particularly if the field trip is to a museum, gallery, architecturally interesting building or sculpture park, can provide useful source material for discussion and consideration in much the same way that use of Internet-based sources would, as outlined above. The benefit of collecting your own bank of images is that they record source material of which the children have first-hand experience, and this makes the material much more engaging. These ideas are relevant to, say, Unit 1C – What is sculpture?, Unit 2C – Can buildings speak? and Unit 4A – Viewpoints (a digital camera will transform this unit!).

Use of digital cameras can also be considered for use in compositional work, such as in Unit 2A – Picture this! where children are encouraged to use montage or collage techniques. Reproductions of digital images may allow them to select more specific images than might usually be available. Images reproduced on an inkjet printer, as available in most primary classrooms, are not especially robust as the inks are water-based and will run when they get wet. As most glues used in the primary classroom are water-based, this can mean that digital images quickly begin to distort if they are cut up and stuck down in collage work. You may consider this to be a negative effect, but it can lead to some very interesting investigations and results.

Modelling: Creating artwork directly on the computer can add a new dimension to the process. Many children find using graphics packages very rewarding, because it is easy to make changes or correct mistakes with a computer-based image, unlike with the real thing. However, another major advantage of working at computers is that they allow you to experiment with colours, tones and effects without the need for drastic reworking of the image. In a good graphics package children will be able to select certain parts of their image and alter its properties without changing the rest of the picture. Of course, they can also change it back again if they don't like what they see!

Such techniques could be useful in several units within the scheme, including Unit 2A – Picture this!, Unit 3B – Investigating patterns and Unit 5C – Talking textiles.

Teachers may consider providing access to far more advanced technology to allow children to create digital works of art, such as digital video or 3D modelling. However, few primary schools have access to significant amounts of relevant equipment and software (both of which are relatively specialised and comparatively expensive) or the expertise necessary to take advantage of what they have to offer. Schools may consider educational visits to places that can offer the necessary equipment and expertise, such as City Learning Centres or local businesses such as newspaper or television and film production companies.

Citizenship

Mapping ICT directly onto the Scheme of Work for Citizenship is complex, as the scheme is written in such a way as to allow very high levels of flexibility in how the units are delivered. Any unit can be delivered at any stage across the primary age range, but the use of ICT is dependent on the skills and abilities of the pupils at the point they study the unit. Suggesting Year 1 children studying Unit 10 – Local democracy for young citizens, should collect and review opinions collected from local children using spreadsheets and complex graphs is pointless, but if they tackle the unit in Year 5, then it would be very useful. Instead, Year 1 pupils could use a digital camera and add speech bubbles to create talking heads to illustrate the range of views that they found. The skills and experience of the pupils you will be working with need to be taken into consideration when planning for the use of ICT in citizenship.

Digital media: The media, and how it represents many issues, is considered in several of the units of work. Some of the units are specifically about considering the nature of the messages that we receive through television, print and the Internet, such as

Unit 11 – In the media – what's the news? or Unit 2 – Choices. Pupils are encouraged to consider issues relating to point of view, bias and motivation, and ICT can provide access to sources of information with different messages to sell in order to illustrate these points. Use of the Internet and research will provide many such sources, but use of digital pictures and video may allow collection and consideration of materials that children have first-hand experience of. You may even want to use digital video to encourage children to illustrate their ideas about bias or bullying by making their own news reports and so on.

Children may also use digital images and videos to illustrate other relevant information within the scheme. Unit 1 – Taking part – developing skills of communication and participation, may provide opportunities for children to illustrate their ideas about how to develop and maintain friendships or resolve conflicts. Unit 6 – Developing our school grounds, could involve the use of digital images and video, too, both to gather information about the current state of the grounds and to show how it might be improved. By superimposing new design ideas over the top of digital photos, you might be able to show what proposed changes will look like.

Research: Using Internet-based sources can be included in most of the units in the citizenship scheme as most relate to issues of social interest. A wide range of social interest groups maintain websites about the subject. The DfES recognise this point and include the following within the scheme the statement:

> Many groups and organisations produce online resources that are relevant to citizenship. QCA has not printed these website addresses as it recognises that they can and do change, often at short notice. So that we can monitor and maintain a reliable and useful resource, the website addresses of the following organisations can be accessed through the key stage 1 and 2 citizenship scheme of work site at www.standards.dfes.gov.uk/schemes

Unit 3 – Animals and us, and Unit 5 – Living in a diverse world, will both benefit particularly from access to Internet-based sources of information.

Communication: Citizenship is all about communication, in the sense that it is about understanding our role within society through talking to and listening to others. Reaching greater levels of understanding about the complexities of society can be done through data handling – using sources of data either to justify your own point of view or to begin to understand the needs of others, presentation of ideas through posters, fliers or interactive presentations and on seeking out and considering other people's points of view.

Viewing information published by public interest groups on the Internet can help children to broaden their understanding of the issues involved in a particular topic, such as in Unit 10 – Local democracy for young citizens, but the Internet can also provide opportunities for asking questions of relevant people. Sending questions to a local councillor or Member of Parliament or other young people in nearby schools can allow children to dig a little deeper into specific issues of concern to them. Unit 5 – Living in a diverse world could benefit especially from such direct communication.

Handling data: As stated above, gathering and/or studying relevant data about people's views and opinions will help children develop a greater understanding of the issues involved in many of the units.

History

The Scheme of Work for History is perhaps rather cautious in describing the use of ICT within the different units, but drives home one main idea: gathering source material through ICT (CD-ROMs and the Internet). Other opportunities are less well considered or developed.

Research: Using ICT to gather source material provides teachers and pupils with a much wider range of opportunities than was available prior to the advent of CD-ROMs and the Internet. Such source material can now include recounts of events or periods, images of artefacts, relevant statistical information and other people's interpretations of available information.

Teachers will find many excellent sources of information and images that will help their pupils engage with the events and ideas being considered. An excellent starting point is the BBCi website (www.bbc.co.uk/history) but most schools will have a CD-ROM collection which you should have a look at. You can also search quickly and easily for relevant sites (see Appendix A for further details).

A few suggestions for units that will benefit from the use of Internet and CD-ROM-based sources and links to appropriate sites include:

- *Unit 6A/B/C – Why have people invaded and settled in Britain in the past?* A Roman case study. A significant amount of useful and relevant information can be found at such sites as www.roman-britain.org/main.htm which includes details about Roman settlements, population and even likely weather patterns 2000 years ago. Also try the British Museum for online information about Sutton Hoo (Unit 6B) www.thebritishmuseum.ac.uk/ or information about the Vikings at www.gettysburg.edu/academics/english/vikingbritain2001/) for Unit 6C.
- *Unit 7 – Why did Henry VIII marry six times?* For source material and background information you might visit the National Portrait Gallery at www.npg.org.uk. When studying Unit 15 – How do we use ancient Greek ideas today?, you can begin to consider some of the relevant points at www.bbc.co.uk/schools/landmarks/ancientgreece/.
- *Unit 4 – Why do we remember Florence Nightingale?* This unit includes the suggestion that more able pupils will: 'use a wider range of sources, *e.g.*

CD-ROMs or children's encyclopedias to find out about her life; use ICT to make their own interpretations of her life'. It may be appropriate here for pupils to create a multimedia presentation about what they have found out using images and information from a range of sources.

A good resource for Key Stage 2 is the National Archives' Learning Curve (http://learningcurve.pro.gov.uk/). This is a teaching resource structured to tie in with the history National Curriculum from Key Stages 2 to 5. It contains a varied range of original sources including documents, photographs, film and sound recordings as well as some games and interactive simulations.

Digital media: Digital images can be used effectively within several of the units in the scheme, and most notably those that try to establish links between life today and life in the past. Taking pictures of houses and buildings in the streets surrounding the school may provide interesting starting points for Unit 2 – What were homes like a long time ago? This would be especially true if there was a mixture of old and new housing in the area, allowing children to compare and contrast architectural styles as well as features indicating age and wear. The following units could all similarly benefit from first-hand source material:

Unit 12 – How did life change in our locality in Victorian times?
Unit 13 – How has life in Britain changed since 1948?
Unit 18 – What was it like to live here in the past?

Communication (including word processing and DTP): ICT can provide many opportunities for developing historical study through classroom resources and displays. Many teachers have a permanent timeline in the classroom and use it to chart significant events as they are studied throughout the year. More often than not, such events are described in printed text but often have a relevant image or two to accompany them. In some instances, pupils are encouraged to bring in their own information to add to the timeline and, almost without exception, the images and pictures will be taken from a computer.

Pupils can use ICT to compile reports and so on, but teachers may also provide more interesting formats for children to write about their historical studies. Word-processing templates, including writing frames, may help children to structure report writing but other templates can also add interest to the task. For instance, providing children with a few pieces of relevant clipart and a template in the style of a newspaper report or poster could provide more interesting contexts for their writing about historical events.

Handling data: Historical study, especially in Key Stage 2, can exploit skills and understanding that the children have developed in relation to handling data. Interpretation of statistical information (including census data), charts and diagrams can be a good way to get children to develop a better understanding of the subject matter and to show what they already know about a subject. For instance, using data about demographic changes in this country since the Second World War, you could begin to explore ideas about population changes, about poverty, transport or the impact of technology. This could be using a thinking skills strategy such as living graphs (see Chapter 11), where statements of fact have to be placed alongside the data to show when and where the children think certain things may have happened, or it may employ a more traditional study of the data and responses to specific questions.

If you dig deeply enough (no pun intended) you will find information about similar issues in Roman, Viking and Tudor times and again, such data could be extremely useful in helping children understand the relative differences between life then and life today. A simple comparison in population numbers between today and any period in history, for instance, gives plenty of food for thought and discussion.

Simulation: Simulation software also has a significant role to play in helping children understand the implications of the historical details they may have read or been told about. For instance, describing life in a Victorian textile mill is very different from taking the role of an 11-year-old boy who works retying broken threads under the weaving machines on a computer simulation. The images, sounds and recounts that such a simulation might offer can have a substantial effect on young children, and not only help them recall significant information but also help them empathise with the situation their character found themselves in.

Simple simulations are also available online, such as those that can be found at the BBCi website, www.bbc.co.uk/schools/famouspeople/, which could relate to study in the following units:

> Unit 4 – Why do we remember Florence Nightingale?
> Unit 12 – How did life change in our locality in Victorian times?
> Unit 20 – What can we learn about recent history from studying the life of a famous person?

Design technology

In the original version of the National Curriculum, ICT (or IT as it was then) was part of the orders for design technology, which points to the fact that the two subjects have a lot in common. ICT lends itself well to various ideas that are central to design technology work, in particular design (graphics and desktop publishing for visualising, making changes easily, drafting and access to specific design tools including clipart etc.), control technology (for designing and managing systems that control events such as making rotating doors rotate when someone is near) and modelling (for trying out ideas, making changes and developing patterns).

Other ICT opportunities, including the use of digital media (to support the design, development and review stages of the process), handling data (relating to gathering ideas for the design process and evaluating feedback from designs and solutions), and research (for gathering ideas and source material) can also be considered.

Desktop publishing and graphics: Several units within the scheme actively encourage the use of ICT within the design and making stages of the work. Unit 3A – Packaging, for instance, suggests that computers are used to investigate surface designs for their packages. This includes experimentation with different fonts and colours (aspects of modelling) as well as use of the computer in the final design. Similarly, Unit 4B – Storybooks, encourages the use of computers for page layout and consideration of different typefaces, font sizes and formats. Units 5B – Bread, and 5D – Biscuits, employ similar ideas.

DTP software could also be used in some of the modelling activities described in other units, such as Unit 2A – Vehicles, where children are encouraged to look at different types of vehicles and decide what they are appropriate for. Collecting images from the Internet and sorting and categorising them on screen might be an effective way to carry out such an activity.

Working with data: Part of the design-and-make process involves the collection of responses to ideas at the initial planning stage and the evaluation stage towards the end of the activity. Several units suggest that ICT may be an effective way to manage this. Units 3A – Packaging, and 3B – Sandwiches, for instance, suggest that children might try ideas out on an audience and record their responses. If this is done directly into a spreadsheet, then charts and graphs can be produced quickly to provide information to help make appropriate decisions. All the Units in Year 5 and Units 6A and 6B suggest a similar approach.

Data is crucial to the design process and developing data-handling skills and understanding through technology work provides a real and relevant context for such work.

Modelling and control: As mentioned above, many of the units of work suggest the use of modelling and of control technology. Since part of the design process is about having ideas and trying them out, modelling ideas can support this work. Modelling can work on a relatively simple level, trying out fonts, styles and colours on a bit of graphics work for instance. The units mentioned in the desktop publishing and graphics section above all use the idea of modelling to try out different possibilities before making a decision.

Unit 1B – Playgrounds, might be a context for modelling using images of play areas. Pupils' ideas or pictures of new play equipment could be drawn or painted on top of the original images to model the effects of adding new equipment and so on. This is a relatively sophisticated idea, but it can be achieved using a 'My World' screen quite easily by children in the foundation stage (see www.granada-learning.com for more information on My World) or by children in Key Stage 1 by using drawing tools with a digital photograph of the play area as the background. Unit 4C – Torches, might provide a context for modelling with simple electrical circuits. This would use specific software such as Crocodile Clips Elementary, which is freely available from www.crocodile-clips.com/m6_4.htm. This software allows children to experiment with a virtual electronics kit and experiment with the effect of adding batteries and bulbs and switches to circuits. Unit 4D – Alarms, could possibly use the same software, though it specifically asks for ICT to be used in other ways.

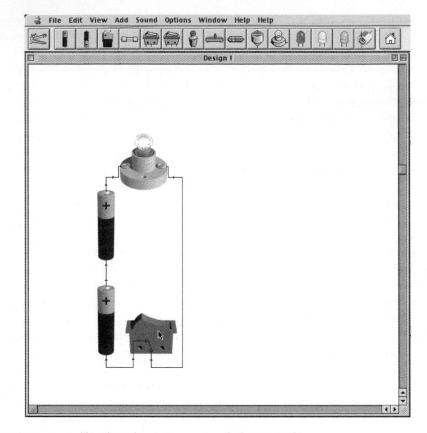

Figure 9.2 Crocodile Clips Elementary – virtual electronics kit

Control technology is mentioned in several units within the Scheme of Work. For the most part, the Scheme outlines opportunities for children to develop an understanding of what control technology is and how it helps (see Figure 9.2). It is not until Key Stage 2 that control technology is incorporated into the units and is only specifically detailed in Unit 4D – Alarms and Units, 6C – Fairground, and 6D – Controllable vehicles. Here, the ICT Scheme is supporting the design technology Scheme effectively, as control technology is not studied in detail in ICT until the upper end of Key Stage 2.

Digital media: Using digital cameras and digital video cameras can be an extremely effective way of collecting relevant information throughout the designing and making process. Digital cameras can be used to collect relevant information in the research phases, such as Unit 1B – Playgrounds, where digital images can be used to discuss the needs of new play areas; Unit 4B – Storybooks, for collecting ideas about different styles and formats for storybooks or Unit 5A – Musical instruments, for the same purpose. Digital media can also be used effectively by recording important and relevant stages quickly and easily. Very often it is the original design and the final product that are reviewed at the end of a project, but the process of making products gets ignored. This is a missed opportunity, as it is children's developing skills in making that have the greatest impact on the quality of and consistency between the original design and final product. By taking a series of pictures throughout the process children not only have something to talk about when reviewing this part of the project, but also see the production process as an important aspect of design technology work.

Digital images of final products also provide a good record of what happened. As often as not, the final product is placed, in all its glory, on a display and slowly, over the course of a term of so, it deteriorates to the point when it is sent home in a polythene bag in several pieces. Digital images make for good records and are much easier to use in assessment paperwork.

In all cases, digital video could be used for similar purposes but with the added advantage that the images could be accompanied by the child's voice, talking about the subject matter. Of course, digital video clips are hard to put into an assessment file, but in all other respects provide excellent opportunities to support design technology work.

Research: Referring to Internet- or media-based sources of ideas and information, especially when starting the design process, can help children generate ideas and become more aware of the possibilities before they start committing things to paper. The use of web pages relating to the subject can be extremely useful and can even become the focus of detailed surveys. In Unit 1D – Homes, it might be worth looking at a few local estate agents' websites. In Unit 2A – Vehicles, looking at different vehicle manufacturers' sites might provide good opportunities for discussing vehicle types and purposes, whereas in Unit 6A – Shelters, Internet searches could be used as a way of compiling information about materials, structures, uses and styles.

Geography

The Scheme of Work for Geography includes the use of ICT in most units and following that guidance would ensure that you exploit the potential of ICT when teaching geography. The main uses of ICT in geography are in gathering source material, locally and further afield, and in studying geographical data.

Research and handling data: Geography can be a very visual subject and accessing maps, charts, aerial photos, landscapes and so on through the Internet can make a real difference to discussions and thinking around geographical ideas (for maps and aerial photos try www.multimap.co.uk). It can also give access to useful demographic information about cities, countries and continents. There is also a helpful section about maps for children on the Ordanance Survey's website: http://www.mapzone.co.uk/.

A more exciting form of data is live data gathered by monitoring stations allowing you to study geographical events in 'real time'. A typical example would be Internet weather services (try www.metoffice.co.uk for really useful up-to-date information but also amazing archives of data and images, including satellite images and video clips of weather systems) (see Figure 9.3) but you can find monitoring stations collecting data about volcanoes, flood warnings, transport (traffic congestion and so on) and public interest issues. (You could try www.volcanoworld.org/ or Stromboli online at www.educeth.ch/stromboli/index-en.html as a couple of examples.)

Figure 9.3   Animated satellite images of weather systems from the Met Office. © Crown copyright, Met Office. Reproduced under Licence Number METO/IPR/2

Units that may benefit from data-handling activities include Unit 2 – How can we make our local area safer?, for traffic surveys; Unit 4 – Going to the seaside, for class surveys and plotting graphs; Unit 6 – Investigating our local area, for investigating land use; Unit 11 – Water, for consideration of the effects of rainfall, and excessive rainfall in some parts of the world; and Unit 12 – Should the high street be closed to traffic?, for survey information.

Units that might use the Internet as a significant element include Unit 3 – An island home (try http://www.virtualhebrides.com/location/coll.htm); Unit 5 – Where in the world is Barnaby Bear?, for sites in countries that Barnaby might visit; and Unit 7 – Weather around the world, for obvious reasons.

Digital media: Digital pictures of field study trips or walks around the local area can make an excellent record of what was seen and discussed and can also provide useful source material for study and discussions once back in the classroom. Pictures taken locally can be compared to images found from wider research (say across the Internet) so that comparisons can be made. With a digital projector in the classroom such discussions can have a very real focus and with an interactive whiteboard the teacher, or pupils, can annotate images as the discussion develops, helping them focus on and recall the important points.

Units that might include the use, especially of digital cameras, include Unit 2 – How can we make our local area safer?, for gathering evidence and information from the locality; Unit 4 – Going to the seaside, to record relevant ideas on a field trip; Unit 8 – Improving the environment, for collecting relevant information but also for illustrating the problems in reports, leaflets and so on; and Unit 13 – a contrasting UK locality, for local evidence.

Music

The use of ICT is only suggested in two of the 21 units in the Scheme for music, Unit 2 – Sounds interesting, where pupils are encouraged to make and listen to recordings to see if they can identify potentially familiar sounds, and Unit 18 – Journey into space, where 'children explore a wide range of sound sources, including ICT, to capture, explore, change and communicate sounds'.

In fact, ICT can, and probably will, be used far more widely in teaching and learning about music than this suggests. If children or teachers use any form of recording or playback, then ICT is being used. Electronic instruments may be used in most of the units that involve some form of compositional work and can be used very effectively by teachers in activities that encourage children's auditory skills. Simple music software is available in many schools and can be effectively used in compositional work, too. Much of this work involves the use of modelling and digital media.

Modelling: Any compositional work involves the use of modelling – trying something out and seeing what it sounds like. When using ICT the modelling aspect is much simpler to use because it is easier to identify and to correct mistakes. In a composition that involves trying out sounds with traditional instruments it is possible that someone will miss their place or play the wrong note. This doesn't happen with a computer, which will play what it has been told to play exactly. This makes the idea of trying things out before making a decision much more accessible, and since trying things out can include changing notes as well as pitch, tempo, volume and even voice (different instruments), children using computers for compositional work could be at a real advantage.

Units that might incorporate the use of music software or programmable electronic instruments include Unit 3 – The long and the short of it, where children listen to and experiment with long and short sounds; Unit 8 – Ongoing skills, for developing aural memory; and Unit 16 – Cyclic patterns, for exploring repeating patterns of sounds and music.

Digital media (recording): Several units suggest that recordings of sounds, singing and compositional work can be made and studied during music lessons. While many might expect recordings to be done on standard audio tape, recording onto a computer or electronic recorder can have some advantages. Editing digital sounds is easy and works much the same as cut, copy and paste does in a word processor; editing on audio tape is practically impossible. While this feature of digital audio harks back to modelling, there are also advantages in terms of using recordings. In a music lesson where children are listening to sounds or pieces of music, having those pieces recorded on CD (digital) makes them extremely easy to use (pick track 10 and off you go). Having those same recordings on tape leads to a lot of searching for the right point on the tape and a much less fluent lesson. By the same token, having recordings made by children available on computer makes them much more accessible (double click on the relevant file to hear it).

Units that might benefit from digital recording include Unit 2 – Sounds interesting, for recording familiar sounds; Unit 10 – Play it again, for exploring rhythmic patterns; and Unit 14 – Salt, pepper, vinegar, mustard, for exploring singing games.

Physical education

As you might imagine, ICT is not mentioned all that often in the Scheme of Work for PE and where it is, it is usually in relation to what might be considered to be cross-curricular links. For instance, several of the units relating to Outdoor and adventurous activities (Units 1, 2 and 3) suggest that ICT might be used to support map-making and route planning activities. Dance activities (Units 4, 5 and 6) suggest the use of ICT for designing stage sets, illustrating stories used as stimuli within dance activities or for stage management (music and lights) while Swimming activities and water safety (Unit 1) suggests the use of ICT to reinforce safety messages by designing posters, and Athletics activities (Unit 3) suggests the use of ICT for storing information about performance and helping set targets.

All are worthy uses of ICT, especially the idea of using ICT to record performance and set targets, as this involves children in the use of ICT in a real and personally relevant way that can be done within a PE lesson and in a short space of time. Filling a time or distance in on a spreadsheet is quick and easy, but using mapping software or designing a poster will take several dedicated lessons in an ICT suite to complete.

Handling data: There are two other aspects of ICT that might be incorporated into PE work – digital media and data logging. Data logging has not been mentioned in this section as it relates most specifically to the schemes for ICT and science and as such is dealt with in other sections of the book. Data logging is the use of computers to take accurate measurements and present data in charts automatically. It has the potential to be used in PE to make accurate recordings in competitive events (in a high-level swimming competition, for instance, the clock is stopped automatically when a swimmer touches the end of the pool, allowing for extremely accurate measurements of time). While few primary schools are likely to have such sophisticated equipment, many do have pressure pads that can be linked to a computer. These pads could be placed at the end of a track to allow similar measurements to be taken. Data logging may also be used to monitor fitness by monitoring heart-rates and recovery times. Again, not many primary schools will have a pulse sensor, but they are relatively cheap and work with other equipment that most schools will have.

Digital media: Using digital pictures and digital video in PE lessons could open up a range of opportunities for encouraging pupils to assess their own performance and improve their skills. Children often find it hard to assess their work in PE unless there is a simple and specific measure. How fast you run or how far you jump is easy to compare with other children or previous performances, but how well you balance or how neatly you roll can be much harder to assess. Taking digital video footage of pupils performing in dance and gymnastic activities can give them evidence that they can view more dispassionately and possibly use to compare with others or with their own previous attempts. Such technology is not often used in PE, but more and more schools are beginning to use such ideas to help children improve their skills.

Modern foreign languages

The Scheme of Work for modern foreign languages (MFL) includes many references to the use of ICT. The principles of using ICT in learning a language are the same whether you are learning French, German or English and for a comprehensive overview of the opportunities that ICT has to offer teaching and learning languages Chapter 6, ICT for literacy and the teaching of English, should be used.

It is worth pointing out that the activities described in Chapter 6 are written specifically for teaching English and therefore won't be directly transferable, but many of the concepts and strategies behind the activities will be useful. Emphasis should be placed on the use of audience and digital audio recording for MFL. ICT offers young language learners a real audience; other classes in the school learning the same language, classes in other English schools and even classes in France, Spain or Germany could be used as an audience for written work (via e-mail etc.) but better still, an audience for their spoken work (audio recordings attached to e-mails or even video-conference). Digital audio recording may be useful for trying out on other people but even better than that, it allows children to listen to their own attempts to speak another language. Many language teachers believe that this is potentially one of the most important things for a child learning a new language to have access to and ICT can be a very nice way to capture and use recorded speech.

Of course, there are also many interactive language-learning programmes on CD-ROM that may be useful and Internet sources can provide early language learning activities (try www.bbc.co.uk/schools/primaryfrench/ for instance). If you are a fluent speaker (or rather 'reader') yourself, you might even find that online games and activities to help young children in other countries could be extremely useful for your classes, too. Many search engines default to the country where the request for the page was made, but these can be changed easily. If you want to use Google in French try: www.google.fr or in German: www.google.de or Spanish: www.google.es.

Summary

ICT can be used in a huge variety of ways. Some are described in detail within the QCA Schemes of Work but many further opportunities are not. The purpose of this chapter was to give you an overview of what is currently possible, but in no way would we suggest that everything described here is a requirement for effective teaching with ICT. A good ICT practitioner will use ICT selectively when they see that it is of value in helping to demonstrate an idea, illustrate a concept, motivate and encourage their pupils or help them focus on the important aspects of learning. As new technological developments emerge, this same practitioner will be able to identify further opportunities to develop their teaching and support their pupils' learning.

This chapter should have helped you to widen your ideas about the role of ICT in effective teaching and learning and helped you to develop a clearer understanding about what it is that ICT is good *for*. A good general rule of thumb when deciding whether or not ICT should be used is to ask yourself whether it will make for a more effective lesson. If it will, then it could be used, but if it won't then it should be left out. Sometimes teachers cite the fact that ICT goes wrong or breaks down, which makes for ineffective lessons. We would suggest that this is not the point. Using ICT with young children can be a frustrating experience when the technology seems to be fighting against you but it can also be extremely rewarding, both for you and for the children, when it seems to be on your side. Patience, persistence and experience count for a great deal when developing your skills in the use of ICT as a teacher. For the benefit of the children you are educating, we would suggest that it is your professional responsibility to take up the challenges that ICT presents. We would also suggest that taking up that challenge does not mean going overboard to incorporate ICT whenever and wherever possible, but making sensible and reasoned judgements about what *you* can achieve and how beneficial it might be for your pupils.

Task 9.2 Using ICT in group or individual work across the curriculum	Plan a specific task where the pupils you are teaching will use ICT as part of a lesson. You will need to assess their skills and may need to discuss aspects of the activity with their class teacher. Base the activity

on one of the suggestions (or QCA Scheme activities) outlined above. Try something that will help develop your own skills (such as the use of a digital camera) and that has a clear purpose that fits with the content of the lesson. Remember the focus of the task is on achieving the specific subject objectives – you should not be spending time teaching ICT skills!

Further information and readings

The QCA Schemes of Work are available from the Standards site at: http://www.standards.dfes.gov.uk/schemes3/.

QCA's NCAction website (http://www.ncaction.org.uk/) has guidance on the *Use of ICT in Subject Teaching* with references to the Schemes of Work and opportunities outlined in the National Curriculum documents.

A good general text that raises issues about teaching and learning with ICT is Angela McFarlane's (1997) *Information Technology and Authentic Learning*. London: Routledge Falmer.

Marilyn Leask and John Meadows' (2000) *Teaching and Learning with ICT in the Primary School*, London: Routledge Falmer, contains a number of chapters relevant to using ICT across the curriculum. In particular see Chapter 7 by John Sampson, History and ICT, and Chapter 10 by Darren Leafe, Managing Curriculum Projects using ICT.

Opportunities to develop the use of ICT across the curriculum are included in the *ICT Connect* series (published by the Heinemann Group) http://www.myprimary.co.uk/.

Nelson Thornes publish a series of Primary ICT Handbooks with ideas for using ICT in different subjects:
Jarratt, R. (2003) *Primary ICT Handbook: Art and design.* Cheltenham: Nelson Thornes.
Mason, D. (2002) *Primary ICT Handbook: History.* Cheltenham: Nelson Thornes.
Pierson, A. (2002) *Primary ICT Handbook: Music.* Cheltenham: Nelson Thornes.

The Geographical Association has resources to support geography with ICT (http://www.geography.org.uk/) and has published *High-tech Geography: ICT in primary schools*, edited by Stuart May (2000). It is based on articles published in Primary Geographer which is aimed at Key Stage 1 and 2 teachers. It is published three times a year and has regular articles and information about ICT to support primary geography.

The Historical Association also has a website: http://www.history.org.uk and a professional journal, *Primary History*, published once a term which has occasional articles on the use of ICT in history in primary schools.

The NESTA Futurelab website (http://www.nestafuturelab.org/research/lit_reviews.htm) has a review entitled *Citizenship, Technology and Learning* by Neil Selwyn. It presents a dual perspective on citizenship education in terms of how ICT can support the current curriculum and how citizenship education itself needs to reflect changes in technology use in the workplace and day-to-day life, and summarises both theoretical and empirical research evidence in the field.

10 ICT in the Foundation Stage

When it comes to ICT, the Foundation Stage is often rather overlooked. There can be a variety of reasons for this, including the fact that young children tend not to be able to use computers when they start nursery or reception with much independence, so the teacher or teaching staff within the setting have a lot of work to do to put the basic skills in place. As a result Foundation Stage staff often feel that the options for using ICT are limited and that the effort required is not outweighed by the benefits offered. Foundation Stage staff are ideally placed to exploit young children's excitement and enthusiasm for ICT and do not need to be highly skilled or have complex equipment to achieve this.

It is, however, desirable that young children have access to up-to-date technology, as it provides so many opportunities for creative teaching and effective learning. It is often easier to use or has better facilities and tools. Text-to-speech, for example, improves all the time and is usually better on more recent equipment. Often in the past the newest equipment was allocated to the oldest children. Thankfully, this situation is changing and most schools recognise that young children can get as much (if not more) out of a new computer and specialist software as older children can. Those schools that have ICT suites will often have timetabled slots for every class in the school, including children in the reception classes, and possibly even for the nursery. Even where this isn't the case, more schools are recognising the value of having appropriate computer equipment in the Foundation Stage and this is usually not machines handed down from older classes.

Documentation for the Foundation Stage (QCA, 2000) includes references to the use of ICT across the curriculum, though instances tend to be fairly general, leaving much to the teacher's professional judgement. The one area of learning that does discuss the use of ICT overtly and in some detail is Knowledge and understanding of the world. Even bearing this in mind, ICT can and does have a much greater role to play in effective teaching and learning in the Foundation Stage than the rest of the document might describe. The purpose of this chapter is to help you to understand how ICT can be used with, for and by young children, to help them acquire appropriate knowledge and skills in all areas of the Foundation Stage curriculum.

Rather than using the titles for the areas for learning used within the Foundation Stage documents, headings used in this section of the book are based around the benefits that ICT can bring to the Foundation Stage and include collaborative work, language development, control, creativity and classroom management. The section on language development attempts to avoid significant overlap with the section on using ICT for literacy (Chapter 8): it may be worth considering both sections together to get a complete picture of the role of ICT in language development in the Foundation Stage.

ICT in collaborative work and language development

One of the most interesting things you notice when watching very young children working collaboratively at computers is the quality of the discussions they have. In many ways this alone is a compelling reason to have plenty of ICT in the classroom. Whether they are working with other children or with adults, the attention to the detail of the conversation is often far more apparent than in other situations. This may have something to do with the abstraction that the computer provides, forcing children to talk more and physically do less, but it must also have something to do with the fact that even very young children are enthusiastic about computers.

Computers in Foundation Stage settings need to be accessible to all pupils and by several pupils at once, if at all possible. Due care to the placing of the monitor, keyboard and printer should be taken. The monitor needs to be at, or just slightly above, eye height for most children and ideally the keyboard and mouse should be positioned just in front of the screen. The idea behind this is that the closer the screen and keyboard are to each other, the less children have to move their heads to focus and coordinate their eye and hand movements between the two. The printer should be placed so that children can see what it is doing and can collect their work easily. It is especially important for young children to see their work emerging from the printer, as it is exciting for them and helps develop their understanding about how computers work.

The advantage of placing computers in areas where several children can see what is going on is the flexibility of modes of use it provides for. Computers can be used very effectively during one-to-one work between the teacher or other adult and one child at a time, or for paired collaborative work and even for small group discussions and review where teachers or other adults work with three or four children at once. Some teachers like to be able to use the computer during whole-class sessions too, and place their ICT areas on the edge of carpeted or group areas to make this easier. As yet, interactive whiteboards and digital projectors are rarely placed in early years settings and this can make working with large groups difficult (for example, in reviewing digital photographs of what the children have done that day in circle time).

Working one to one with children at the computer can provide useful opportunities for introducing basic skills of computer use but can also provide useful contexts for wider discussion. Many pieces of software designed for use in the Foundation Stage try to develop basic concepts such as colour or shape recognition, positional language, comparative measurement and so on. Spending time with an individual child working with such software can provide teachers with useful baseline assessment information and provide opportunities for the teacher to help develop these ideas. Of course the point of such software is that it should help pupils do this for themselves, and this is worth considering when purchasing appropriate software. However, it should be noted that such programs can have disadvantages as well as advantages, as young children can develop misconceptions about what the software is trying to teach them. It is important to check that young children are actually learning the ideas and skills that you have planned. Many teachers comment that computer-based activities can hold young children's attention better than more traditional table-top resources and as a result encourage greater interaction and evidence. This is often considered to be especially true when working with boys, though it also depends upon the kind of activity or type of ICT that is made available. Again it is essential that you monitor the learning that is actually taking place.

More open-ended or creative software, such as paint programs or modelling activities, will also provide contexts for discussion but in a less prescriptive form. As children create things on screen, their talk will be about what is going on and what they are trying to achieve. As the activity is more creative, the language will be more creative too, and this can give a good insight into children's linguistic abilities and provide contexts for helping them develop their vocabulary and their speaking and listening skills.

Teachers often find that working alongside children at the computer provides useful opportunities to model effective use of software and management of programs, but more importantly to model appropriate behaviour when working collaboratively, too. Children need to learn how to discuss events on screen and share responsibility for controlling the computer. Modelling these processes with children can help them develop these skills quickly, much as it would do in the role play corner or learning to share other equipment.

Of course, children will spend a great deal more time working at the computer with their peers where they will learn (with constant encouragement and reinforcement) the skills you have modelled for them. ICT tends to be an extremely useful focus for developing collaborative skills, of turn-taking and discussion. When working with a paint program, young children will spend a great deal of time in discussing colour and shape as they produce pictures. With appropriate contexts and sufficient relevant experience, these discussions can be extended to include other work. For instance, children may use a paint program to make a record of other activities, perhaps an investigation they have recently completed. In these cases, the discussion will include ideas about colour and form, but will also include negotiations about which details should and should not be included, a review of the findings and the sequence of events.

Using ICT as a focus for reviewing ideas and events can be effective with small groups of pupils. Again, using a paint package, ideas about a recent topic can be discussed, reviewed and recorded as a group. Not only does this give the teacher a chance to check what each child has learnt about the subject, but it also provides contexts for group discussion, reflection, extension and consolidation of vocabulary and helps pupils clarify their ideas.

If you have access to a digital camera even more possibilities for reflection and review are open to you. A series of images of a task undertaken with a group, perhaps a baking activity, can be displayed on screen and used to discuss what was done and to consider why. Images can be sorted into the correct chronological sequence and stored as presentations on the computer. Young children tend to respond extremely well to seeing pictures of themselves, and the fact that the record is of first-hand experiences means that the quality of talk and the ability to recall events can be markedly improved. Since images can be downloaded from the camera to the computer very quickly, ICT is providing the opportunity to carry out reviews within the same work session, something difficult to achieve with traditional photography.

Once familiar with the use of a digital camera, young children can start to make decisions about when to use it to record their work or points of interest around the classroom. Again, in paired or group work the use of the camera can be negotiated and the subject matter discussed. Digital pictures make excellent source material for discussion, reflection, display, evidence of attainment and communicating with parents about what goes on in the Foundation Stage. Some Foundation settings are beginning to use digital video in similar contexts and are discovering that some simple digital video cameras can be used effectively even by children of nursery age. Digital evidence tends to have as marked an effect on parents as it does on children. Many Foundation Stage teachers find it difficult to convince parents that their children do little more than 'play' at school but digital pictures or video clips of investigations, role play, collaborative work, artwork, trips and visitors can help teachers explain the worth of constructive play.

Foundation Stage documentation suggests that pupils should be encouraged to interact with adults and ask questions of them or seek their support. Many teachers report that children who are reluctant to interact with adults in this way in many contexts will seek this sort of support when relating to ICT. This motivation factor can be enormously powerful and should be exploited for the benefit of the children, even to the extent of pursuing questions they may bring with them from outside the setting. If you have access to the Internet, this may provide opportunities for you to work with children on things they are interested in. In one account of such an experience, a young boy became extremely curious about caravans when his parents told him they would be staying in one for their summer holidays. The teacher agreed to look for caravans on a search engine and spent some time with a small group looking at pictures of different caravans and discussing the features of each.

Case study

A reception class have been studying the growing of seeds and have had a garden centre as a role play area where they have been planting and caring for seeds, seedlings and young plants. The class teacher uses role play to do a great deal of topic-based teaching and often works in the role play area alongside the pupils, asking questions and encouraging investigation.

The class has a computer and a digital camera and children are encouraged to use the camera to capture evidence of things they think are interesting. Children have used the camera many times to take pictures of the seeds they have planted and the seedlings as they have grown. Many of these pictures have been printed out to be studied in group-review sessions and are also used in displays around the garden centre.

At the end of the project, the teacher gathers groups of up to four pupils around the computer and, using a simple paint program, asks the children about what they have learnt about growing plants. They discuss what plants need to grow and what they look like. As children mention different ideas, that child is asked to come to the computer and draw the relevant details on the screen. As the discussion continues the drawing on the screen builds up to show soil, water, sunshine, warmth and the plant's roots, stem and leaves. The teacher helps the group to label the parts of the flower and the images are printed out and used in displays and in pupil records.

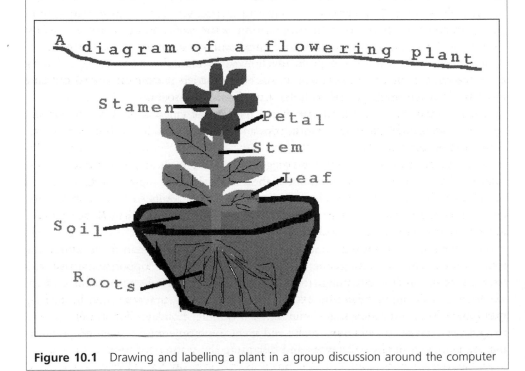

Figure 10.1 Drawing and labelling a plant in a group discussion around the computer

Task 10.1 Observing ICT in the Foundation Stage	When observing children working in the Foundation Stage, take note of the types of interaction they have with technology. If ICT is being used proactively, take

the opportunity to listen to the quality of the discussions taking place around the activity. It may be instructive to listen to the types of interactions taking place around other activities within the setting and compare the two.

Taking control (*fine motor control as well as controlling technology*)

'Cause and effect' is a central part of the section of Foundation Stage guidance entitled Knowledge and understanding of the world, though the term is not actually used. Teachers are encouraged to provide opportunities for children to investigate and ask questions about why and how things happen. ICT provides a wealth of opportunities for investigation and is specifically detailed within the guidance – 'Find out about and identify the uses of everyday technology and use information communication technology and programmable toys to support their learning.'

Learning to use and control a computer is only a part of this process, but the use of all kinds of technology are part and parcel of young children acquiring skills and familiarity with the breadth of learning about ICT. Children should be given opportunities to work with equipment in the setting, such as listening centres (audio tape players), video recorders, perhaps digital cameras and video cameras where appropriate, microwave ovens, cookers, perhaps telephones and washing machines. They should also be given opportunities to investigate and discuss the use of technology outside the setting, such as in supermarkets (rotating doors, barcode scanners, fridges and freezers), on public transport (ticket machines, barriers, automatic doors) out and about (pelican crossings, parking tickets, street lights) and so on.

Using a computer or investigating and controlling programmable toys encourages the development of hand–eye coordination and fine motor controls, both significant in themselves. As children work with these resources, they also begin to understand a lot more about cause and effect – 'if I press this button, the car goes forward'. Some young children need to reinforce these ideas several times. The fact that ICT is (usually) consistent in its responses to inputs, means that children have the opportunity to experiment and test out their ideas, developing their understanding of the process and improving their ability to control events accurately.

The learning environment in a Foundation Stage setting is key to making these opportunities valuable. Children should have access to resources in both formal and informal ways. Sometimes activities will be planned around the listening centre, when the teacher will work with the children on controlling the tape and modelling appropriate behaviours (book and tape match, turning pages and/or following text along with the tape, cooperation with peers etc.). At other times, the listening centre and the tapes and books will be organised in such a way as to ensure that they are as accessible to children as possible. Independent use of the resources will be encouraged by placing a green sticker on the play button and a red sticker on the stop button of the tape deck and by organising tapes and books so that they can be matched up easily.

A very effective way of encouraging pupils to use controllable devices is by incorporating them into role play. If the role play area is set up as an office, the computer may be included so that children can play at typing letters and printing them out. An old telephone or two and a phone book may be included to encourage children to act out looking up and dialling numbers (cause and effect) and holding relevant conversations. Granada Learning produce a range of software designed specifically for use in role play and based around well-used role play scenarios, such as the Vet or the Doctor (see www.granada-learning.com/school/ for more information and look for the 'At the . . .' range). If you can't spare the class computer for role play, an old screen and keyboard can still provide useful props to help children act out the things they have seen.

When using video tapes or television programmes it might be worthwhile to allow the children to use the remote controls. You might have the digital camera in a place where, with permission, pupils can collect it for themselves. You could encourage them to help program the oven or the microwave. Having programmable toys available for use in construction or role play areas is always popular and will help develop knowledge and skills about controlling technology, as well as providing opportunities for developing skills and concepts across the curriculum.

Task 10.2   Using ICT in the Foundation Stage   Plan a simple activity to introduce to a piece of controllable equipment that children in your next placement have not used before. You may try this out with a single child or small group. Pay particular attention to the 'cause and effect' element of using the resource, and encourage the children you are working with to discuss what they do and the results of their actions.

Using ICT creatively

ICT is a creative medium, but beyond the obvious paint package on the computer, what additional opportunities does it offer in the Foundation Stage? Basic modelling activities can be extremely effective on computers in the nursery or reception class with the right software and prepared activities. Granada Learning (www.granada-learning.com) distribute a piece of software called My World 3. My World has been used in primary schools for probably 10 years and is well established for one simple reason – it's good! My World comes with lots of prepared activities based around the idea of sorting, matching, investigating and discovering things (it is difficult to be more specific as the range of topics covered in prepared activities for My World is restricted only by what people are prepared to develop). Activities usually include a collection of on-screen objects that can be dragged around the screen and sorted or used in different ways. One activity may have a range of map symbols and children use the symbols to recreate maps of journeys they have been on, or to map out the progress of Little Red Riding Hood as she went to Granny's house and so on.

Another activity might have a teddy bear and clothes that children have to put on Teddy in the right order, or a range of shapes or numbers or letters that they have to group according to set criteria and so on. These activities aren't creative in themselves, but if you allow children to experiment and solve problems they set themselves with the resources the creative potential is vast (and creative across a range of issues from language to art, design, mathematics and storytelling . . .).

Again, digital cameras can provide great resources for creative work. Allowing children to experiment with photos of themselves or their surroundings, to work over the top of the images in a paint package or to use an image as the stimulus for some writing (emergent or otherwise) will produce impressive results and resources that they will be keen to share and discuss. Allowing children to use the camera to capture images they find interesting will provide even more opportunities for discussion, record keeping and assessment.

Away from the computer, ICT resources such as photocopiers and overhead projectors can be used to provide creative opportunities for young children or to enhance the experiences you are already providing for them in the classroom. For instance, if you have access to a photocopier in your setting, try arranging collections of objects on the glass plate of the copier and investigating what happens when you make a copy (taking care not to drop anything heavy or put too much weight on the glass, of course). This can produce interesting effects in itself and can be enhanced by playing with the shade controls on the copier to produce lighter and darker images. Objects on the glass can be rearranged or changed to see what happens to the image. One really nice example of this idea was the use of fuzzy felt-like characters on the plate, which produced images, a bit like in an Indonesian shadow-puppet theatre, tying in well with recent project work about storytelling in different cultures. Since the process is so quick many children who otherwise aren't especially interested in creating pictures can be persuaded to get involved and this provides opportunities for discussion about making pictures and studying images, making changes, reviewing and making representations. Talking about the images, making comparisons between the subject matter and the image and discussing how different effects were created all help to enhance the experience and extend children's appreciation of being creative. Of course, photocopies can also be used to make records of work and, as with access to digital cameras and computers, it might be possible to allow children to decide when making a photocopy of their work would be a good idea. Their use also encourages development of vocabulary and decision-making associated with texture, shape and composition etc.

Overhead projectors (OHPs) can be very versatile pieces of equipment, too. Not only do they provide a means to demonstrate and present pictures, but they can also be used to share the creation of pictures. You may be prepared to allow children to use OHP pens and draw onto acetate sheets, enjoying the way the projector magnifies the image and discussing the effects and content. Some pens that are not designed to be especially used with OHPs can produce interesting marks. Water-based markers don't actually draw lines on acetate sheets but produce trails of blobs of colour instead. When using water-based ink pens spraying a little water onto the acetate can make wonderful smudging effects and allow children to discuss colour mixing as they see the inks mix together (NB this is a potentially messy activity and you will need to ensure that the children are suitably protected). Of course, using OHPs in more conventional ways can also be valuable. Many bubble-jet printers can print directly onto special acetate sheets which means you can print digital photos onto sheets for projecting. These acetates could be used in review sessions, but some teachers have also used them to provide backdrops for role play areas (an image of a fire appliance standing outside a fire station was used when children were learning about 'People Who Help Us').

Supporting creative play through ICT should always be considered: allowing children access to controllable or programmable toys might be appropriate to help them act out scenarios with construction equipment; encouraging them to make decisions about when and where the computer could be used in role play allows them to explore the creative potential of the equipment; providing a microphone so that they can record themselves (either on audio tape or on the computer) might encourage them to listen to themselves talking and to talk more clearly and with greater thought and planning. All provide excellent learning opportunities and may provide interesting evidence and records of what they do and how they do it.

| **Task 10.3   Using ICT to develop creativity in the Foundation Stage** | Make a list of the ICT resources that are available in the early years setting in which you are placed. Find out what experiences of these resources the children have had so far. Select one resource that you think has further potential and plan a short creative task that can be carried out with a small group of children. Pay particular attention to the discussion and vocabulary you want to try to develop through this task. |

ICT for classroom organisation and management

Supporting young children in working safely, but with independence and confidence, is a major priority in Foundation Stage settings and ICT can be an extremely powerful tool in helping teachers setup and manage their classrooms. Through clipart, digital pictures and clearly printed simple instructions teachers can provide young children with strong visual clues about what they are supposed to do and how they should do it. One early years setting used simple images of figures (rather like those seen on toilet doors) alongside the appropriate numeral to indicate how many children were allowed to work in each area, ensuring children could work safely and sensibly (as well as promoting practical counting skills). Another used digital images of all the children to act as a self-registration board: as children entered the nursery they found the picture of themselves and placed it over their space on the register mounted on the wall. Another adopted a labelling system that put the same image and child's name onto labels appropriate for indicating who owned what in the classroom. These labels were used on drawers, coat pegs, gym bags, lunch boxes and so on, but were also used on milk bottles, handwriting cards, planning boards and personal possessions. Reinforcing name recognition was one benefit of this approach, but it also supported the children in achieving simple tasks independent of adult help because the systems enabled them to do so.

Using ICT is especially efficient for this sort of task, because it allows you to create templates so that similar resources can be produced for every area or every child quickly and simply. Once you have made (or found) templates, preparing for a new intake is much less time-consuming and making adaptations as children come and go throughout the year is relatively straightforward.

Shadowing shelves is standard practice in Foundation Stage settings. Again, the idea is simply to support pupils in carrying out required tasks independently. If a container is clearly labelled with a representation of what it contains, then children can work out for themselves where they should put resources when it is time to tidy up. If there is a space on the shelf that bears the same symbol then the container can be put in the right place, too. Once again, ICT is a good way to provide and manage labels for this sort of organisation and management. Through clipart, scanning images of resources or taking digital pictures, the use of a computer helps teachers to adapt images to fit requirements and support their pupils in working independently (see Figure 10.2). (Note here that scanners are really good for capturing images of resources, even 3D resources, as the image remains the same size as the original. If

Figure 10.2 Using ICT to develop sorting, planning and matching activities for young children

taken with a digital camera it can be a lot harder to provide a printed image that is exactly the same size.)

ICT can be used to provide resources that help with planning, carrying out and reviewing tasks in the Foundation Stage, too. For instance, many Foundation Stage settings or units place a great deal of emphasis on helping children plan what they are going to do each day. Some use planning boards where symbols of activities in the classroom are used to help children map out their intentions for the session. These symbols could be prepared using clipart or digital pictures and can easily be replicated to provide resources for several planning boards at once. Digital pictures can also be an excellent way of managing and organising group and guided tasks such as baking. Images of ingredients and processes can be used to record initial discussions, so the teacher talks to the children about what they are going to do when making biscuits and places images representing the ingredients and the processes of mixing, rolling, cutting and baking onto a sequence board. This sequence board is then used as a reference point for carrying out the activity and also provides useful prompts for reviewing the activity later.

Taking the idea of using digital images a stage further, they provide excellent evidence of pupil attainment for use within the Foundation Stage profiles, and could easily be used as first-hand evidence of what pupils achieve – perhaps in an investigation – but can also provide excellent source material to review what children do and what they understand about what they have done. The sequence boards suggested above could be used at an individual level to check what children recall and understand about their experiences and could then become the record of the conversation between pupils and teacher (especially if the sequencing is done on the computer, as suggested in the section on developing collaborative and language skills above).

At a slightly more mundane level, ICT can be used to help manage the process of planning, record keeping and assessment at various levels, from providing standard templates that help you record your planning or the evidence you need to databases that coordinate the information-handling process regarding all the work undertaken in school. (Simple tick-lists, label and planning templates and assessment proforma would be enough for most teachers.) With access to the Internet, teachers can get hold of recent and relevant documentation relating to their professional practice from the DfES (www.dfes.gov.uk/foundationstage/ and www.standards.dfes.go.uk) or resources developed by other teachers to help them plan and prepare interesting and relevant learning experiences for their pupils (www.teachernet.gov.uk, www.bbc.co.uk/schools/preschool/). Such resources may involve activities to use with pupils on and off screen and will include resources such as pattern and matching games, board games, puzzles and paper-based activities.

Display is an important part of any learning environment, and ICT can help by providing clear, consistent labels and headings as well as evidence of work, from digital photos to images created on the computer. Displays not only celebrate achievement and celebrate success but can also be used as stimuli for discussion or review and can help inform parents about what goes on in your setting. Clear labelling and activities that get children to consider the content of displays can help develop vocabulary and help recollection of facts.

Summary

In all, ICT has an important role to play in teaching very young children. It can support you as a teacher in organising and managing your planning, teaching and assessment. It is also a valuable tool to support the development of young children's understanding of their experiences. It can be tempting to allow access to ICT to be a passive experience, using software that effectively runs itself and entertains the children, but ICT has so much more to offer young children. You will find that young children pick up ideas about ICT very quickly and become confident and competent users of the technology they see around them in no time. Given half a chance, they'll be teaching you new things about the technology!

Further information and readings

The use of ICT in the early years is a contested issue, with some believing that such technology is inappropriate for young children. Others suggest that ICT can be helpful in supporting young children's learning depending on how the technology is used. This issue is discussed by Elaine Hall and Steve Higgins (2002) 'Embedding computer technology in developmentally appropriate practice: engaging with early years professionals' beliefs and values'. *Information Technology in Childhood Education Annual 2002* (1), 301–320. Norfolk, VA: Association for the Advancement of Computing in Education (AACE). Also available online at http://www.dl.aace.org/9115.

You might also want to have a look at what is happening north of the border, where there is a strategy emerging for the use of ICT in the early years in Scotland: see http://www.ngflscotland.gov.uk/earlyyears/ICTstrategy.asp for more information.

For more detailed accounts of research into the use of ICT in early years education see Marshall, G. and Katz, Y. (2002) *Learning in School, Home and Community: ICT for early and elementary education.* London: Kluwer Academic Publishers.

There are also a number of books specifically aimed at early years teachers:

Parton, G. (2000) *ICT: Early years activities to promote the use of information and communication technology.* Dunstable: Belair Early Years Series.

Farr, A. and Brown, J. (2001) *Using ICT (Skills for early years).* Leamington Spa: Scholastic.

O'Hara, M. (2003) *ICT in the Early Years.* London: Continuum International Publishing Group.

Poulter, T. and Basford, J. (2003) *Using ICT in Foundation Stage Teaching.* Exeter: Learning Matters.

11 ICT and thinking skills

Thinking skills are an important part of the National Curriculum. Since the review undertaken by Carol McGuinness (1999) and their specific inclusion in National Curriculum documentation there has been increasing interest in the teaching *of*, *for* and *about* thinking. The headings under which 'thinking skills' are grouped are as follows:

- **Information-processing skills** – These enable pupils to locate and collect relevant information, to sort, classify, sequence, compare and contrast, and to analyse part/whole relationships.
- **Reasoning skills** – These enable pupils to give reasons for opinions and actions, to draw inferences and make deductions, to use precise language to explain what they think, and to make judgements and decisions informed by reasons or evidence.
- **Enquiry skills** – These enable pupils to ask relevant questions, to pose and define problems, to plan what to do and how to research, to predict outcomes and anticipate consequences and to test conclusions and improve ideas.
- **Creative thinking skills** – These enable pupils to generate and extend ideas, to suggest hypotheses, to apply imagination and to look for alternative innovative outcomes.
- **Evaluation skills** – These enable pupils to evaluate information, to judge the value of what they read, hear and do, to develop criteria for judging the value of their own and others' work or ideas, and to have confidence in their judgements.

Whilst there are many other ways of thinking about thinking skills, these headings are a good starting point and can help you to plan a range of activities which demand different types of thinking across a range of different subjects. In this chapter we will look at how ICT can be used to support you as a teacher to plan, prepare and teach lessons and activities to challenge and develop pupils' thinking under these broad headings.

What are thinking skills?

At a basic level thinking skills are aspects of cognition or thinking that are teachable. This might be at a level of learning how to observe and listen (perception), recalling and applying historical information (knowledge), finding a solution to a technology challenge (problem-solving) or to reflecting and thinking about your own thinking (metacognition). Although we learn many such cognitive 'skills' automatically or implicitly, it is important to consider what aspects of thinking might benefit from more explicit development through teaching and discussion. Sometimes particular types of thinking are called 'higher order' thinking skills, such as *analysis*, *synthesis* or *evaluation* (following the work of Benjamin Bloom and colleagues (1956), who categorised thinking into different types in a widely-used taxonomy of cognitive abilities). However, whilst these may be more complex or more demanding types of thinking they are not necessarily *better* kinds of thinking; it all depends on the context in which thinking is required. It may be more appropriate to remember and apply a solution to a problem than work out a new one from scratch (think of throwing a lifebelt to someone in a river as opposed to considering and evaluating a range of possibilities to effect their rescue, for example). At the heart of thinking skills approaches, however, is a belief that learners can get better at thinking and that thinking is teachable. This involves the learner taking some strategic or reflective view of their thinking. Sometimes you may set up opportunities which allow children to apply and use their cognitive skills: teaching *for* thinking. On other occasions you might specifically want to develop a particular skill, such as problem-solving in mathematics: teaching *of* thinking. On further occasions you might want to develop pupils' understanding of the way that they think, their metacognitive skills or teaching *about* thinking. A more complete classification of thinking skills might therefore look like the model shown in Figure 11.1.

Developing thinking and understanding

Another common emphasis in many teaching thinking approaches is the development of thinking in order to develop understanding, so that the learner can develop their knowledge or take more responsibility for evaluating the effectiveness or appropriateness of their own thinking. A basic starting point from this perspective might be John Dewey's definition 'to understand is to grasp meaning' (Dewey, 1933: 132). ICT can help pupils in grasping meaning through a variety of teaching activities and to make their learning more meaningful.

Dewey elaborates upon his definition of understanding with a typically pragmatic extension which develops this relationship with thinking:

> To grasp the meaning of a thing, an event or a situation is to see it in its *relations* to other things: to note how it operates or functions, what consequences follow from it, what causes it, what uses it can be put to.
>
> (Dewey, 1933: 137)

This definition of understanding as seeing relations or relationships is a useful one for teachers. It helps us identify one aspect of ICT that is particularly powerful. ICT can

Strategic and reflective thinking	Value-grounded[1] thinking (including critically reflective thinking)		
	Engagement with and management of thinking and/or learning (metacognition/self-regulation)		
Cognitive skills	Information-gathering	Basic understanding	Productive thinking
	Perceptual skills (seeing, hearing) Accessing stored or recorded knowledge (recognising, remembering, recalling)	Adding to and representing meaning (e.g. features and functions) Working with patterns and rules Concept formation Organising ideas	Reasoning Understanding causal relationships Systematic enquiry Problem-solving Creative thinking

Figure 11.1 An integrated model for understanding thinking and learning (adapted from Moseley *et al.*, 2003)

be used as a teaching tool to focus pupils' thinking on the relationship between particular ideas.

It immediately raises an issue about ICT, as studies suggest that when pupils use computers in school they are very unlikely to develop their thinking. First, there is very little actual use of computers by pupils (once or twice a week for no more than a hour or so) and these computer activities are separated from or unconnected with other teaching and learning activities. Developing particular ICT skills or drill and practice tasks and typing up of 'a best copy' of a piece of writing are the main activities (Chalkey and Nicholas, 1997). There are, however, a number of ways that ICT can support your teaching of the whole class when you want to focus on developing particular aspects of their thinking. If you have access to a data projector and a large screen you can display text or pictures that you can ask the children specific or detailed questions about. This can be helpful as your questions can then refer to things that the children can see, rather than them having to remember what you said. Showing a slide show of different animals can help younger pupils focus on similarities and differences in living things, or displaying a paragraph of text and asking for suggestions for improvement in the range of adjectives or verbs may elicit more creative responses. You can also ask similar questions about different pictures such as properties of shapes in mathematics, where the pupils can see examples of the quadrilaterals you are referring to. It becomes easier to ask more searching questions or follow up responses from the pupils with such technology. If you also have access to interactive technology (such as an electronic whiteboard or tablet PC) you can make changes on the large screen that focus pupils' attention on specific aspects of what is being presented.

Task 11.1 ICT and children's thinking

When you see computers being used by pupils in school, reflect on what thinking the pupils have to do. Is the activity demanding or is it routine? Are they just practising skills (particularly keyboard skills) or do they have to think about what they have to do?

Plan an activity using ICT where you believe the pupils will have to think. Try it out and see what happens.

Case study: Thinking in mathematics

As part of a mathematics lesson, the teacher uses an interactive teaching program, 'Number Grid' on an interactive whiteboard, to get pupils to identify patterns in a hundred squares (see Figure 11.2). She asks the Year 5 class to identify the numbers

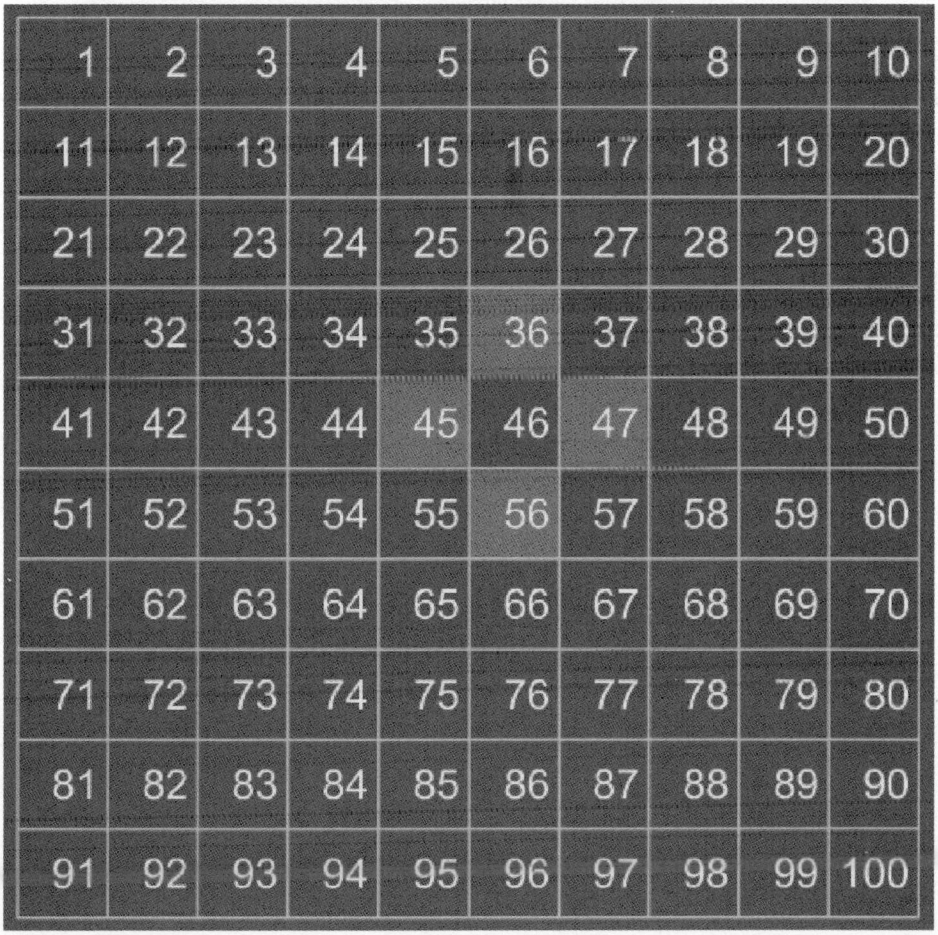

Figure 11.2 A screen from Number Grid

that form a cross around the number 46; above (10 less), below (10 more), right (one more), left (one less).

She then asks them to predict which numbers would make the same pattern (a cross) if the grid had only eight columns. She asks the children to provide reasons for their choices (such as 'the one to the right will still be just one more and the one to the left will be one less' or 'but the one above will now be eight less, so that's 38'), highlights them on screen on the 100 square (where they do not make a cross) then reduces the number of columns to eight so that the pupils can see if they now make the required shape.

The class then have a go at making predictions about patterns in a grid with 11 columns. The activity provides strong visual feedback from the patterns on screen

1	2	3	4	5	6	7	8
9	10	11	12	13	14	15	16
17	18	19	20	21	22	23	24
25	26	27	28	29	30	31	32
33	34	35	36	37	38	39	40
41	42	43	44	45	46	47	48
49	50	51	52	53	54	55	56
57	58	59	60	61	62	63	64
65	66	67	68	69	70	71	72
73	74	75	76	77	78	79	80

Figure 11.3 A further screen from Number Grid

to support pupils' mathematical reasoning (in particular identifying, explaining and predicting patterns in number).

The teacher then asks if any pupils can describe a general rule to identify what number will be above or below a given number in any sized grid (i.e. the number above the target number above is *minus* the number of columns in the grid; the one below is *plus* the number of columns).

This example illustrates how ICT can support teaching thinking by providing a context where pupils can use the visual presentation (in this case the number grid) to help them focus on the relationship between the numbers in the grid. The added advantage of being able to alter the grid by increasing or reducing the number of columns helps the teacher to get the children to think of a more general principle by seeing the relationship between a number of examples.

Task 11.2 Using ICT to develop thinking with the whole class	Plan an activity where you could use ICT to lead a session with the whole class to develop a particular aspect of thinking. You could:

1 Use an interactive teaching program to develop mathematical thinking (there are a number of examples on the numeracy section of the Standards site).
2 Design a PowerPoint presentation to help children classify living things or materials in science (such as with a Venn diagram).
3 Prepare a short piece of text that needs improving so that pupils can evaluate the impact of changes to the text and justify their reasons as to which version is the best.

NB If you try out this activity with your class make sure you practise using the data projector or (if your school has one) interactive whiteboard. Doing the activity on a desktop computer and on a large screen or on an interactive whiteboard is not the same thing!

There are a number of programs which have been developed as tools explicitly to support, develop and explore aspects of thinking. The following example describes how a teacher might use ICT to develop understanding in geography by identifying connections between geographical ideas. The example refers to a particular piece of software which has been designed to make concept mapping easier using a program aimed at younger learners called Kidspiration (produced by Inspiration: http://www.inspiration.com). This software enables links to be made on screen between pictures and text boxes. It also has the facility to 'read' words and instructions on screen with a text-to-speech facility. The case study is set in a mixed-age class of Year 3 and Year 4 children who were comparing two geographical locations: their own village and locality around the school and contrasting locality which was a village in India.

Case study: Using concept mapping software

The teacher's aim was to capitalise on the benefits that the particular tools in the software offered to sort information and make links on screen, in order to identify similarities between the localities and classify the kinds of similarities. As the children had already used the software and were familiar with using concept maps in other subjects, they quickly had some good ideas as to how concept maps could help them to sort and organise the geographical information. They were keen to show that there were many links between information and eager to explain how it could be presented.

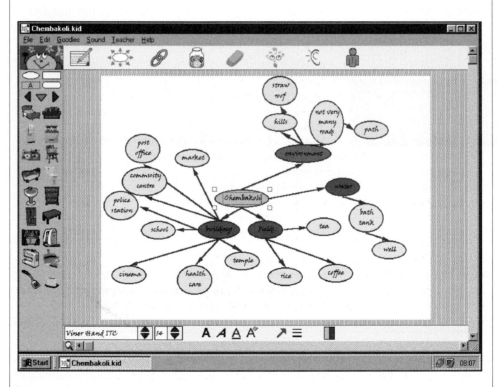

Figure 11.4 A child's mind map created with Kidspiration.

Presenting information in text boxes as separate statements generated a high level of discussion as the pupils could focus on key terms (see Figure 11.4). Children were able to point at boxes and explain why certain statements fitted together. An interactive whiteboard would be a bonus here to demonstrate joining statements or creating groups using colours or by dragging and moving the boxes. Children were able to justify their choices with reasons such as 'these are all buildings so we could group them and link them together, then these two are for leisure so they could link'.

Using the template on the screen as a guide they began creating their own concept maps working in established pairs. Starting with their own locality seemed logical, as they didn't have to refer to the map very often to check ideas. A class discussion helped to draw out links between the history of the two villages. The Year 4 children had looked at the history of their own village in depth and they knew there used to be a cinema and more shops. This led to a discussion on their knowledge of the history of the village in India. This level of discussion came from the links the children had been making and the connections that they were able to make due to the way the information was represented on screen. One of the benefits of working with concept maps is that they not only enable children to make links between ideas but also to find reasons and justifications by labelling these links.

| **Task 11.3 ICT as a tool for thinking** | Find an open-ended program designed to promote or develop pupils' thinking (such as those for mind-mapping or concept mapping) and learn how to use it. Explore how |

the tools that it offers could be used to support or develop pupils' thinking or understanding.

Make a list (or use it to create a mind-map) of the opportunities that the program offers across the primary curriculum.

ICT and small group work

ICT can also provide valuable opportunities to develop pupils' thinking and learning through work in small groups. However, evidence suggests that it is important to ensure that children can work together effectively before using computers in such collaborative activities. One approach that has been developed uses preparatory activities or 'Talk Lessons' in which classes establish ground rules for collaboration such as listening with respect, responding to challenges with reasons, encouraging partners to give their views and trying to reach agreement. These activities are not only concerned with improving the quality of children's working relationships, but also with developing their use of language as a tool for reasoning and constructing knowledge. That is, the Talk Lessons encourage teachers to create a 'community of enquiry' in their classrooms, in which children are guided in their use of language as a tool for both individual reasoning and collaborative problem-solving. Computers are used not only for stimulating effective language use but also for focusing children's joint activity on curriculum tasks. This embedded and catalytic role for computers in primary education is distinctive (for more details see Wegerif, 1996; Wegerif and Scrimshaw, 1997; Wegerif, Mercer and Dawes, 1998). The evaluations of the Talk Lessons programs have shown that computer-based activities can be used to stimulate reasoned discussion *and* focus joint activity on curriculum-related learning and that the increased use of explicit, reasoned discussion improves children's thinking (at least as measured by individual scores on Raven's Progressive Matrices test – a test of reasoning). This is persuasive evidence that the use of ICT can support the development of children's thinking and understanding.

Some software is aimed specifically at developing pupils' thinking by offering a series of activities or challenges. One of the best of these is the Zoombinis Maths Journey[2] (and the follow-up Zoombinis Mountain Adventure and most recent Zoombinis Island Odyssey). These programs contain a series of captivating logical thinking puzzles designed around the theme of escape and adventure. The puzzles in the programs require the use of logical and deductive reasoning and thinking. Each of the puzzles are different and have different levels making it suitable for a range of ages, though in our experience pupils aged eight and older will benefit most from collaborative working and explicit teaching of strategies based on the software. Whilst this program is not new, there are few other programs to rival the range of thinking challenges and engage the interest of primary age learners. The example that follows illustrates how such a program can be used to develop thinking and reasoning, both when using the program and by making connections with other learning.

Case study: Using 'thinking skills' software to develop logical thinking and reasoning

In this program each 'Zoombini' has one of five different types of hair, eyes, colour of their nose, and feet. These features form the basis for many of the tasks in the first program, the Maths Journey. Once you have chosen your group of Zoombinis, you have to help them to overcome a series of different obstacles using deductive logic and creative reasoning. For example, the first obstacle in their path is a pair of rope bridges at the Allergic Cliffs. One of the two guardians of these cliffs sneezes if a Zoombini with the wrong feature (or combination of features) tries to cross his bridge. If you make too many mistakes, the bridge collapses. This requires children to use evidence to work out how to get all of their group of Zoombinis across without the bridge collapsing.

Because the pupils understand the context of the game, they quickly become involved in the program. The disadvantage of this is that they do not automatically see the links with the mathematical logic and reasoning that they are using. It is possible to make two different links with mathematical diagrams with explicit teaching about this first puzzle. A Venn diagram can be used to analyse the common features of the Zoombinis who have crossed the bridges. This is powerful because as each Zoombini is successful the two sets increase in size, and it is possible to use the language of hypothesis and testing from science here to describe what is happening. With a data projector or an interactive whiteboard, the puzzle can be analysed with the class and this language reinforced. The disadvantage of this approach is that some children then think that both of the groups have some connecting feature. In fact, one group has a feature in common and the other group lacks that feature. One of the guardians is allergic to something and the other is allergic if they do not have it. So an alternative is to use a decision tree (a flow diagram with 'yes' or 'no' options) to identify which bridge each Zoombini should cross. This has the additional advantage of asking the pupils to identify the question that they need to ask such as 'Does this Zoombini have sunglasses?'. If 'yes' then use the top bridge, if 'no' then use the bottom bridge. This enabled the teacher to ask pupils 'What do you think the question is?' as he observed and supported pupils working on this puzzle.

Other activities in the program include arranging the creatures on Captain Cajun's raft in a correct sequence where each Zoombini must have something in common with their neighbour. One pupil described this as 'like dominoes'. The teacher was then able to use this description of the strategy to help other pupils to solve it. Other puzzles lend themselves to other mathematical diagrams. The puzzle at Stone Cold Caves can be visualised as a Carroll diagram. To get past the Fleens you can use a mapping diagram to show which attributes of the Zoombinis correspond to the attributes of the Fleens.

Figure 11.5 The Zoombinis meet the Fleens. Reproduced by kind permission of Sunburst Technology Inc.

One of the most impressive features of this program is the potential it has for repeated use, across a broad range of ages. Each of the puzzles increases in complexity if you get all of your Zoombinis through. At the simplest level, five- and six-year-olds have completed the puzzles through trial and error. The hardest levels of the hardest puzzles challenge any adult! The disadvantage of this is that it is difficult to keep the class together and discuss strategies or solutions to particular puzzles. However, the program also has a practice mode where the puzzles can be tried at four levels of difficulty. This can be useful for setting a specific challenge to teach particular skills and discuss successful strategies. One teacher used this approach with a data projector in the ICT suite. Each session started by looking at a particular puzzle in practice mode. Each of the pairs and small groups tried it, then discussed their strategies as a class. The groups then returned to the game mode to continue their logical 'journeys'.

In this example the key feature is using challenging but motivating software where pupils have to make their thinking and reasoning explicit, both in small collaborative groups and in whole-class discussion. The teacher's role is to draw out the learning that happens when the pupils are using the software and connect their thinking with other activities in (or out of) school.

Task 11.4 'Thinking skills' software	Find a program which aims (or claims) to develop thinking skills.

- Does it describe what kind of thinking (reasoning, creative, etc.)?
- Does it explain how it should be used (by the teacher, by individual pupils or in groups)?
- Try it out with some pupils – do you think it lives up to its claims?

ICT for thinking

ICT offers teachers a range of ways to challenge and stimulate learners' thinking. This could be through whole-class demonstration and discussion, by planning activities which use existing software creatively, by using particular software tools such as those for concept or mind mapping, or by using games and adventures which aim to develop aspects of thinking. Certain features or functions of ICT (TTA, 1999) may well lend themselves to supporting effective demonstration by the teacher, facilitate changing and evaluating information either by the teacher or by pupils, or support communication of ideas. The impact of the use of such technology will depend upon the context of how the ICT is used and the teacher's skill in making the connections meaningful for learners. If Dewey is correct then this will also require active participation on the part of learners:

> things gain meaning when they are used as means to bring about consequences . . . or as standing for consequences for which we have to discover means. The relation of means–consequence is the center and heart of all understanding.

(Dewey, 1933: 146)

This suggests that just planning activities and guiding learners through the tasks may not be enough. You may need to provide opportunities to discuss what has been learned or to review how skills and strategies could be applied elsewhere. No matter how well you prepare an activity or a lesson, you cannot guarantee that it will develop pupils' thinking or understanding in the way that you intended. Teaching for thinking will always require active monitoring and assessment from teachers about the meaning that pupils find in the different educational activities that they undertake. There is plenty of evidence that learners will find the easiest way that they can to make a task easier or less demanding. Understanding requires active construction on the part of pupils and this can be hard work:

> There is a challenge to understanding only when there is a desired consequence to which means have to be found by inquiry, or things . . . are presented under conditions where reflection is required to see what consequences can be effected by their use.
>
> (Dewey, 1933: 147)

ICT can present and re-present information and ideas in a range of different forms, so that it can be manipulated and exchanged quickly and easily. It is a tool that can be used by teachers for this purpose in their teaching so that the relationship between ideas can be highlighted and explored. Pupils can also benefit from this tool by exploring these ideas and their consequences for themselves as they see, listen and experiment with these ideas purposefully. It is therefore an essential option in any teacher's toolkit of choices for developing thinking and understanding.

Notes

1   This term is not meant to imply that values and beliefs are rigid or static.
2   Originally released as the Logical Journey of the Zoombinis.

Further information and readings

You can (or could) download a Word version of the 1999 DfEE report by Carol McGuinness *From Thinking Skills to Thinking Classrooms* (www.dfee.gov.uk/research/re_brief/RB115.doc), which was part of the thinking behind the revision and inclusion of thinking skills in the National Curriculum.

A project team based at Newcastle and Sunderland Universities undertook a review of taxonomies and classifications of thinking skills on which the model in Figure 11.1 is based. See Moseley, D., Baumfield, V., Elliott, J., Gregson, M., Higgins, S., Lin, M., Miller, J., Newton, D. and Robson, S. (2003) *Thinking Skill Frameworks for post-16 Learners: An evaluation. Research report to LSRC.* Newcastle upon Tyne: Newcastle University.

The DfES Standards site has a section on thinking skills and information about a range of resources appropriate for primary schools, including software reviews (http://www.standards.dfes.gov.uk/thinkingskills).

For an overview of teaching thinking and teaching strategies to develop thinking see Steve Higgins' (2001) *Thinking Through Primary Teaching*. Cambridge: Chris Kington Publishing.

For more information about the development of concept mapping have a look at Novak, J.D. and Gowin, D.B. (1994) *Learning how to Learn*. New York: Cambridge University Press.

Many of the software companies which make concept or mind-mapping software have free downloads (e.g. http://www.inspiration.com/ for Inspiration (older primary pupils) and Kidspiration (younger children).

The 'Talk Lessons' to develop effective collaboration are described in Dawes, L., Mercer, N. and Wegerif, R. (2000) *Thinking Together: A programme of activities for developing thinking skills at KS2*. Birmingham: Questions Publishing. See also their website http://www.thinkingtogether.org.uk.

For an overview of thinking skills and ICT generally see the report by Rupert Wegerif, *Thinking Skills, Technology and Learning* on the NESTA Futurelab website (http://www.nestafuturelab.org/research/lit_reviews.htm). The review examines the role of technology in supporting the teaching of thinking skills under different headings, summarising research into the use of technology as a 'mind tool', as a tutor and for developing collaboration and communication.

There is also a report by Avril Loveless, *Creativity, Technology and Learning*, on the same site. It examines specifically the relationship between ICT and creativity. The report maps out the different perspectives on creativity, and the teaching and learning of creativity, and brings together recent thinking in this field. The review summarises some of the implications of existing research and thinking in this area for the design of software and learning environments which might foster creativity amongst learners.

PART III

ICT and your own professional learning

This third section of the book provides an overview of how ICT can support you as a teacher more broadly. The aim of this is to help you to address the requirements in the professional standards for qualified teacher status (TTA/DfES, 2002) to 'know how to use ICT effectively . . . to support their wider professional role' (2.5 p. 8). As part of your progress towards attaining the professional standards for QTS you will need to keep a record of your learning. This section also describes how ICT can support you in this task.

The chapters in this section are organised as follows:

- Chapter 12 Managing your professional responsibilities with ICT – In this chapter we look at how ICT can support you as a teacher in your broader professional responsibilities such as with planning and preparation, teaching and assessment and continuing professional development.
- Chapter 13 Becoming a reflective practitioner – This chapter considers wider professional issues in terms of developing as a teacher. This means accepting responsibility for improving yourself by reflecting on your experiences in the classroom and seeking to improve as part of your approach to teaching.
- Chapter 14 Applying for jobs and coping with interviews – We offer some practical information and advice and on getting a job and look at how ICT can support you with this part of your career.

As with the other parts of the book, we can only offer you some general principles and advice on how ICT can support your professional learning. You will still need to undertake and keep a record of your learning. This will include trying things out, experimenting and practising both with and without ICT. As you do so you will have opportunities to think about how to develop your skills to improve your teaching, and, most importantly, ensure the learning of your pupils.

Tracking your own learning

At this point in the book (if you are working through it section by section) you should have a clear idea of the areas in which you need to develop your skills so that you can meet the standards for qualified teacher status (QTS).

You should also have an idea of how ICT can support you as a teacher and how you might use it with pupils to support their learning. Most of the chapters contain tasks that you could undertake; however, there are more tasks than you could accomplish. Our suggestion is that you use the list at the beginning of the book and identify perhaps five or six key tasks that will enable you to develop your skills, knowledge and understanding of ICT. You could keep a formal record of what you do in each task as part of a portfolio of your professional development. This may even come in handy when going for job interviews (see Chapter 14 for further advice in this area). You should at least be aware of and be able to talk about what you have done as part of your training to develop your use of ICT. It is not an area you can ever finish. Technology changes all the time, and as it changes new opportunities open up for how ICT can support teaching and learning. As a professional teacher it will be your responsibility to be aware of developments that you may be able to benefit from in your professional life.

The tasks can be classified as follows:

- Developing your own ICT skills (such as learning how to set up a database).
- Using ICT to fulfil your professional responsibilities (such as for preparation and planning, record keeping or access to information about your work).
- Developing your teaching skills where *you use* ICT (such as using a digital projector and presentation software).
- Developing your teaching skills where your *pupils* use ICT.

Our advice would be that you choose a task from each area, unless you already have advanced ICT skills, in which case developing your understanding of how to use them in the classroom will be most valuable.

As an interesting aside, in our experience it is not always the trainees with the most developed skills who use ICT best in the classroom. Sometimes their knowledge is so automatic that they miss creative or innovative ways that ICT can be applied in the classroom, whereas when you learn something new, you may be closer to how your pupils will experience ICT and can see the potential for learning in what seems like ordinary software and equipment.

Further information and reading

The Standards site is an essential resource for any primary teacher. It has information on national policies and the national primary strategy, with overview and background information as well as more detailed guidance which aims to support your teaching. This includes examples of planning over the medium term as well as lesson plans with suggested activities and resources.

http://www.standards.dfes.gov.uk

Evidence from inspections and advice from the Office for Standards in Education (Ofsted) about aspects of the curriculum as well as broader issues about teaching and learning can be found on their website.
http://www.ofsted.gov.uk

The General Teaching Council also offers information and advice on professional aspects of being a primary teacher. You will find resources and information on a wide range of professional issues.
http://www.gtce.org.uk

The Teacher Training Agency website also has essential information for you about induction and professional development.
http://www.tta.gov.uk/

12 Managing your professional responsibilities with ICT

The use of ICT in education has developed rapidly over recent years. It is therefore an exciting time to be using such technologies as a teacher. Not only are new teaching and learning opportunities emerging as the technology develops, but the range and quantity of information that is available with and through ICT is increasing dramatically. You will, however, need to keep learning if you are to benefit from these developments. This is for two main reasons. First is the rapid development of technology itself. Each year computers and other forms of educational technology evolve. New machines and new equipment create new opportunities. Sometimes these have been developed especially for education; on other occasions a new development offers new opportunities for the classroom. One example of this is digital video. It is a relatively new technology and challenging to manage in the classroom. However, reviewing learning when you have access to a video recording of, say, a technology project, is really powerful. As new video equipment is developed that can exchange information easily with computers it is possible for young learners (even in early years settings) to record what they have done. Schools have only just begun to explore how such opportunities can be exploited to support learning.

The second reason is current possibilities in the use and management of information. As noted above in Chapter 3, databases are probably underused in schools. Their power is in the way that information can be related to other pieces of information. At present most of the information available on school networks (or on the Internet for that matter) is unrelated. You have to find the content that you need and make the connections yourself. Recent developments suggest that new tools are being developed that may make this process easier. Web pages with planning information could link to a range of activities and assessment opportunities. This information could then be connected automatically with schools' record keeping and pupil profiles. So-called 'intelligent' search engines can already 'learn' from tracking patterns of use what other information you are likely to be interested in. These and other developments will make it valuable to keep up to date with professional tools that ICT can offer as you begin your teaching career.

ICT can therefore support you in a wide range of ways as a teacher in training (and once you start with your own class). In the short term it can help you to manage meeting the requirements of the course, particularly in terms of the planning, preparation, teaching and assessment you will need to undertake for your teaching practices. If you already use ICT to complete your planning and make some of the resources that you use for teaching, you will have started to accumulate invaluable information and materials. Over the longer term ICT can also support you in meeting your developing professional responsibilities in keeping up to date with information and research and finding (or even taking courses) for your continuing professional development. It also has the potential to manage some of the more routine aspects of professional life more easily, though a cynic might observe at this point that the potential of ICT is often unfulfilled!

Planning and preparation

The Internet is a vast source of information and with computers you can easily develop, adapt and store resources to use in the classroom. The challenge is in knowing when it is a good use of your time to look for information and materials that might help you, and when it is a better use of your time to make something yourself from scratch. There is a considerable amount of official information available for you in electronic form that you should already know how to find and use:

- National Curriculum documentation;
- National Literacy Framework (with Unit plans and activities);
- National Numeracy Framework (with Unit plans and activities);
- QCA Schemes of Work.

There are also huge quantities of resources that you can use in the form of lesson plans, downloadable resources and ideas for activities (many of them free). Searching for materials may take some time, but it is a skill you will quickly develop. You will need to be critical about such resources (there are some excellent materials; there are also many examples of rather dull activities too). A good idea here is to team up with someone else on the course and exchange websites and resources that you can develop (especially if you have easy access to e-mail).

Another important strategy is to plan how any activity or resource could be reused when you design it. Don't create one-off resources (unless you really need to). Most ideas can be adapted and developed to be used on another occasion. Templates are a good idea here. If you regularly complete a planning sheet or prepare resources make sure you create a template with the font size and styles that will make preparing other resources easier (or at least make key resources 'read-only' and use the 'Save as . . .' feature to stop you losing or overwriting your original document – as we discussed in Chapter 6).

Managing the files that you use will quickly become an issue. You will have to work out a means to store and organise the materials that you use and create. This can be challenging, as file sizes can become large quickly and with a few colour photos as illustrations they will not fit on a floppy disk. This is a particular challenge if you are working between college or university and home and school. E-mail can help (though again there may be restrictions on the size of files you can attach) as can access to computers with CD writers.

Another issue is organising the files and information that you have. Some resources can be used with different age groups, or can be adapted for use in other lessons, so it is not easy to decide how to classify and store what you have created and used so that you can find it again easily. One idea that may be useful is to make sure that you name (or rename) the files that you use consistently so that when you see a file name it jogs your memory about what it contains.

At the heart of this area is the realisation that making decisions about ICT helps you to be more efficient or more effective. This will depend on your current level of skills. It is worth investing time and energy in developing your skills further, but only with the aim of being able to benefit in the long run. Developing resources with ICT often takes longer than other means, particularly at first. The reason to choose to use ICT is because of the longer-term benefits it offers through being able to reproduce or develop further resources, or because your skills develop so that producing resources over time becomes quicker and easier.

Task 12.1 Organising your resources	Think of the range of ways that ICT can support you in your planning and preparation.

Organise (or reorganise) your work in a way that you can easily classify and find information you need (this might be by subject or by year group) that you have downloaded and developed. Don't forget that you can use shortcuts to 'point' to files.

Identify where there are some gaps between what you have and what you need. Search for and download information and materials you could use. Develop a further resource to help you with your next teaching placement.

Teaching and assessment

ICT can also help with the teaching and assessment of pupils that you need to undertake on your course. If you have access to presentation technology it is easy to develop a range of presentations that you can use, or you could collect copies of specific teaching programs (such as the interactive teaching programs for mathematics) that you will be able to use again. At a more basic level you can create teaching resources for you to use to help you present a particular idea, or examples of texts that you could print out large enough for the class to see or as a focus for a plenary discussion.

ICT is also invaluable as a support for assessment. Although primary schools do not generally have an integrated administration, teaching and assessment system, your planning should link with the assessments that you need to undertake and you should at least be able to create assessment sheets efficiently with pupils' names on. You might want to store such information on a computer (though see also Appendix D for an overview of data protection issues).

| Task 12.2 Assessment and recording | Review your current planning for teaching. Design an assessment and recording sheet for one of these object- ives (perhaps using a spreadsheet or a table) to use |

with your class. Print out a copy and undertake the assessment you have planned. Decide if you need to keep an electronic version of the assessment (this might be the case if you plan to update it regularly, or where you are keeping a num- erical record, such as marks or scores).

Professional development

ICT can also support your ongoing professional development. You should be able to find current relevant information on the Internet. This might be in terms of develop- ments with the National Primary Strategy or reports and information from organisa- tions like Ofsted or BECTA, as well as more general information about teaching and learning in schools.

In terms of your ICT skills and knowledge you should also have opportunities to continue your professional learning. This might be from a number of possible sources:

- School-based INSET;
- LEA courses;
- Online continuing professional development;
- Master's courses at your local university (or through distance learning);
- Courses and conferences from other organisations such as teacher unions or national organisations;
- Classroom-based research.

You will be offered opportunities in the first few years of teaching, but you may also need to create some opportunities of your own by finding information about courses or conferences or new developments in educational technology and pursuing them yourself. There never seems to be time to do everything you want to in teaching. However, it is also helpful to have some idea of where you want to get to in terms of your professional development. If you want to continue to develop your effectiveness as a teacher, ICT is one area you should probably not ignore.

| Task 12.3 Extending your professional knowledge | Think of a piece of research about schools or an area of teaching and learning you are interested in. |

Search for this information and see if you can find more details on the Internet.

What are the implications of this research for you in the classroom?

Wider professional role

As part of the professional standards that you need to achieve in order to obtain Qualified Teacher Status you need to demonstrate that you know how to use ICT effectively to support your wider professional role (TTA/DfES, 2002: 2.5 p. 8). If you undertake the tasks in this chapter you will be able to provide evidence of this through your use of ICT to find information to help you with your preparation, planning, teaching and assessment, as well as finding more general information about teaching and learning to develop your effectiveness as a teacher.

Summary

ICT has the potential to help you as a professional teacher. However, you will need to develop your knowledge and skills in finding and using such information to help you with your work.

Suggestions for further information and reading

The National Grid for Learning is a collection of websites and resources for teachers in the UK. It includes the Virtual Teacher's Centre and links to regional 'grids' or other websites with resources to support you.
http://www.ngfl.gov.uk

The British Educational Technology Association (BECTA) has extensive information about the use of ICT in schools, professional development opportunities and research and development work in the UK. It provides downloadable help sheets written in jargon-free language covering both technical and pedagogical issues.
http://www.becta.org.uk

A number of other organisations offer support, information, advice and courses. The National Union of Teachers (NUT) (http://www.teachers.org.uk/) run courses in a range of areas including ICT; Micros and Primary Education (MAPE) (http://www.mape.org.uk/) specifically covers ICT in primary schools and the Association for ICT in Education (ACITT) (http://www.g2fl.greenwich.gov.uk/acitt/) has helpful resources. See also the organisations listed in Appendix B for further information.

For further general information about the use of ICT in primary schools you could have a look at:
Ager, R. (1998) *Information and Communications Technology in Primary Schools*. London: David Fulton.
Leask, M. and Meadows, J. (2000) *Teaching and Learning with ICT in the Primary School*. London: Routledge Falmer.
McFarlane, A. (1997) *Information Technology and Authentic Learning: Realising the potential of computers in the primary school*. London: Routledge.

13 Becoming a reflective practitioner

| **Task 13.1   Why do I want to teach?** | Think of the reasons why you want to become a primary teacher. Jot down the first three that you thought of. |

Classify your responses as:
   focused on children;
   focused on yourself;
   focused on teaching subjects/content;
   other reasons.

When you were first interviewed for your place on the initial teacher training course you have been following, you were probably asked, among other things, why you wanted to teach. Your answer probably included reference to liking children, enjoying their company and gaining pleasure from helping them to learn. By now, you should realise that nothing in education is that simple. If all that was needed to be a teacher was the liking of children and pleasure gained from being with them and helping them, anyone could do it. You now know that there is much more to it than that. As Pollard (1997) explains, teaching is '. . . a complex and highly skilled activity which, above all, requires classroom teachers to exercise judgement in deciding how to act' (1997: 4).

Your initial teacher training course is just the first rung of a long professional ladder. It has laid the foundation for your teaching career. It will have raised your awareness of the complexity of your role as teacher, the skills you need, the judgements you will make and the decisions you will need to take. You will have had opportunity to practise all of these but you will be by no means expert at them. Your training does not equip you for the rest of your life as a teacher, it simply starts you off on that life. You have begun the process of *Continuing Professional Development*. Once you start teaching and have the hectic first few years behind you, you should be asking yourself, How can I improve as a teacher? How can I progress in my career? Pollard goes on to say that you need to develop the skills of reflecting on practice – to become a reflective teacher. 'Reflective teaching is seen as a process through which the capacity to make such professional judgements can be developed and maintained' (Pollard, 1997: 4).

He has introduced the idea of the reflective practitioner. So what does this mean?

Moving on in your teaching

You will not gain your first teaching post if you cannot teach. Indeed, you will not pass your school placements and gain Qualified Teacher Status. So, QTS indicates that you can do the job. You have reached at least a minimal level of competence deemed appropriate for someone at the end of the training programme. Is this enough? Those of us who have been teachers for a long time know that there are some teachers out there who have been teaching over twenty years but can be described as having one year of experience twenty times over. They are competent teachers but they have stood still in their thinking and practice. On the other hand, the majority of teachers have moved on. Twenty years of experience really does mean twenty years of thought, learning, change, adaptation and personal development. This notion of the reflective practitioner is not new. Dewey (1933) contrasted *routine action* with *reflective action*. Routine actions are guided by factors such as tradition and habit (*I do it like this because I always do it like this . . .*) and authority (*. . . and it works . . .*) alongside unchanged institutional definitions and expectations. This is the teacher with one year's experience twenty times over. Reflective action, on the other hand, indicates a social and educational awareness and is a willingness to carry out self-evaluation and develop necessary skills to develop and be flexible. As Pollard suggests:

> teaching concerns values, aims, attitudes and consequences as well as skills, knowledge and competence . . . there is a constructive relationship between the state of classroom competence and the processes of reflection through which competence is developed and maintained.
>
> (1997: 4)

Task 13.2 Reflecting on teaching with and about ICT

Think through your preparation to teach with ICT and to teach the ICT National Curriculum to your pupils. Try to make explicit:

1 Your own values, aims, attitudes about ICT and ICT education and the possible consequences of these.
2 The skills, knowledge and competences you are acquiring which will help you to be effective in teaching with ICT and in teaching ICT to primary children.

How do you feel the first will influence the second, if at all?

Developing competence

The competence mentioned by Pollard develops with time, opportunity and experience and in your teaching career you will exhibit different levels of competence, as you travel along the road from *novice* (the student teacher at the beginning of your training), through *competent* to *expert* (the teacher who is thoughtful, adaptable, searches for ways to move the teaching and learning forward and for ways to move his or her own thinking on, and draws on experience to apply new ideas in the classroom). During your training the level of competence is defined by the government's requirements in meeting the standards. You have to meet the standards and the training course is designed to support you in doing so. When you finish your course, you take with you into your first teaching post your career entry profile. This identifies your experiences during training and your particular strengths and areas for further development. During your induction year you will be supported both within the school (by the headteacher or a designated mentor) and by the LEA with a programme aimed at meeting your personal development needs. This support will help you to deal with the challenges of classroom life. You will have to deal with a range of issues.

From a study of three schools Berlak and Berlak (1981) identified a lengthy list of common dilemmas faced by teachers which included:

- Organisational issues – children, resources, tasks, space, time . . .
- Interpersonal issues – relating to children, other staff, other adults . . .
- Delegation/control issues – how much freedom to give children, flexibility . . .
- Motivational issues – children's involvement, relevance, expectations . . .
- Curricular issues – integration, subject teaching, time on each area . . .
- Standards issues – quality control, focus on skills/knowledge/understanding . . .
- Individual needs – differentiation, individual programmes, special needs . . .
- Whole curriculum issues – personal/social/moral development, equality . . .

Pollard (1997) sums these up as challenges relating to:

- practicalities
- teaching competences
- personal ideals
- wider educational concerns.

This means that as a teacher, to prove your competence, you must rise to the challenge, reconcile numerous demands and make complex decisions. To resolve the dilemmas, you must use your professional judgement to assess the situation, make decisions on how to act and have the skills to carry out those actions. If you do so effectively, you will be exhibiting the characteristics of the next level of competent practitioner – the experienced and reflective teacher. As such, you go through a cycle of reflective teaching: planning actions, organising for action, carrying it out, collecting evidence of the consequences, analysing and evaluating it, reflecting on the evidence and feeding the reflection into the next planning cycle.

Dreyfus (1981) considered the stages of development of teachers' competence, and suggested that to show evidence of understanding and be able to make judgements teachers need four basic skills:

- the ability to recognise issues;
- the ability to identify which of those issues are important;
- the ability to understand the situation as a whole; and
- the ability to make appropriate decisions.

With these four capacities in mind, you can see that a *novice* teacher, a student teacher and a teacher in her or his first few years of teaching, would tend to recognise issues out of context (having no real experience to work from). As a consequence he or she would be unable to select the important ones (all tend to loom large and be seen as important). He or she will probably be analytical in understanding the whole situation (building it from individual components) and make decisions rationally (using logic and reasoning).

A *competent* teacher, on the other hand, after a few years of teaching experience, would tend to recognise issues in context (drawing on prior experiences of similar events) and select only the important ones (he or she knows which are minor and can be ignored). Such a teacher would still tend to understand the whole situation analytically and make decisions rationally.

Finally, an *expert* teacher, who has both experience and further reading, research and training to draw upon, will tend to recognise issues in context, select the important ones, understand the whole situation holistically (viewing the integrated whole rather than the individual component parts) and make decisions intuitively (drawing on experience and practice).

Task 13.3 Developing an action plan	Think of your own development as a teacher who needs to use technology and to teach ICT to your pupils.

1 What level of competence do you bring to the start of your teaching career?
2 What are your weaknesses as far as teaching with and about ICT is concerned?
3 If given a free choice in your first three years of teaching, what continuing professional development support or courses would you like to participate in to develop your skills and competence further?
4 Draw up a personal action plan, listing a timescale for what you would like to achieve and how you might achieve it.

As with any model, this is simplified and there are always exceptions, but you should be able to see how your professional development as a teacher is a continuing process. It is at this point that your continuing professional development is crucial. Remember that you cannot stand still. Children, curricula, environments all change. This is especially true of ICT! You must be flexible and adaptable in order to develop appropriately. Eventually you will probably want promotion in some form or to develop your responsibilities as a professional teacher. Keeping yourself up to date with developments in ICT and information and courses on the Internet is a good first step.

Suggestions for further reading

If you would like to explore further some of the issues touched upon in this chapter, the following books should be of interest to you.

Pollard, A. (ed.) (2002) *Readings for Reflective Teaching in the Primary School.* London: Continuum International Publishing Group.
In this book, Andrew Pollard brings together over 100 readings from experts in education across the whole spectrum of educational pedagogy. He does not limit himself to contemporary writers, but includes writings from the past to show how ideas in education have changed and developed. The whole is intended to support the primary teacher in the process of reflecting on his or her own practice.

Pollard, A. (2002) *Reflective Teaching: Effective and research-based professional practice.* London: Continuum International Publishing Group.
This is a companion volume to the *Readings* . . . above, but is much more focused on actual classroom practice and supporting the student teacher and new practitioner. Again, it is a large volume which covers a wide range of educational skills and ideas and which has a supporting website.

14 Applying for jobs and coping with interviews

Your initial teacher training programme will secure your confidence and competence as far as teaching and learning generally is concerned, and your ICT skills and knowledge in particular. Your next challenge is to look ahead. You will begin applying for teaching posts around the January or February of your final year, and probably begin the interview cycle around March to April. This means that you have to be thinking about your future before you have even finished the training programme. Although applying for jobs and interviews are not elements included in the standards: everything that you do in terms of meeting the standards can be seen as part of your preparation for this next stage in your professional development. In this chapter, we will finish by considering how to apply for your first teaching post and what to expect at interview and how using ICT may be able to help you.

Applying for teaching posts

Good classroom practitioners who have performed well during their training programme, both professionally and academically, are not necessarily good at 'selling themselves'. Yet that is what the interview game is all about. There are a few basic rules which can help you with this.

First, in the autumn term begin to think about where you want to teach: do you want to stay in the area where you are training, go back to your home area, or go somewhere completely new? Begin scanning various newspapers and publications (like the *Times Educational Supplement* or the National Union of Teachers' *The Teacher*) to get a feel for the way posts are advertised. You will find that at the primary level, there are likely to be two ways of doing things. Schools may advertise directly. These are likely to be larger primary schools. These schools often offer posts for one year in the first instance. Don't be put off by this – it is a way of ensuring the school is getting the right person for the job. At the end of the year, if you have proven yourself an effective teacher you are likely to be made a permanent member of staff. (This is something you could explore with the headteacher if called for interview.) Alternatively, many primary schools work with their Local Education Authority (LEA). In this case, a pool system may be operated. The LEA would have a rough idea of how many primary teachers would be needed by the authority in the following September and organise to do blocks of interviewing over several days. Successful interviewees would then be placed in the LEA pool, which means that headteachers would look through the application forms, curricula vitae and interview reports held by the LEA then choose someone from the pool for their school. You would then be offered a post at that school at a later date.

Once you have spotted the post or the LEA pool you wish to apply for, you would need to send off to the address provided (either the school or the LEA office) for the details and an application form. What exactly is asked of you varies, but usually you are asked to include three things:

1   **A letter of application** – Some schools or LEAs will ask you to include a short letter of application. Even if not asked to do so, it is always wise to include one; applications may not be considered without one. This should be a short, personal statement about your interest in the post, school or area, your suitability for the job – you could identify two or three strengths that you would bring to the situation and your potential (again, two or three points only). Normally, a letter of application should not run over one, or at the most two, sides. In a way, it is pulling out the key points you want to emphasise from the formal application form or curriculum vitae.

    Sometimes you are asked explicitly to write your letter of application in your own handwriting. It is important to comply with this, as it will be used in the decision-making procedure. Take care with presentation, spelling, grammar and punctuation. If you are not asked to write it freehand, then stick to word processing. You could always redraft on a word processor and copy out the final version!

2   **A completed application form** – This normally includes brief biographical details to provide a personal and academic context, qualifications and experience before and during your training programmes, and your different and varied experiences in schools. With respect to the latter, if you identify the schools where you have had placements, it is possible that the headteachers may be contacted, so it is always polite to check with them first that they don't mind you identifying the school. You may be asked to submit a curriculum vitae (CV) in addition to the application form. However, you should not omit sections on an application form because they are included on your CV.

    If it is a school or LEA application form, there is usually an open section which asks you for a personal statement. You can also include such a personal statement with your curriculum vitae. Link your personal statement to what you know about the school. Write confidently about your experience and expertise – your strengths and developing interests in terms of primary teaching and learning. Also, indicate your agenda for your future professional development – what you would like to do, if given the chance. Finally, indicate how you would fit in with the philosophy of the school and help to meet the needs of the children. This might include references to a portfolio which you would take along to the interview, if invited to attend (see below).

You may be able to get an electronic copy of an LEA application form. This can save you a lot of time if all you have to do is update it and print it out for the next application. Where electronic copies are not available, a good tip is to complete as much general information as possible in a black fibre-tipped pen on the paper form, but omitting the name of the school and particular post applied for, then make a few photocopies of the form so that it looks like the original (use a copy bureau to get a professional finish if necessary). Complete the form with the specific details as you apply for posts (using the same fibre-tip pen – it should be almost indistinguishable from the photocopy). This can save you valuable time in sending off subsequent applications.

3   **Names of at least two, possibly three, people who will provide references** – Never give names without first contacting the relevant people for their permission. One referee should be someone from your training course (usually your course director or personal tutor – you could use both). This person can comment on both your academic and professional profile. A second person should be able to comment on you as a person. This may be a tutor, but could also be someone who has known you in other contexts – for example, a family friend, a club or association leader if you are a member of a relevant organisation, or someone from your place of worship if you have a religious affiliation. Finally, whoever you use, give them some information about the post you are applying for and some brief pointers about any specific things you would like them to refer to in their reference. This helps them to tailor the reference a little.

If you have sent for details, you should have been sent some general information about the school with the details of the post and the application form. Do your homework about the school. At the very least, look up the most recent Ofsted report on the Internet. This will give you a feel for the 'official' face of the school. If the school is local, try to visit it on an evening or weekend, to get a feel for the area and the environment. If you like what you see, then go ahead and apply for the post. If you were invited to go on a visit prior to an interview, try to do so. It not only gives you a chance to look around the school and meet staff and children, but also to ask some informal questions. It enables you to go into the interview feeling confident that you like what you see and would like to teach there.

On very rare occasions, the reverse can happen. You find this is not the right school for you, and you can save everyone time and effort by withdrawing before the interview with good grace. This really is better than going through an interview and possibly being offered the post, just to turn it down. That creates ill-feeling and if you are applying for other posts in the same area you can put yourself at a disadvantage. The headteachers' grapevine is formidable! You were probably asked beforehand if you were still a serious candidate for the post anyway, and that makes the situation even worse.

Task 14.1   Applying for jobs

Look in a recent issue of an education newspaper like *The Times Educational Supplement* for the posts available in the Key Stage for which you are training.

Choose one of the posts which attracts you. Draft a letter of application and a CV on a word processor as if you intended to apply for the post.

Show your application to your tutor or mentor for comment and advice on how to improve it. Update the letter and CV accordingly and save as a new version to update as you apply for jobs.

Completing forms and writing letters is a time-consuming and onerous task. Do not underestimate how long it will take you. Start early and give yourself plenty of time to do the job well – to gather information, contact referees and to prepare the materials you must send off. The professionalism with which you do this shows through and when shortlisting for interviews is being carried out, the quality of the application itself can make the difference between you and someone else with similar experiences and qualifications. Information technology has made the task of writing personal statements and letters of application and CVs much easier. It is possible to change them and adapt them to school-specific contexts relatively easily, again a plus when choices are being made. Make sure you keep copies of the application documents that you send!

Another advantage you can give yourself is to prepare a *personal portfolio*. Refer to this in your letter of application and/or your personal statement and take it along for interview.

Good quality personal portfolios take time to prepare. They are not something that can be left to the weekend before. This is something you can begin at the start of your course to show progression in your own skills, knowledge and understanding as a teacher as well as your best qualities. Most importantly, make sure you bring it to the attention of the interviewing panel. Offer it to the chairperson when you go in to the interview and offer to leave it with them and collect it later. Do not be upset if they choose not to look through it, they may want to treat all candidates equally.

Task 14.2 Creating a portfolio

In order to 'sell yourself' well, you need to be thoroughly prepared for your interview. This includes preparing a personal portfolio to show to the interview panel so they can gain a feeling for you in the school and classroom context.

Use a file with plastic wallets to collect positive, high-quality evidence to show at interview. This could include:
- a brief CV;
- an overview of your experiences in schools and with children;
- some examples of your planning produced on computer which you feel shows your thoroughness, imagination and professionalism;
- examples of activities or worksheets you created (particularly some showing evidence of differentiation);
- photocopies of observation reports by your tutors or mentors;
- photocopies of report forms from previous school placements;
- photographs of any displays you created in schools;
- photocopies of children's work, showing the quality you maintained and how you marked it;
- examples of some lesson evaluations;
- evidence for assessment purposes;
- samples of recording and reporting procedures you used.

There are more things you could include – it is up to you to choose what will show you at your best. Remember to label your samples.

Create (using your DTP skills!) a front page which is both attractive and contains some brief biographical information, perhaps even a photograph of yourself. This could be followed by a contents page, to guide the reader through your portfolio.

Attending for Interview

Usually, far more people apply for posts than can possibly be interviewed and so a shortlisting panel is set up. In school, this is usually the headteacher and the chair of the governing body and perhaps a local primary adviser. A parent governor or a member of staff from the school may also be present. For the LEA it may be a primary adviser with one or two headteachers. The task is to weed out those applicants who are unsuitable for the post and to select from those who are thought suitable a manageable number for a morning or afternoon of interviewing – normally about five or six people.

Unfortunately, interviews have a habit of occurring during teaching practices. This is not usually a problem with your college or university – time away to attend for interview is allowed. But it does mean that you are not necessarily at your best – feeling tired and very busy. Try to organise things in advance, both with the school and with your personal life. Organise with your class teacher for what she or he will need to do while you are away. Try to get all your planning, preparation, marking and so on up to date a few days in advance of the interview. This means the night before you can concentrate on preparing for the interview. This doesn't mean just reading through what you said on your application and rehearsing your answers to possible questions. You need to plan your route to the school and the times of local transport (a dummy run is always a good idea, if possible). Prepare in terms of your physical appearance as well. Decide what to wear. Make sure everything is ready, clean and pressed. While you may not be able to afford new clothes, you can look smart in an existing outfit. Remember that the latest fashion statements can reflect your personality but may also count against you in a professional context. Try to relax and have a reasonable night's sleep and a decent breakfast. Appearances really do matter and you will need stamina to get through the day. Give yourself plenty of time so that you do not have to rush.

You may be asked to prepare and teach a short demonstration lesson. Try to use a lesson or activities that you have taught before. Make sure you bring any resources or materials with you. This is a good opportunity to demonstrate your use of ICT in preparation and planning – bring a few copies of your planning to give those observing the lesson. If you intend to use ICT as part of your demonstration lesson (such as a digital projector or teaching in an ICT suite) we urge caution. School networks have peculiarities that can make this challenging for even the most experienced user and you will need to have tried and tested everything first. This is sometimes difficult to do – make sure you have a plan for when something does not work!

At interview the aim is to find out what experience and expertise each candidate has to offer the school. The emphasis here is on balance. While schools want committed and conscientious practitioners, they also want balanced human beings with a sense of humour and signs of interests wider than just the school. Today's primary practitioners have to be multi-talented. You will have to manage and organise the learning for a diverse group of demanding pupils, across the full range of National Curriculum subjects plus religious education. You will be expected to contribute to the extra-curricular life of the school – not just parents' evenings, but clubs and events. You will also be expected to be a member of a team who work together for the good of the school – the whole being greater than the sum of the parts. And you will need to remember that there is life after work. To stay healthy and balanced you will need to maintain your own personal and social life. This will help to keep you a less stressed teacher.

Each member of the interview panel is likely to ask a question. Make sure you address your response to them, but include the other panel members by speaking to them too. If you are not sure that you understood the question, don't be afraid to clarify. Also be prepared to ask if they would like you to extend your answer. Also be specific: if you can give an example of something you have done, make reference to it appropriately. With these points in mind, the focus at interview will probably be on a number of themes.

You as an individual

Why are you an interesting person? What are your personal interests? What do you do outside of school? Will you fit in with the existing team? What life experiences do you bring to your career? Where do you see yourself in five/ten years' time?

You as a potential primary teacher

What attracts you to teaching as a career? Why do you want to work in that area/school/with that age range? What is your own personal philosophy of education? How do you see yourself in the classroom? How would you organise/manage/assess the teaching–learning situation? How would you deal with specific situations (for example, bullying or bad behaviour)? What extra-curricular experiences could you bring to the school? What is the best lesson you have taught so far? What made it effective?

You as a potential subject coordinator or leader

If you were asked to lead an area of the curriculum, what would it be? Why? What sorts of things would you need to think about?

A final point – do not become disheartened if you don't get the first post you apply for. Very few students do! If there are six candidates being interviewed for one job, then your chances are only one in six. It usually takes four or five interviews before you are successful, and for some people, they can even have to persevere into double figures. This reflects the current economic situation in education, the high standards which are being set by governing bodies and the high standard of competition out there in the market. However, learn from the experience. Take opportunities offered to you to be given feedback on your performance at interview and act on the advice given. It pays to do so. It should also help you improve your chances.

Task 14.3 Planning for interviews   At interview you are likely to be asked questions which will help the interview panel make comparisons between you and other candidates. Remember, they are looking for the best person for the post. In the context of ICT, how might you answer the following questions? They are in no particular order but are typical of the kinds of questions asked at interviews.

1   How do you feel ICT contributes to the all-round education of primary school pupils?
2   What methods have you experienced for organising and managing children and classrooms to use ICT effectively?
3   Use specific examples from your school placements to give us a feel for how you would plan for, teach and assess ICT in the pupils' National Curriculum.
4   Do you think there should be more time for ICT in the primary school curriculum? Give your reasons for your answer.
5   How will you manage the ICT experiences for a class of 35 pupils, all with very different needs and abilities?
6   How would you assess children's learning in ICT?
7   How could you link ICT with other areas of the curriculum?
8   What do you feel is the most serious problem facing you when teaching with ICT?

9 How would you make the ICT you use explicitly relevant to the needs of the pupils in this school?

10 What are your main strengths and weaknesses as a user of ICT? How will you address the latter?

Choose three or four of the questions and draft your responses.

Suggestions for further reading

If you would like to explore further some of the issues touched upon in this chapter, the following books should be of interest to you.

Moyles, J. (1995) *Beginning Teaching, Beginning Learning in Primary Education*. Buckingham: Open University Press.
This book covers the main educational issues you need to think about as a teacher, in chapters that are clearly organised and well illustrated with practical examples. Particularly useful is Chapter 15, 'Don't make a drama out of a crisis! Primary teachers and the law' (p. 244 onwards).

Proctor, A., Entwistle, M., Judge, B. and McKenzie-Murdoch, S. (1995) *Learning to Teach in the Primary Classroom*. London: Routledge.
Like Janet Moyles' book, this book covers all the main educational topics relating to classroom practice and pedagogy. It is one which can be dipped in to in order to refresh your memory of things covered on your training programme.

The Times Educational Supplement

This weekly newspaper is the main source of information about teaching posts around England, Wales and Scotland. In addition, occasional special sections are aimed directly at students applying for their first teaching posts, and focusing on how to apply, what to expect at interview, what to expect in your first year and so on.

Appendix A
Finding information
on the web

It is easier to look for information on the Internet than to find it. Searching is easy, discovering something useful is rather harder. It is perfectly possible to spend an hour of two (or even a week or two) getting absolutely nowhere. Undertaking effective searches is something you will need to learn for yourself, as well as teach your pupils, to make sure you get the information you need as quickly as possible. What follows are suggestions and some information which might help to make your searches more productive.

Search 'engines' and indexes

It is worth learning how to use a search 'engine' that suits you and sticking with it. To find anything on the WWW, if you don't know its URL (web address) already, you will need to use a search engine. This is a page you can type keywords into and get a list of 'results' with pages that should contain the words you specified (if not the information you wanted). These search engines are basically huge, usually automated databases that you can use to search for keywords, topics and so on. If you find one that makes sense to you, stick with it: the chances are that as you delve deeper, it will have more features than you notice at first.

It is also worth experimenting with some index-based searches and bookmarking a few 'favourites'. Index-based searches, such as 'Yahoo', are a way of moving from broad topics to more specific topics, so if you are searching for something about the Spanish Armada you might start from a broad topic such as 'History'. This will give you a series of headings from which you might choose 'European', which will give a series of headings from which you might choose 'Famous Battles', and so on. Once you have found a site that is useful, bookmark it (or add it to your 'favourites' list).

Using search terms

If you want to find information on the Internet you have to think carefully about what words you could use to find the information you need. Bear in mind that the search is automatic and literal. The computer matches patterns of letters, not meanings of words (though some searches are more 'intelligent' than others and may guess what you are looking for based on what other people have searched for before). Try to be precise and use as many keywords as possible at first. It is easy to get a message such as 'Matches 1–20 out of 1,726,432 possible matches for search: "famous, Spanish, battles".' The computer then displays the first 20 or so sites that it has found with these words in, and would then show you 86,322 lists of 20 sites until you'd seen all 1,726,432! The more keywords you use, the more likely you are to find what you are looking for.

If you feel like you are wasting too much time, try an advanced search. Ten minutes is a good rule of thumb for most searches. If you have not found what you are looking for in that time, change your strategy. This might mean changing the words you are using, trying an index, or using a more advanced or precise search. Almost all of the search engines on the web have an 'advanced search' option which can help you search more efficiently, but only if you know how to use it. Some of them use + or − so that you can specify words that must or must not be on a page it finds. Others use logical commands similar to those used in database programs, such as AND, OR and NOT (Boolean logic) or use brackets like in mathematics so that you can be more precise. You will have to check the details for each search engine you use (hence why it is helpful to learn one you like in detail). Most will let you search by putting things in quotation marks so that you can find that sequence (or 'string') of letters and words. So 'National Literacy Strategy' will find pages with those three words in that order, whereas putting in the same words without the quotation marks will find you pages that have the words 'national' 'literacy' and 'strategy' on them somewhere, but not necessarily in that order.

Some suggestions:

- **Be focused** – Even in the early stages of using the web you will learn more if you search for something specific than if you just try something and see where you end up.
- **Ignore adverts** – Banners and adverts offering all the riches of the orient (or more salacious products) will probably take you somewhere totally useless and try to keep you there by opening up extra windows you don't want. Some adverts are a little more subtle and try to lead you to sites by offering you a more intellectual reason to try it. If a link looks a little out of context with the rest of the page, it's probably best avoided.
- **Look at the web address** – Before visiting a site mentioned in the results of a search, check its URL. The URL is that string of words and letters with lots of slashes and dots. The last part of the URL gives some indication of the sort of establishment running the site. For instance, if it ends in '.edu' it will be an American educational establishment, if '.ac' it may be a British (or

Australian/New Zealand, or others) university or college, if '.com' it will probably be a commercial company, if '.org' it will probably be a non-profit or governmental institution and '.uk' indicates a British site. With a little experience you can second guess what the content will be like.

- **Practice makes perfect** – There are no easy solutions when searching for sites. The best way is a little practice on a regular basis and try to become an expert in one way of working, using a range of different tactics each time. There are usually a hundred routes to the same place, it's just a question of finding the sort of route that suits you best.

Some general search 'engines' that you might find useful are listed below. Please note that (as with all websites) the pages and addresses may change.

Google

http://www.google.com
Google has a well-deserved reputation as the first choice for those many who search the web. The automatic 'crawler-based' service seems to offer as comprehensive coverage of the web as you can get along with results that are usually relevant. Google also has a 'safe search' facility which makes using it with pupils in schools rather less stressful (you can find it among the advanced search options). A good place to start in your hunt for whatever you are looking for.

AllTheWeb.com

http://www.alltheweb.com
If you had a go on Google and didn't get what you wanted All The Web should probably be next on your list. Some people prefer it as a first choice. Again it is based on an automated database from 'crawling' web pages. It seems to provide both comprehensive coverage of the web and highly relevant results. In addition to web page AllTheWeb.com offers the facility to search for news stories, pictures, video clips, MP3s and FTP files.

Yahoo

http://www.yahoo.com
Yahoo is the web's oldest 'directory', or list of sites organised by people rather than automatic 'web crawlers', and has been going since 1994. However, more recently it has also added Google's crawler-based listings for its main results and combines the power of an automatic database with more readable information and categories compiled by humans! A good choice if you have a general question (rather than looking for a specific page or address) as the category listings can help you refine your search.

Metacrawlers and metasearch engines

http://www.metacrawler.com/
Unlike search engines, metacrawlers don't find the information directly but send a query to the databases of several search engines all at once. The results are then blended together onto one page. This way you compensate for the strengths and weaknesses of the different sources of information.

Vivisimo

http://vivisimo.com/
Enter a search term, and Vivisimo will not only find matching responses from the major search engines but also automatically organise the pages into categories or clusters that you can investigate further. Neat, quick and easy to use.

EZ2WWW

http://www.ez2www.com/
This meta search engine provides results from an impressive number of major search engines: AllTheWeb, AltaVista, Google, Open Directory, Teoma, Wisenut and Yahoo. Again it clusters the results by type so that you can see what kind of results it has found. The advanced search option offers access to more than 1,000 specialised resources which are searchable by category.

Kartoo

http://www.kartoo.com/
If you want to get a visual image of what your search results look like, try this meta search engine which provides a 'map' of the results with sites interconnected by keywords.

Search Engine Watch

http://searchenginewatch.com/
If you have a geekish streak and want to know more about how search engines work or get the latest details on the fastest and most accurate metacrawler, try the 'Search Engine Watch'. It has more information than you can reasonably deal with on a regular basis, but is good as a source of links to different types of search engines, along with information about how each search engine finds (and funds) its valuable resources.

Appendix B
Other sources of information

This appendix contains a list of websites to the main government and official organisations that we think are most likely to be useful during your training and as you start your teaching career. Occasionally web addresses change so we have usually referred only to the main or 'home' page for a site. You may have to do some digging to find the resources that you want. Our suggestion is that you have a look at the sites during your training and bookmark or add the sites to your favourites (depending on your browser). The list could have been much longer; however, we recognise that a printed list of websites can be a bit frustrating . . . it is likely that your training institution will have a page of useful links too which may save retyping the URLs.

Government and official websites

www.standards.dfes.gov.uk/

The Standards site managed by the Department for Education and Skills is a valuable repository of official information, guidance and support. You will need to refer to it regularly in your training and become familiar with what is available, particularly for the Primary Strategy.

www.teachernet.gov.uk

TeacherNet, the DfES teacher's portal, aims to provide easy access to the full range of relevant government information and services and to National Grid for Learning approved classroom resources (beware – not all are free). The main DfES site is at: www.dfes.gov.uk/.

www.tta.gov.uk/training/

The **Teacher Training Agency** website has information specifically aimed at those training to teach in England with details about the Skills Tests and the Standards for Qualified Teacher Status.

www.justforteachers.co.uk

Just for Teachers offers support for newly qualified teachers (NQTs) and teachers in the areas of good practice, career guidance and teaching resources. You can send in your particular problems and receive free advice from a trained career adviser, educational psychologist and legal adviser. You also may be interested to investigate the history of how this site developed and how it is maintained as this should help you evaluate the information and support offered.

www.becta.org.uk

The **British Education Communications and Technology Association** (BECTA) provide a wealth of information on ICT and teaching and learning in schools. They offer a range of helpsheets on using ICT in different topics (such as portable computers or keyboarding skills) and different subjects (such as using ICT in the core curriculum at Key Stage 2) as well as research summaries about the use of ICT for teaching and learning.

www.qca.org.uk

The **Qualifications and Curriculum Authority** (QCA) is responsible for standards in education and training. They aim to maintain and develop the school curriculum and associated assessments, and to accredit and monitor qualifications in schools. Curriculum guidance for the Foundation Stage as well as the schemes of work (for ICT science, history, geography, music, PE) can be found on QCA's website.

www.ncaction.net

The **National Curriculum in Action** website provides practical examples of children's work using ICT. This official exemplification site is produced by QCA and offers general guidance on the use of ICT in subject teaching related to the opportunities in the National Curriculum and schemes of work.

www.ofsted.gov.uk/

The **Office for Standards in Education** (Ofsted) was established in 1992 as a non-ministerial government department. They claim that their main aim is to help improve the quality and standards of education and childcare through independent inspection and regulation; they also provide advice to the Secretary of State. You can download copies of school inspection reports from the website. They also produce reports based on inspection evidence, such as the 'ICT in schools' series.

www.gtce.org.uk

The **General Teaching Council for England** is the professional body for teaching and provides an opportunity for teachers to shape the development of professional practice and policy as well as to maintain and set professional standards. The site contains a 'Research of the Month' section which offers a useful digest of a piece of recent or relevant research.

www.ncsl.org.uk

National College for School Leadership site offers a range of information sources and interactive tools to all school leaders.

ICT organisations

acitt.digitalbrain.com/acitt/

The **Association for ICT in Education** (ACITT) Membership of the Association is open anyone interested in ICT coordination and the specialist teaching of ICT in the 4–18 age range.

www.mape.org.uk/

MAPE (Micros and Primary Education) aims to support the effective use of ICT in primary education. Their website contains a section that pupils can use (KidsMAPE).

www.naace.org/

National Association of Advisers for Computers in Education (NAACE) is a professional association for those concerned with advancing education through the appropriate use of ICT.

Main subject or primary associations

Although many of the subject associations which support teaching have a strong secondary focus, most also have primary teachers who are members or offer support to subject coordinators in primary schools.

The Association for Language Learning: www.languagelearn.co.uk/
The Association for Science Education: www.ase.org.uk/

The Association of Teachers of Mathematics: www.atm.org.uk/
The British Association of Advisers and Lecturers in Physical Education: www.baalpe.org/
The Centre for Information on Language Teaching and Research: www.cilt.org.uk/
The Design and Technology Association: www.data.org.uk/ (see also Nuffield Primary Design and Technology: www.primarydandt.org/home/)
The Geographical Association: www.geography.org.uk/
The Historical Association: www.history.org.uk
The Humanities Association: www.hums.org.uk
The Mathematical Association: www.m-a.org.uk/
The National Association for Primary Education: www.nape.org.uk/
The National Association for Special Educational Needs: www.nasen.org.uk/
The National Association for the Teaching of English: www.nate.org.uk/
The National Association of Music Educators: www.name2.org.uk
The Professional Council for Religious Education: www.pcfre.org.uk/

Teacher unions

It is likely that you will be a member of one of the teaching unions. All of them offer information and support over the web and can be a valuable source of information about teaching as a profession from a perspective other than that of the government.

The Association of Teachers and Lecturers (ATL): www.atl.org.uk/
The National Association of Schoolmasters Union of Women Teachers (NASUWT): www.teachersunion.org.uk/
The National Union of Teachers (NUT): www.teachers.org.uk/
The Professional Association of Teachers (PAT): www.pat.org.uk/

Software for teaching in primary schools

There are a number of companies and suppliers of software and ICT resources for primary schools. You should be able to find further information by searching on the WWW or looking at the different companies' websites. The following are offered as a starting point and, where specific mention has been made, to programs in the book. The list is in alphabetical order of the supplier's name.

Another valuable source of information is the local LEA which may well have an ICT resource centre where you can go and look at software or get advice while you are on a placement in a local school. This can be particularly helpful, as they are likely to have computers set up similar to what you will find in schools in the area.

2!nvestigate, Modelling Toolkit, Infant Video Toolkit

2Simple Software
2–4 Sentinel Square, Brent Street, Hendon, London, NW4 2EL

Tel: 020 8203 1781
www.2simple.com

Counting Pictures, PickaPicture, Talking WriteAway

BlackCat Educational Software
Granada Learning, Granada Television, Quay Street, Manchester, M60 9EA
Tel: 0161 827 2927
www.blackcatsoftware.com
Pictogram and word-processing programs.

Clicker

Crick Software Ltd
35 Charter Gate, Quarry Park Close, Moulton Park, Northampton, NN3 6QB
Tel: 01604 671691
www.cricksoft.com
An essential tool for the primary school. Create grids and set up words and sentences for pupils to select for recording or to support work across the curriculum.

FlexiTREE, FlexiDATA

Flexible Software
PO Box 100, Abingdon, OX13 6PQ
Tel: 0845 2300 330
Fax: 0845 2300 340
www.flexible.co.uk
One of the few producers of branching tree software for schools.

Dazzle, Granada Branch

Granada Learning
Granada Television, Quay Street, Manchester, M60 9EA
Tel: 0161 827 2927
granada-learning.com
A painting program for children. Granada Learning also sell a branching tree database and supply a range of curriculum resources (see also BlackCat).

Inclusive Writer

Inclusive Technology Ltd
Gatehead Business Park, Delph New Road, Delph, Oldham, OL3 5BX
Tel: 01457 819790
Fax: 01457 819799
E-mail: inclusive@inclusive.co.uk
www.inclusive.co.uk/

DataSweet, Pictogram, DataPlot, Splosh, Retreeval, Ask Oscar

Kudlian Soft
Nunhold Business Centre, Dark Lane, Hatton, Warwickshire, CV35 8XB
Tel: 01926 842544
www.kudlian.net/
Data handling (graphing), branching database and painting software for schools.

Junior ViewPoint, PicturePoint, Imagine LOGO

Longman Logotron
124 Science Park, Milton Road, Cambridge, CB4 4ZS
www.logotron.co.uk/

Kid Pix Deluxe 3

Riverdeep Interactive Learning Ltd
Styne House, 3rd Floor, Upper Hatch Street, Dublin 2, Ireland
Tel: 353 1 6707570
Fax: 353 1 6707626
www.kidpix.com/

Number Magic, Talking First Word, Easiteach, Starting Graph

RM plc
New Mill House, Milton Park, Abingdon, OX14 4SE
www.rm.com

Sherston Software
Angel House, Sherston, Malmesbury, SN16 0LH
Tel: 01666 840433
www2.sherston.com/
A good source of curriculum software and primary school clipart.

TextEase

Softease Ltd
Market Place, Ashbourne, Derbyshire, DE6 1ES
www.textease.com

Software suppliers

REM (Rickitt Educational Media)
Great Western House, Langport, Somerset, TA10 9YU

Tel: 01458 254700
Fax: 01458 254701
E-mail: Info@R-E-M.co.uk
www.r-e-m.co.uk/
Supplies most of the software listed above.

TAG *Software Developments*
25 Pelham Road, Gravesend, Kent, DA11 0HU
Tel: 01474 357 350
Fax: 01474 537 887
E-mail: sales@taglearning.com
www.taglearning.com/
An excellent source of information, software and resources for schools.

Appendix C
Glossary of educational ICT terms and abbreviations
or A Guide to Modern Geek for Teachers

The world of ICT has a language all of its own. You often recognise the words, but not the meaning. On other occasions you don't have a clue what the word could possibly mean. It is all part of the 'geek-speak' of the computer world. Learning all of these terms is clearly unnecessary unless you need to communicate with technicians, understand manuals or enjoy the nerdy thrill of incomprehension on the faces of friends or colleagues.

Most of the words and terminology listed below are part of current educational ICT jargon. We hope all of the definitions are helpful to someone at some time. Even if this is only to help you keep a sense of perspective or to relieve stress with wry smiles. . . . If the word or term you are looking for is not here, try the web-based 'hyperdictionary' which should have a definition: http://www.hyperdictionary.com/, though be warned, most of these are in geek and you may need a translation.

@   Actually means 'at' and is usually part of an e-mail address. It sits between the user name and the domain name, the user being the person who receives the mail and the domain being the part of the server that is dedicated to that person.

Adventure program   A program which usually puts the player or user in an imaginary situation. The player is required to take decisions to control the way the adventure progresses. One of the early educational adventure programs was Granny's Garden (produced by 4mation), a current example would be the Logical Journey of the Zoombinis (Brøderbund) or SimCity (EAGames).

Application   The software which makes your computer do something useful for you, as opposed to doing things useful for itself. An application is a program which lets it carry out particular tasks, such as word processing, desktop publishing, running a database, creating a presentation or e-mail program. It *applies* the computer to a particular task, but unlike glue, it may not stick at it: this is then known as a **crash**.

Archiving   Storing old files which you don't want to get rid of permanently but which take up valuable space on a hard disc. This involves backing up or saving to a separate hard disc, floppy disc or CD. Can be a handy technobabble excuse: 'I'm sorry I can't come to the local *Star Trek* fan club meeting with you tomorrow night because I'll be *archiving* my lesson plan files.'

AUP (Acceptable Use Policy)   An agreement which explains the rules of Internet use for an institution. All schools should have such an agreement, both to have clear guidelines for pupils to use and so that parents and governors understand how access to the Internet is managed.

Back-up   To make a copy of the information held on a computer, a software application, or individual files (usually on a hard disc backed up to a floppy disc). A back-up should be made regularly and stored away from the original, for reasons of safety and security. You won't back up regularly enough until you lose a crucial file or program and then it is TOO LATE!

Bandwidth   A nerd-word used to describe how much data you can send through a connection to the Internet. Think of it as how big the pipe is allowing information to come gushing in to your computer. (If you are using a telephone line to get access to the Internet think of a small pipe, letting in a trickle of data; no, better still, think of a straw and a thick milkshake . . .) Broadband networks, the basis of the information superhighway, allow video signals to pass at high speed (visualise the Hoover dam bursting); narrowband networks tend to be text-only and are slower (think of sucking on a half frozen vanilla milkshake through a bent straw). For example, a voice over the telephone network requires a bandwidth of 3 kHz, while uncompressed video requires a bandwidth of 6 MHz. Glastonbury is much more fun.

Baud   A unit of data transfer speed ('baud rate'). One baud equals one bit in most instances and is measured in bits (or Kbits) per second. A baud is one single event per second, and so it can also be a character, digit or byte. Geek-speak for the speed of a modem (measured in bits per second). It is interesting that the computer world is as obsessed by capacity and speed as car fanatics or train spotters. 56Kbps (kilobits/sec) is currently a typical modem speed. You should never need to use the word in the real world. It is pronounced 'bored' for obvious reasons . . .

Bit   An abbreviation for BInary digiT. It is the basic unit of information in the computer world. A bit is a binary number and has one of two values, 0 or 1. Computers can only count to one as they have no fingers.

Bookmark   When using the Internet, this is a method of saving addresses (URLs) of sites or pages that you frequently visit in a list. Netscape uses the concept of a 'bookmark', whilst Microsoft Internet Explorer uses the term 'favorites' instead. The word 'hotlist' is also used.

Boolean operator (also known as 'logical operator')   An operator which defines a logical relationship between two conditions. This relationship can be 'AND', 'OR' or 'NOT'. They are used by some search engines to limit or combine search terms.

Broadband   The informal meaning is 'faster than commonly occurring networks', and so the actual meaning depends on what is commonly occurring at the time. BT defines broadband as 'a connection of 500 kbps or more'; the important thing is to think of that pipe delivering data and broadband is supposed to be more like a firefighter's hose than a garden sprinkler.

Browser   An application used to search and retrieve information. Netscape Navigator and Microsoft's Internet Explorer or Apple's Safari are browsers which you can 'point' at URLs and view WWW pages. As with most things in the computer world you never have the latest version which lets you hear the latest whistles and bells. It is interesting to note that the names conjure up the vision of exotic foreign travel when in all probability you are stuck in your living room or a school classroom as you 'voyage' through 'dataspace'.

Bug   An error in a computer program which may cause the computer to 'crash' or behave in an otherwise inexplicable manner. Of course, if the computer's behaviour is usually inexplicable it can be difficult to tell.

Byte   A single computer character, generally eight bits. Each letter displayed on a computer screen occupies one byte of computer memory – 1000 bytes, 1 kilobyte (k), 1000 k = 1 megabyte (Mb), 1000 Mb = 1 gigabyte (Gb); now that's a real mouthful.

CD-ROM (compact disc read-only memory)   A CD which looks like a music disc but contains computer information – such as words, graphics and sound rather than simply sound. CD-ROMs have a large storage capacity (up to 250,000 pages of text) and require a specific CD-ROM drive which may be built into the computer or available as a separate item. Some CD-ROMs will only work on computers of a particular type (e.g. Apple Macintosh or Microsoft Windows); many now use a common format and will work on a range of computers and other machines. See also **DVD-ROM**.

Clipart   Pictures (usually copyright-free) stored on computer disc or CD-ROM, often as a library, useful for importing into art, multimedia or desktop-published files. These clipart libraries almost always have a picture very nearly like the one you are looking for.

Compression   A range of techniques which reduce the amount of space required to store a specific amount of data. There are general compression techniques using mathematical algorithms which can reduce the space files take up on a computer, but better results are obtained when the compression techniques use characteristics of the particular type of information, such as text, audio, image or video. Names of programs like Winzip, Stuffit or Zipit give you a good general idea. Think of a sleeping bag or a stuffed sack and forget the maths.

Concept keyboard   An A4- or A3-sized slab connected to the computer on which paper overlays can be placed. By pressing different areas of the slab, actions can be made to happen on the computer (sounds; letters, words, phrases of text; pictures; animations; the control of output devices such as a turtle or robot).

Content-free programs   Open-ended programs which permit more control of the computer by the user. A word processor, database and spreadsheet are all 'content-free' in that the person using it decides what the content of the file will be. By contrast a drill-and-practice program has predetermined content and a set way to progress through that content.

Control interface   A box which has a number of output and input sockets, and plugs into a computer. Lights, buzzers and motors are plugged into the output sockets, and can be turned on and off by a set of instructions defined by the user. These instructions may respond to environmental changes detected by sensors (such as a thermometer or light meter) plugged into the input sockets. Something that has no face you will not be able to control.

CPU (central processing unit)   Generally means the actual chip or processor inside a PC – the part of a computer system which does all the work. Commonly used to refer to the 'box' the monitor sits on which contains the CPU and all the other gubbins inside. (NB do NOT refer to the delicate and sophisticated circuitry inside a computer as 'gubbins' when there are ICT enthusiasts around, you will hurt their wirings.)

Crash   What the computer does when you are stressed.

Cursor   The flashing mark which appears on the screen to show where text will appear when a key is pressed on the keyboard. A cursor's shape can be changed. Depending on its shape, a cursor is also called an 'I' bar, a caret, an insertion point, or a mouse pointer! If all else fails try cursing the cursor . . . it is guaranteed not to work but may make you feel better.

Data   The 'raw' information which a computer handles. Data can take the form of text, numbers or pictures. If your first thought was Commander Data, from *Star Trek* NG, award yourself two extra nerd points . . .

Database   A structured store of conceptually related information or data files organised and stored permanently in a computer system. A relational database is a hierarchical database that has extra links between data in different files. Data is stored in a series of tables allowing access from any point, therefore making searching more effective. Think of a library card index in lots of little boxes but on a computer and you will have the general idea.

Data logging   The use of sensors to measure and record environmental changes – for example, the changes in temperature of water in a pond over the period of several hours. Not something you do with a chainsaw in Kielder forest, though you may feel like taking an axe to the computer as you try to get the equipment working. If you can teach all of the required aspects of the National Curriculum for primary age pupils you will be a data logger and you're OK!

Data projector   A device which connects to a computer and projects what you see on the computer screen onto a wall or large screen like a film or slide projector. More economical and capable of making a bigger picture than an interactive whiteboard, though not as versatile.

Desktop publishing (DTP)   A computer application which allows the user to create page layouts which combine words, graphics and images with different sizes and styles of type. DTP software is used for the production of materials such as newspapers, magazines and leaflets.

Dialog(ue) box   A window which appears on screen giving information which requires a response. In fact no dialogue is possible. You are usually forced to do what is required, a bit like a consultation document in the education world.

Digital camera   A camera which takes still or video pictures as digital images, which can then be transferred to a computer for printing or playing with (or 'manipulating' in Geek) in a painting program. Saves all that waiting around for your photos to be lost by the developers.

Digitised speech   An electronic way of recording, storing and reproducing human speech, similar to using a tape recorder. Digitised speech is increasingly used in electronic communication aids as well as or in place of synthesised speech. It has advantages over the robotic quality of synthesised speech, although each word or sound takes up a great deal of computer memory.

Domain name system (DNS)   The Internet is divided up into domains on a hierarchical basis. A domain is an individual network. The domain name system maps Internet protocol (IP) addresses to individual computers within the domain. Internet e-mail addresses include domain name information such as:

.ac   academic (UK higher education)
.edu   education (US)
.com   commercial (US)
.co   company (UK)
.gov   governmental or public
.mil   military
.net   network resource
.org   an organisation (usually not a commercial one)

For example, a Newcastle University web and e-mail address will contain the domain identifiers .ncl (for Newcastle) and .ac (for an academic university).

Download   The term describing the transfer of information from one computer to another (such as through a modem or from an Internet site). To upload is to send a file to another computer.

DPI (dots per inch)   Refers to resolution or quality, often in association with printers or monitors. The higher the dpi the finer the quality. 300 dpi used to be a high quality printer, now you can get 1400 dpi printers cheaply which print pictures at near photograph quality.

DVD-ROM   Digital Versatile Disc Read-only Memory (sometimes Digital Video Disc). It looks like an audio CD but is capable of holding lots more information (as computer data, video or audio files).

Electronic mail (e-mail)   E-mail is a relatively simple form of communication and very easy to get to grips with. Everyone who has an e-mail account (usually given free with any Internet connection) has an e-mail address and therefore can send and receive e-mail. E-mail works in principally the same way as conventional mail. You write a message, address it to the person who you want to send it to, and then 'post' it using your computer! Precisely how it gets there can remain a mystery to all but the most ardent anoraks; all that is important is that it is quick, easy and amazingly reliable! It is also very inexpensive. It is also quite addictive! Think of it as texting with a computer for free.

E-mail attachment   A file attached to an electronic mail message carrying more complex information, such as a document with formatting codes, a spreadsheet, graphic image, sound or video sequence. Often frustrating as you will not be able to 'open' the attachment unless you have a copy of the program that created it.

FAQ (frequently asked questions)   Files on the Internet containing common questions and answers, usually online and posted to Usenet lists or on help sites.

Who reads them? More common is the response 'Oh FAQ' when someone tells you the answer is on their website.

Favourites   A method of saving WWW addresses (URLs) of sites or pages that you frequently visit in a list. Microsoft Internet Explorer uses the term 'favorites', while Netscape uses the concept of a 'bookmark' instead.

File transfer protocol (FTP)   A common method of transferring files from one computer to another over a TCP/IP network. Anonymous FTP is a way of copying files from an FTP server without having an account on the system in your name. Nerdy or what?

Files   Organised collections of related data, usually in a folder or directory on a disk. These can be pieces of work created in an application such as a word processor (for example, a document) or a spreadsheet of database records. Each file needs a unique label (name) in order to be accessed. Most pupils build up a collection of files either called by their name Steve1, Steve2, Steve3, or 'untitled'. These names are therefore almost completely indistinguishable and it means much time can be fruitlessly spent in locating previously saved work.

Flame   To send a sharp, critical or downright rude e-mail message to another person. If you get one, just delete it otherwise the flame spreads . . . One e-mail program even has a chilli pepper rating for messages that might be too 'hot' to send . . . See also **Netiquette**.

Floor turtle   A programmable device, sometimes called a floor robot, controlled by LOGO or LOGO-like languages. The turtle has a pen holder which can be lifted or dropped to trace the turtle's movements on paper.

Floppy disc   A portable, hard, plastic, rectangular envelope in which flexible, round, 3.5-inch magnetic disc is hidden. It therefore appears neither floppy, nor round: cunning name . . .

Font   A typestyle. Each font has a name and can be displayed in different sizes. Many fonts are available in different weights and variations, such as Times Medium, Times Bold, Times Medium Italic and so forth. Do not confuse a font with a font and try to baptise a small child in Arial Bold Italic.

GIF (graphics interchange format)   Digitised pictures are often stored and exchanged in this format (.gif as the file type), as most popular software can cope with it. It is very popular for pictures on the web because of the small file size.

Grammar checker   Purports to inform you when you use incorrect grammar in your writing. In practice it tends to recommend rephrasing things which are perfectly clear and displays a shocking ignorance of the difference between 'that' and 'which'.

Graphic calculators   A calculator which enables graphic displays of information on a little LCD screen; no blood, no violence but still graphic.

Graphical user interface   (GUI pronounced 'gooey' in the land where anoraks are worn)   A system, such as Microsoft Windows or the Macintosh OS, in which an on-screen pointer is moved, usually with a mouse, and 'clicked' on pictorial representations or icons in order to make the computer do things. If we didn't have GUIs we would have to type instructions into the computer all the time to tell it what to do.

Graphics program   An application which enables the user to create or manipulate images on screen. However sophisticated it is, it will not automatically draw graphs (see **Spreadsheet**).

Hard disc or disk   A rigid disc, usually made from aluminium, coated with magnetic material and hermetically sealed, and generally fitted internally in a personal computer. It is hard and disc shaped, but you can't see it either (see floppy). Schools computers may use floppy, hard and optical (CD-ROM) disk drives, some may even have zip and jaz drives (not nearly as exciting as they sound).

Hardware   The bits you can feel as opposed to the bits and bytes you can't. The physical parts of a computer or a communications system, including both mechanical and electronic parts: the processor, memory, keyboard, screen, mouse and printer.

High density disc (HD)   A disc capable of carrying double the data of a normal disc. With 3.5-inch discs, the high-density kind are usually marked 'HD' and have two square holes one at each corner where you hold it.

HTML (hypertext mark-up language)   A type of programming code or language used to create documents or pages on the WWW. HTML files are read by a web browser which interprets codes determining the format and size of text where tables or pictures should appear and where links to other files are to be placed. It is in the process of being superseded by DHTML, or Dynamic HyperText MarkUp Language, which offers greater flexibility.

HTTP (hypertext transfer protocol)   This is the process by which HTML is transferred from one Internet computer to another. You will see it at the beginning of most website addresses.

Icon   A small symbol or picture on the computer screen, for example representing a computer program or a data file. The religious overtones of the word add to the mystery that is ICT.

ICT (pronounced 'icy tea')   Information and Communications Technologies, used to be just IT (information technology).

Input device   A device which is capable of entering programs and data to a computer system, such as a keyboard, mouse, scanner or microphone.

Integrated learning system (ILS)   A computer-based practice system with assessment capability that monitors and manages the delivery of curriculum material to students so that they are presented with individual programmes of work.

Integrated package   A suite of application programs which have a consistent interface and include, at least, a word processor, spreadsheet and database, bundled together. Other programs may be included, such as graphics and communication modules. Information can be transferred easily between the applications. They may be parts of a single program or a collection of individual programs. Integrated packages tend to be cheaper and less fully featured than the individual applications when purchased separately.

Interactive video (IV)   A computer linked by software to a video system which allows the user to control a video disc and explore the information on that disc; choices can be made about the order in which the exploration takes place.

Interactive whiteboard   A whiteboard and digital projector that is connected to a computer so that you can stand in front of the board (and the class) but still control the computer by touching the whiteboard (usually with a special pen or just a finger).

Internet   The intercommunicating set of computer networks which provide access to the World Wide Web, online databases, file transfer, electronic mail, news and other services across the globe. The Internet is basically a global network of computers, connected by various forms of telephone line (various as in ordinary telephone cables, higher speed ISDN phone lines, very high speed optical cable and slightly more mind-boggling technologies such as satellite and microwave!). But more importantly, it is also a way of communicating and cooperating with people from all over the globe. This communicating and cooperating can take a few different forms, outlined below.

Internet relay chat (IRC)   Internet users world wide logged in simultaneously can 'talk' to each other by sending text messages. This is real-time or 'synchronous' communication – i.e. the other person or people need to be there at the same time. Most IRC chatting is no substitute for going down the pub with your mates, or even just sitting on your own watching TV!

Internet service provider (ISP)   An organisation with a direct connection to the Internet providing connections to the Internet for other users.

Intranet   An internal website set up to serve a closed group such as within a school, which contains pertinent information such as school documents, bulletin boards, health and safety information etc.

IP   Stands for Internet Protocol and any computer linked to the Internet needs an IP number or 'address'. This number ensures that pieces of information that are sent across the Internet get to where they were going.

ISDN – Basic Rate   A version of ISDN which which allows a total of 144 Kbits per second to be transferred between two points. This 144 Kbits is split into three different channels to allow for simultaneous transfer of different types of data. The split for speech or data, for example, is 2 × 64 Kbits/sec channels (B-channels), plus a 1 × 16 Kbits/sec channel (D-channel) used for signalling and control purposes. We guarantee you will never need to know this.

ISDN – Broadband   A version of ISDN allowing greater data transfer at a faster speed (essential for large data transfer such as video, for instance, in video-conferencing). Currently defined as 34 Mbits/sec +, it is proposed that broadband ISDN rates will grow to 150 Mbits/sec or 600 Mbits/sec. Just think of it as moving from narrow pipes to wide ones . . .

ISDN (Integrated Services Digital Network)   International telecommunications system for sending data over the telephone network. The data can be text, graphics or voice and is transferred in digital form at high speeds.

JPEG   Pronounced jay-peg in Nerdish. A data compression standard designed by the Joint Photographics Experts Group to store digitised colour or black-and-white photographs. The file type is .jpg.

Justify   Text is said to be justified when the words line up along a margin. Most text is left-justified but it can also be justified to the right margin.

Key words   These are particularly associated with 'free text' databases. Important words within descriptions are 'tagged' to ease the retrieval of the information. A search using a key word will display each individual record which has been given that particular tag.

Keyboard overlay   A sheet placed over the touch-sensitive membrane of an overlay keyboard. The overlays can contain pictures, maps, diagrams, words or objects. Pressing on any part of the overlay causes a message relevant to that area to appear on the computer screen. The messages may already be defined in the software, or they may be defined by the user. Messages may be vocabulary, pictures, sounds, instructions, questions or information of varying complexity.

Keyguard   A rigid frame placed over the keyboard. It is raised above the keys and has holes in it to allow access to the individual keys through the holes. With a keyguard, children with less well developed fine-motor skills may access the keyboard more accurately. An overlay keyguard works in the same way for use with an overlay keyboard.

LCD   Liquid crystal display screen: a thin form of monitor screen (about the thickness of two pieces of glass). Electrical charges cause different areas of the screen to change colour. Most calculators use LCD display to show the numbers.

LOGO   A simple computer programming language where instructions are written to control the actions of the computer. LOGO was written by Seymour Papert (among others) to provide a 'low floor, high ceiling' programming language – easy enough for infants to grasp, potentially complex enough to challenge graduates. In its simplest form (turtle graphics) it allows the user to control the movements of a screen turtle to draw pictures.

Memory   The storage medium used by computer systems to hold programs and data. Usually **RAM** (a form of volatile or working memory, which is erased when the system is switched off) and **ROM** (which is a form of semi-permanent memory).

Menu bar   A section of the screen (usually across the top) on which little lists of things you can do appear when you click on the words or icons. None so far serve alcohol (or even a cheese toastie).

Model   A representation of a real or imagined situation governed by certain rules which are managed by a computer program. The rules or data can be changed by the user and the outcome of the changes viewed on the computer screen. Mathematics is used to model reality (e.g. when three objects are placed with four objects, there will be seven objects all together; the model for this is $3 + 4 = 7$). A computer uses mathematical patterns and algorithms to model quite complex situations (e.g. global weather patterns, and gets these wrong too).

Modem (MODulator–dEModulator)   A device which translates digital signals into analogue signals (and vice versa) so that information can be carried over ordinary telephone lines. Modems operate at different speeds depending on the model and available bandwidth. Seek a geek for the numbers you want for the speed you need. Fax modems enable faxes to be sent and received by a computer.

mp3   A file format commonly used to store music files on computers. Sadly it refers to the 'Moving Pictures Expert Group (MPEG) 1 audio layer 1' compression algorithm (which you will be glad to hear enables files to be about 12 times smaller) rather than anything to do with music. Sounds good though.

Multimedia   A combination of still or moving images, graphics, text and sound. A multimedia machine is fitted with hardware such as a sound card and a CD-ROM drive to allow the full use of a multimedia product.

Netiquette   Network etiquette: the conventions of politeness recognised in e-mail communications (such as short messages without attachments unless the receiver is expecting your holiday high-resolution digital photographs) and on Usenet or in mailing lists, such as not (cross-) posting to inappropriate groups and refraining from commercial advertising outside the biz groups. An odd word which makes you think of correct behaviour in nightclub toilets, but an important concept as it is all too easy not to think through the consequences of what you do in the electronic world (see also **Flame**).

Newsgroup   A Usenet bulletin board topic such as 'films', 'recipes' or 'education'. An excellent way of meeting other people with similar interests, particularly if you like model railways or discussing the internal workings of your computer.

Online database   A remote database which can be accessed using the Internet or via a modem via a telephone line.

Operating system (OS)   Software usually held on a ROM chip or loaded in from a disc which provides all the basic control functions to supervise the computer system. Not all computers use the same operating system. The main ones are Windows, Macintosh and Linux.

Optical character recognition (OCR)   Recognition of printed or written characters by a computer. Each page of text is converted to a digital image using a scanner. This image is then converted into a text file using complex image-processing algorithms. It rarely achieves 100 per cent accuracy so manual proof reading is essential.

Peripheral   Any hardware device which can be plugged into the computer to perform some additional function such as a disc drive, a printer, an overlay keyboard or VDU.

Procedure   Ordered and structured commands to perform a particular task. For example, a LOGO procedure for turning two lights on and off in order might be: TURNON 1 WAIT 10 TURNOFF 1 WAIT 10 TURNON 2 WAIT 10 TURNOFF 2. Something of a turnoff.

Programmable toys   Toys which will obey a sequence of stored instructions entered by the user through a keypad – for example, floor turtles.

RAM (random access memory)   The memory used whilst executing a program such as a word-processing package. It can both read and write (record) information, but when the power is removed from RAM its contents are lost. The easiest analogy is that it is the computer's working, thinking or operating memory.

ROM (read-only memory)   A form of memory whose contents are permanent and cannot be altered, and which does not lose data when the power is switched off. Used by hardware manufacturers to incorporate programs and data that must be permanently available. One advantage of applications in ROM is that they cannot be accidentally deleted or corrupted.

Scanner   A peripheral device by which pictures and text can be imported into a computer. Small hand-held devices work by rolling the scanner head across the picture. Larger flatbed scanners work rather like a portable photocopying machine. With a speech synthesiser, it is possible to scan text into the computer and hear it read aloud. Can also be used to read bar codes and convert them into numeric data. **OCR** and OMR are types of scanner and associated software.

SCSI card (Small Computer Systems Interface card)   This card provides the computer with the standard (SCSI) used to connect high-speed peripherals such as hard discs to personal computers. Now largely replaced by **USB**.

Sensor   A device used to measure environmental changes such as light, temperature and movement. Sensors may be connected to control interfaces or data-logging devices.

Simulation   A predefined computer model of a situation which may allow the user to try different strategies and see what happens as a result. A type of software which enables the learner to take part in experiences which would be difficult or impossible in real life. This could be motor racing at Silverstone or exploring potentially dangerous situations. It includes role play and adventure games which imitate a real or imaginary situation. They can help decision-making by simulating situations such as moving house.

Software   A generic term for all computer programs associated with a computer system. Software falls into two major types: applications programs such as spreadsheets or databases, and systems programs such as MS-DOS or Windows. In addition, there are utility programs.

Spam   The electronic equivalent of junk mail. To indiscriminately send large amounts of unsolicited e-mail meant to promote a product or service. The link back to Hormel Foods Corporation's coinage of the term in 1937 for 'spiced ham' (now officially known as 'SPAM luncheon meat') is intriguing only to those with nothing better to do.

Spellchecker   An electronic dictionary, usually part of a word-processing application which scans text on the screen and highlights any word it does not recognise. The writer is given the option to correct, ignore or add the word to the dictionary. The spellchecker can be set to offer alternative spellings to the writer. Harry Potter fans may be disappointed to discover it does not check spells. See also **Grammar checker**.

Spreadsheet   A computer program which allows words and figures to be entered into cells on a grid format. Cells can be linked by formulae, so that altering numbers in individual cells will produce an alternative set of results. Spreadsheets may be used to model situations whose rules are governed by mathematical relationships such as numerical series like Fibonacci or the management of a budget account. Nothing to do with quilting . . .

Synthesised speech   Electronic speech produced by a computer or speech synthesiser from text rather than from a real voice. The vocabulary that can be spoken is not limited to the available memory (as with digitised speech), but the accuracy and clarity of the speech may be affected, as the computer pronounces speech according to a set of rules stored inside the machine. Often you can adjust the spelling of a word to improve its pronunciation. As with most synthesised things, nearly but not quite like the real thing (think of nylon and polyester).

Tablet PC   A computer that looks a bit like an 'Etch-a-Sketch®' but is a fully functioning computer that has a touch screen which you can 'write' on with an electronic 'pen' to control the computer. You may still have problems if you pick it up and shake it to delete what is on the screen.

TCP (Transmission Control Protocol or Transfer Communications Protocol)   A sort of Esperanto for computers that lets them talk to each other. You may need the antiseptic version after you damage yourself and the computer when it refuses to communicate via any transfer protocol. A collection of networking standards which underpin the Internet.

Tele-conferencing   This involves the use of telephone and/or computer links to connect people in a meeting who are in different locations. This is also known as audio-conferencing or video-conferencing depending or whether you can hear or hear and see the other parties involved.

Telnet   Telnet is a system by which you can connect to someone else's computer over a network or phone line. It tends now to be for services such as weather watching or checking library catalogues and is rapidly becoming an Ancient Geek dialect.

Touch screen   A particular kind of computer screen where pressure on the screen enables you to interact directly with what you see without having to use a mouse or keyboard.

Trackerball   An alternative pointing device sometimes used in place of a mouse. The device is rather like an upside-down mouse and the user moves the ball which in turn moves the pointer on the screen. Selections are made by pressing the buttons on the device, and this is especially suited to pupils who find small hand movements difficult.

Trojan horse   A malicious program that overcomes your computer's defences by being disguised as something innocuous, such as game, word-processing file or weblink.

URL (Uniform/Universal Resource Locator)   A unique reference system locating a file on the WWW or in other words a fancy abbreviation for a website address or file location. The URL is that weird string of letters and symbols that goes something like http://www.wonderful.brilliant.com/index.html – there is no full stop right at the end. You should be able to identify various parts of this URL from this glossary.

USB (Universal Serial Bus)   In Geek: 'an external peripheral interface standard for communication between a computer and external peripherals'. In English: an easy way of plugging different things into your computer.

User group   A collection of like-minded people who get together to discuss a particular product or technology. Each of the main computer manufacturers has one or more associated user groups. Think of the connotations with addiction and you will not be far wrong.

Video-conferencing   This involves the use of video links to hold meetings between people who are in different locations. This might even be pupils at remote sites who can see and hear the teacher working in another school. Video-conferencing is a rather more complex form of communication via the Internet (or between a networked series of computers or terminals called an intranet). It involves a few pieces of extra hardware (such as a webcam) and additional software but principally allows two people or small groups, who are connected to the Internet to link up in a one-to-one or one-to-a-few situation and 'talk' to one another in what techies call 'real time'. Currently the verb 'talk' has to be used loosely as 'talk' can really mean 'type' unless you both have a very high-speed link to the Internet. Even with supposedly high-speed connections, talking is far from a reliable method of communicating using all but the most expensive video-conferencing. But its advantage over e-mail is that, as long as all parties have access to a digitising camera, you can actually see the person you are talking to!

Virtual reality (VR)   The presentation of a 3D scene on a computer or special goggles, creating an environment with which users can interact in real time with the use of sensors, gloves and/or helmets.

Virus   A program written with the deliberate intention of corrupting files which stores and sometimes replicates itself without the user's knowledge. Some viruses affect only particular programs (e.g. Word macro viruses), others affect particular operating systems. See also **WORM** and **Trojan horse**.

Webcam   A small video camera which plugs into your computer so that you can send pictures and live video. A number or permanent webcams are set up so you can watch what is happening at a particular place in a city (such as the Tyne Bridge – http://www.tynebridgewebcam.com/webcams.htm) or a waterhole in a safari park (http://africa-web-cams.com/). You can use a webcam on messenger services to set up home video-conferencing.

World Wide Web (WWW)   This is the bit that has all the web pages and sites that you hear so much about. Basically, anyone with an Internet connection can have a website. People and institutions that have websites publish, and make available, information pages and downloadable software, that contain information about almost anything and almost everything for anyone to get at. To help you find what you want, various companies have set up vast databases of websites. These are called search engines. WWW information is viewed by a piece of software called a browser, such as Microsoft's Internet Explorer or Netscape. The system was developed at CERN, Europe's centre for research into particle physics, in Switzerland, so that physicists could exchange the results of their experiments easily. And you thought physicists were boring! Also known as the World Wide Wait for those who do not have a broadband connection.

WORM   A worm is a type of virus which can 'worm' its way into your computer. In an obscure geek dialect it can also refer to optical discs on which information cannot be erased or changed once it has been recorded or written (Write Once Read Many). Never to be used in polite conversation, unless you are in the company of like-minded individuals receiving therapeutic care.

Write protect   To make a disc or a file so that its contents cannot be altered or erased 'read-only', usually by altering the file's properties or by moving a notch on the disc casing.

WYSIWYG   What-you-see-is-what-you-get (or 'whizzywig' if you want to irritate your friends). Used to describe programs that accurately represent on the screen what is printed out such as in desktop publishing. In our experience with Microsoft Word it is what you see is nearly (but not quite) what you get when you print it out.

Zip drive A proprietary disc (and disc drive) made by Iomega – it will not help you when Wayne jams his zip on his shirt during playtime.

Appendix D
Legal, ethical and health and safety issues

The intention of this appendix is to outline some of the legal, ethical and health and safety issues involved in the use of ICT in schools. It is not intended to give definitive advice, but rather to flag up issues where you may need to clarify the position with your university or college during your training and school where you undertake teaching practices (as well as issues you need to be aware of as you embark on your teaching career). Information should also be available through the school or Local Education Authority where you are placed as well as advice from professional bodies and teaching unions.

Internet safety

Internet safety is an issue which concerns parents, schools and teachers. The issue is exposure to offensive material (particularly of a racist and pornographic nature) or making personal information public which could be exploited by someone who might want to harm a child. You should also be aware of illegal or fraudulent use of personal information and offensive communications in an electronic environment. Of a lesser concern (but nonetheless real) is exposure to computer viruses which can damage or destroy information on computer networks.

You should follow the agreed guidelines on Internet use in whatever educational establishment you are working. If you intend to let pupils use e-mail or the Internet it is essential that you find out what is allowed, what is recommended and what is considered good practice. Unsupervised access to the Internet for primary pupils is inappropriate, though you should also be helping pupils to learn to be responsible for their own actions too. Beware if you use university or college computing facilities with school children. Schools usually have some kind of protected or filtered access to the Internet, facilities for adults often do not.

If you publish web pages there are further guidelines on pictures and information about pupils that you will need to follow. You should never put up photographs which have pictures of pupils on without getting permission first. The general rule is that only first names of pupils should be used and that it should never be possible to identify a pupil individually on a web page. Some schools have more restrictive policies that do not allow any photographs of children to appear on their website, or only profile or back-of-head shots. The concern is about providing a stranger with sufficient information to start a conversation with apparent knowledge about them that might create a false sense of confidence.

Most schools will have some kind of virus protection software on their networks. All computers that are connected to the Internet or share information with other computers (by CD or floppy disks) need to be protected. It is simply not worth the risk of losing files because your computer does not have anti-virus software. These days you are most likely to be 'infected' by getting an e-mail which tells you to open an attached file. Be careful as some of the most cunning ones copy themselves by using the e-mail program's address book so it may look like it is from a friend. In addition you will get hoax e-mails warning you that there is a virus around and to look at or delete various files on your computer then to pass on the information to everyone you know. Don't! If you think it is a real threat, ALWAYS check it out first before adding to e-mail traffic by forwarding the hoax. Have a look at one of the anti-virus software companies' sites for up-to-date information on virus threats (such as http://www.symantec.com) which often contain information on hoaxes too.

Copyright

Anything published (in print, music, artwork, pictures, films) is subject to copyright. This means that you are not free to copy or use the material without the permission of the copyright owner (usually either the originator of the work or the publisher). This may involve paying a fee. Whilst studying you are entitled to quote from or use sources that are covered by copyright as part of your personal study and research (covered by the Copyright, Designs and Patents Act of 1988). This is referred to as 'fair dealing'. However, making multiple copies of material for pupils in your class is **not** permitted unless what you want to copy is printed material covered by the Copyright Licensing Agency (CLA). Most British publishers allow copying (usually photocopying) of small extracts or sections of books if your school or university has paid a licence fee to the CLA. You will, however, need to check exactly what you are entitled to copy.

Computers and copyright

Material on the Internet is still covered by copyright. There is an implicit understanding that this material is then freely available, but you still cannot use it in any way that you choose. Computers make it easy to copy things; however, just because it is easy does not mean that it is legal or ethical. If someone else has put the time and effort into making information available you should not exploit this. If in doubt, contact the website owner (many sites have an e-mail address you can use).

You must have a licence for each piece of software that requires it on your computer. Some software companies have 'take-home' rights which allow teachers to install a copy on their home machine of a program that the school has a licence for. However, it is your responsibility to ensure that you comply with the legal requirements. You should not make copies of software other than as a legitimate back-up as allowed in your licence agreement.

Data protection

Schools must keep any information that they hold on individuals (including children) confidential. The current version of the Data Protection Act which took effect in March 2000 sets eight key principles into law. Those holding personal information must ensure that data is:

1   fairly and lawfully processed;
2   processed for limited purposes;
3   adequate, relevant and not excessive;
4   accurate;
5   not kept longer than necessary;
6   processed in accordance with the data subject's rights;
7   secure;
8   not transferred to countries without adequate protection.

(Data Protection Commissioner, 2000)

In addition individuals have a right of access to any data held about them and can insist on it being corrected if there are any errors.

Heath and safety

The Professional Standards for Qualified Teacher Status require those preparing to teach to be 'aware of, and work within the statutory frameworks relating to teachers' responsibilities' (1.8 p. 6) and specifically to 'select and prepare resources, and plan for their safe and effective organisation' (3.1.3, p. 9) and to 'organise and manage the physical teaching space, tools, materials, texts and other resources safely and effectively' (3.3.8 p. 12). The current health and safety legislation is extensive and is covered by documents issued by the Heath and Safety Executive, though you should also consider what is believed to be good practice alongside such more formal advice, as well as the limitations on what it is possible to achieve within the school environment. The legal responsibility for health and safety issues lie with your employer (usually the

Local Education Authority); however, as a teacher you also have a responsibility to your pupils to ensure that they are safe and so have a duty to check and report any issues you are aware of (such as worn or damaged cables).

The main issues are:

- electrical safety (no liquids near computers which should also not be near to taps);
- visual issues (positioning screens or monitors to reduce glare and make safe posture possible);
- lifting and handling heavy equipment (you should not ask pupils to move heavy equipment and you should know how to lift it safely if necessary);
- hazards from trailing wires or equipment that is not positioned correctly;
- excessive heat in a computer suite (particularly on sunny days in rooms which have been made secure from break-ins!).

You should also know about good posture and taking breaks whilst using computers (though it is more likely that you will suffer problems yourself as you prepare lessons into the small hours of the morning, than your pupils who are unlikely to be using computers for extended periods). The ideal position is to sit with your feet flat on the floor and the top of your legs parallel to the floor. Your forearms should not rest on the desk or keyboard and again should be parallel to the floor. The monitor should be adjustable to accommodate different users. Encouraging pupils to position themselves correctly may help them get used to adopting a good posture.

Further information

BECTA has an information sheet on health and safety issues, 'Health and safety: the safe use of ICT in schools' (http://www.becta.org.uk/infosheets/html/general.html) and on copyright, 'Copyright involving electronic materials: advice and issues for schools' (http://www.becta.org.uk/infosheets/html/copyright.html).

The Copyright Licensing Agency (CLA) have their own website (http://www.cla.co.uk) and there is information on the Copyright website at: http://www.bendict.com/.

Data Protection Commissioner (2000) *Data Protection Principles* (http://www.dataprotection.gov.uk/principl.htm) (dated 26 June 2000).

Federation against Software Theft (FAST) not only polices the use of software but offers advice and guidance (http://www.fast.org.uk/).

Heath and Safety Executive has its own website with information and advice. See, for example, 'Working with VDUs' at http://www.hse.gov.uk/pubns/vduindex.htm.

References

Ainsworth, S. E., Bibby, P. A. and Wood, D. J. (1997) Information technology and multiple representations: new opportunities – new problems. *Journal of Information Technology for Teacher Education*, 6, 93–106.

BECTA (2000) *A Preliminary Report for the DfEE on the Relationship Between ICT and Primary School Standards*. Coventry: BECTA (available on the web at: http://www.becta.org.uk/news/reports/).

Berlak, A. and Berlak, H. (1981) *Dilemmas of Schooling*. London: Methuen.

Blyth, A. (1998) English primary education. Looking backward to look forward. In C. Richards and P. H. Taylor (eds) *How Shall We School Our Children? Primary education and its future*, London: Falmer Press, pp. 3–16.

Breese, C., Jackson, A. and Prince, T. (1996) Promise in impermanence: children writing with unlimited access to word processors. *Early Child Development and Care*, 118, 67–91.

Chalkey, T. W. and Nicholas, D. (1997) Teacher's use of information technology: observations of primary school practice. *Aslib Proceedings*, 49, 97–107.

Central Advisory Council for Education, England (1967) *Children and their Primary Schools*, Volume 1. London: HMSO.

Davies, J. (1998) The standards debate. In C. Richards and P. H. Taylor (eds) *How Shall we School our Children? Primary education and its future*. London: Falmer Press, pp. 160–172.

Dawes, L., Mercer, N. and Wegerif, R. (2000) Extending talking and reasoning skills using ICT. In M. Leask and J. Meadows (eds) *Teaching and Learning with ICT in the Primary School*. London: Routledge.

DfEE (Department for Education and Employment) (1997a) *Excellence in Education*. London: HMSO.

DfEE (Department for Education and Employment) (1997b) *Preparing for the Information Age: Synoptic report of the education department's superhighways initiative*. London: DfEE.

DfEE (Department for Education and Employment) (1998) *Teaching: High status, high standards – requirements for courses of initial teacher training* (Circular number 4/98). London: TTA Publications.

DfEE (Department for Education and Employment) (1999) *The National Curriculum for England*. London: DfEE.

DfES (Department for Education and Skills) (1989) *The National Curriculum Non-Statutory Guidance*. London: HMSO.

Dewey, J. (1933) *How We Think*. Boston, MA: D.C. Heath.

Dreyfus, H. L. (1981) From micro-worlds to knowledge representation: AI at an impasse. In J. Haugeland (ed.) *Mind Design*. Cambridge, MA: MIT Press, pp. 164–204.

Eidson, S. and Simmons, P. E. (1998) Microcomputer simulation graphic and alphanumeric modes: examining students' process skills and conceptual understanding. *Journal of Computers in Mathematics and Science Teaching*, 17.1, 21–61.

Eraut, M. (1995) Groupwork with computers in British primary schools. *Journal of Educational Computing Research*, 13, 61–87.

Fitz-Gibbon, C. T. (1995) *Monitoring Education: Indicators, quality and effectiveness*. London: Cassell.

Fletcher-Flynn, C. M. and Gravatt, B. (1995) The efficacy of computer-assisted instruction (CAI): a meta-analysis. *Journal of Educational Computing Research*, 12, 219–242.

Harrison, C., Comber, C., Fisher, T., Haw, K., Lewin, C., Lunzer, E., McFarlane, A., Mavers, D., Scrimshaw, P., Somekh, B. and Watling, R. (2002) *ImpaCT2: The impact of information and communications technologies on pupil learning and attainment*. Coventry: BECTA.

Hativa, N. and Cohen, D. (1995) Self learning of negative number concepts by lower division elementary students through solving computer-provided numerical problems. *Educational Studies in Mathematics*, 28, 401–431.

Hattie, J. A. (1987) Identifying the salient facets of a model of student learning: a synthesis of meta-analyses. *International Journal of Educational Research*, 11, 187–212.

Hattie, J. A. (1992) Measuring the effects of schooling. *Journal of Education*, 36, 5–13.

Hattie, J., Biggs, J. and Purdie, N. (1996) Effects of learning skills interventions on student learning: a meta-analysis. *Review of Educational Research*, 66.2, 99–136.

Higgins, S. (2001) Identifying feedback in mathematical activities using ICT. *Education 3–13*, 29.1, 18–32.

Higgins, S. (2003) *Does ICT Improve Learning and Teaching in Schools?* Nottingham: British Educational Research Association.

Higgins, S. and Moseley, D. (2001) Teachers' thinking about ICT and learning: beliefs and outcomes. *Teacher Development*, 5.2, 191–210.

Jackson, A. and Kutnick, P. (1996) Groupwork and computers: task type and children's performance. *Journal of Computer Assisted Learning*, 12, 162–171.

Jonassen, D. (2000) *Computers as Mindtools for Schools: Engaging critical thinking*, 2nd edn. New Jersey: Prentice Hall.

Kirkwood, M. (2000) Infusing higher-order thinking and learning to learn into content instruction: a case study of secondary computing studies in Scotland. *Journal of Curriculum Studies*, 32.4, 509–535.

Kramarski, B. and Feldman, Y. (2000) Internet in the classroom: effects on reading comprehension, motivation and metacognition. *Educational Media International*, 37.3, 149–155.

Lewin, C. (2000) Exploring the effects of talking books software in UK primary classrooms. *Journal of Research in Reading*, 23.2, 149–157.

Lynch, L., Fawcett, A. J. and Nicolson, R. I. (2000) Computer-assisted reading intervention in a secondary school: an evaluation study. *British Journal of Educational Technology*, 31.4, 333–348.

Mann, W. J. A. and Tall, D. (eds) (1992) *Computers in the Mathematics Curriculum*. London: The Mathematical Association.

Marzano, R. J. (1998) *A Theory-based Meta-analysis of Research on Instruction*. Aurora, CO: Mid-continent Regional Educational Laboratory (available on the web at: http://www.mcrel.org/).

McClain, K. and Cobb, P. (2001) Supporting students' ability to reason about data. *Educational Studies in Mathematics*, 45.1–3, 103–129.

McGuinness, C. (1999) *From Thinking Skills to Thinking Classrooms: A review and evaluation of approaches for developing pupils' thinking*. London: DfEE (Research Report RR115).

Miles, M., Martin, D. and Owen, J. (1998) *A Pilot Study into the Effects of Using Voice Dictation Software with Secondary Dyslexic Pupils.* Exeter: Devon Education Authority: occasional paper.

Mioduser, D., Tur-Kaspa, H. and Leitner, I. (2000) The learning value of computer-based instruction of early reading skills. *Journal of Computer Assisted Learning*, 16, 54–63.

Moseley, D., Baumfield, V., Elliott, J., Gregson, M., Higgins, S., Lin, M., Miller, J., Newton, D. and Robson, S. (2003) *Thinking Skill Frameworks for Post-16 Learners: An evaluation. Research report to LSDA.* Newcastle upon Tyne: Newcastle University.

Moseley, D., Higgins, S., Bramald, R., Hardman, F., Miller, J., Mroz, M., Tse, H., Newton, D., Thompson, I., Williamson, J., Halligan, J., Bramald, S., Newton, L., Tymms, P., Henderson, B. and Stout, J. (1999) *Ways Forward with ICT: Effective pedagogy using information and communications technology in literacy and numeracy in primary schools.* Newcastle upon Tyne: University of Newcastle upon Tyne (available on the web at: http://www.ncl.ac.uk/ecls/research/project_ttaict/).

Olson, R. K. and Wise, B. W. (1992) Reading on the computer with orthographic and speech feedback. *Reading and Writing*, 4, 107–144.

Pollard, A. (1997) *Reflective Teaching in the Primary School: A handbook for the classroom.* London: Cassell.

Sandholtz, J. H. (2001) Learning to teach with technology: a comparison of teacher development programs. *Journal of Technology and Teacher Education*, 9.3, 349–374.

Snyder, I. (1993) Writing with word processors: a research overview. *Educational Research*, 35, 49–68.

Somekh, B. and Davis, N. (eds) (1997) *Using Information Technology Effectively in Teaching and Learning.* London: Routledge.

Subhi, T. (1999) The impact of LOGO on gifted children's achievement and creativity. *Journal of Computer Assisted Learning*, 15, 98–108.

Torrance, H. (1997) Assessment, accountability and standards: using assessment to control the reform schooling. In A. H. Halsey, H. Laude, P. Brown and A. S. Wells (eds) *Education: Culture, economy, society.* Oxford: Oxford University Press, pp. 320–331.

TTA (1998) *Teaching – A guide to becoming a teacher.* TTA: Chelmsford: Teacher Training Agency.

TTA (1999) The Use of ICT in Subject Teaching: Expected Outcomes for Teachers in England, Northern Ireland & Wales. London: Teacher Training Agency.

TTA/DfES (2002) *Qualifying to Teach: Professional standards for qualified teacher status and requirements for initial teacher training.* London: Teacher Training Agency (TPU 0803/02-02).

Underwood, J. and Brown, J. (1997) *Integrated Learning Systems: Potential into practice.* Oxford: Heinemann.

Van Dusen, L. M. and Worthen, B. R. (1995) Can integrated instructional technology transform the classroom? *Educational Leadership*, 32.9, 28–33.

Weaver, G. C. (2000) An examination of the National Educational Longitudinal Study database to probe the correlation between computer use in school and improvement in test scores. *Journal of Science and Technology*, 9.2, 121–133.

Wegerif, R. (1996) Using computers to help coach exploratory talk across the curriculum. *Computers and Education*, 26.1–3, 51–60.

Wegerif, R. and Scrimshaw, P. (eds) (1997) *Computers and Talk in the Primary Classroom.* Clevedon: Multilingual Matters Ltd.

Wegerif, R., Mercer, N. and Dawes, L. (1998) Integrating pedagogy and software design to support discussion in the primary curriculum. *Journal of Computer Assisted Learning*, 14.1, 99–211.

Wild, M. (1996) Technology refusal: rationalising the failure of student and beginning teachers to use computers. *British Journal of Educational Technology*, 27.2, 134–143.

Wood, D. (1998) *The UK ILS Evaluations: Final report.* Coventry: BECTA/DfEE.

Index

Abacus Maths 81
Access 33
ActiveStudio 44
Advanced Learning Systems 78, 85
art 107–108, 110, 112–114
assessment 57, 62, 85, 138, 157, 159–160
asynchronous communication 44
audit grid 20

BECTA 53, 60, 160, 180
bitmap images 25–26, 107
Bloom's taxonomy 141
Blyth, A. 2, 5
Branch 183
branching tree database 33, 35–36
British Museum 116

calculators 56, 85
Capacity and range of ICT 26, 37, 47–48
Carroll diagram 84, 107, 149
categorical data 34
CD-ROMs 27–28, 37, 67, 91, 98, 102
citizenship 10, 108, 114–116, 127
Clicker 66, 106, 183
clip art 136, 188
collaborative use of ICT 56, 130, 147–149
Colour Magic 17, 184
community of enquiry 147
computer-assisted instruction 53
computer-based learning 53
Concept Cartoons 98
concept mapping 71, 145–147

continuous data 34
control technology 120, 133
copyright 201–202
Counting Pictures 183
creative play 136
creative thinking 85, 134, 140, 150
critical thinking 28
Crocodile Clips 99, 119–120
Curriculum Online 73, 90, 101

data protection 202
Data Protection Act 202
databases 34–36, 40, 94–95, 107–108, 157
data-logging 92, 124, 189
Davies, J. 4
Dazzle 17, 183
design technology 107–108, 118–121
desktop publishing 24
Dewey, J. 141, 150
digital cameras 17, 93, 95, 113, 120, 131
Digital Frog 97
digital images 95, 110, 115, 117, 121, 131
digital projector 25, 65, 67–68, 81, 96, 100, 110, 154
discrete data 34
display (classroom) 138
drawing software 25

Early Years 128–139
Easiteach 44, 81
editing 69–70
Education Reform Act 1

effectiveness of ICT 52–60
electronic whiteboard 25, 46, 57–58, 129, 142, 192
e-mail 43, 45–46, 48, 50, 69, 111, 125, 190
English 65–75
ethical issues 200–203
Excel 33

feedback 26, 37, 55, 65, 85
FlexiDATA 183
FlexiTREE 17, 183
Foundation Stage 16, 29, 38, 48–49, 61, 128–139
foundation subjects 61, 104–127
Framework for Teaching Mathematics 8, 17, 38, 85
Fresco 44

Geography 29, 41, 121–123
graphical calculator 56
graphics 107

Health and safety issues 200
higher-order thinking 56, 141
history 29, 108, 116–118

ICT and attainment 53–54
ICT capability 15, 17–18, 63, 104
ICT skills 20–22, 30–31
Inclusive Writer 17, 183
Individual Education Plans 55
Integrated Learning Systems 54, 58
Interactive Teaching Programs (ITPs) 47, 78–80, 83, 89
interactive whiteboard 25, 46, 57–58, 129, 142, 192
Interactivity of ICT 26, 37, 47–48
Internet 27–28, 37, 57, 87, 98, 102, 111, 120–121
Internet Explorer 44, 46
Internet searching 102

job interviews 167–174
Junior Pinpoint 17, 184

Key Stage 1 29, 38, 46, 48–49, 115, 119
Key Stage 2 29, 39, 48, 102, 107, 115
keyboards 16, 106, 129
Keynote 44, 67
Kid Pix 17, 184
Kidspiration 145–146

legal issues 200–203
Logical Journey of the Zoombinis 148
LOGO 191, 194

Mathematical Journey of the Zoombinis 148
mathematics 77–90, 143–145
Meteorological Office 97
microscopes 99
microwaves 134
mind-mapping 71, 145–147
modelling 108, 114, 119
Modern Foreign Languages (MFL) 125
multimedia 24, 55, 110, 195
music 123–124
My World 119, 134

NASA 97
National Curriculum x, 1–4, 12, 38, 61, 73, 86, 158
National Grid for Learning 9, 52
National Literacy Strategy 1, 8, 12, 65, 68, 73, 158
National Numeracy Strategy 1, 8, 12, 35, 47, 77–90, 158
National Portrait Gallery 112
Number Magic 17, 184

painting software 25
personal portfolio 95, 169–170
physical education 92, 110, 124–125
PickaPicture 17, 183
Pictogram 17, 183
Plowden Report 2
Pollard, A. 163
Powerpoint 44, 46, 67, 70
Professional learning and ICT 17, 153–154, 157–161, 162–166
programmable toys 17, 134, 136, 195
Provisionality of ICT 26, 37, 47–48
Publisher 70, 82, 84

QCA 8, 16, 39, 158, 180
QTS skills tests 21–22
Qualified Teacher Status x, 5–8, 19, 161

record-keeping 62, 138, 157
Relational database 35
Religious Education 61, 111
Research (using ICT) 111
Research (about ICT) 52–60

Safari 44
science 41, 91–103
search engines 45, 125, 175–178
self-audit grid 20
sensor 92, 124, 196
simulation 109, 118
Special Educational Needs 16, 70, 106
Speed and Automatic functions of ICT 26, 37, 47–48
spreadsheets 34–35, 40, 81, 87, 92, 94–96, 107, 109, 196
Stephenson Report 43
synchronous communication 44

tablet PCs 47, 197
talking books 55, 101
Talking First Word 17, 184
Taxonomy 35, 141
Teacher Training Agency 6, 26, 54, 180
templates 16, 74, 137, 158
Textease 24, 67, 70

text-to-speech 55, 65, 74, 105
thinking skills 118, 140–152
tutoring programs 55

URL 44, 175, 197

vector graphics 25–26, 31, 107
Venn diagram 107, 148
video 27–28, 92, 94, 96, 110, 115, 120, 131, 157
video-conferencing 43, 48, 125, 197
virus 198, 201
visualisation tools 56

Word 24, 66
Word bank 65
World-processing 24, 105
World Wide Web 44, 67, 175–178, 198

Zoombinis 148–150
Zoombinis Island Odyssey 148